LIBERTY OF CONSCIENCE

This book sets out a novel account of the conceptual foundations of liberty of conscience based on John Rawls's concept of moral personality.

Liberty of conscience (often called religious freedom) is a notoriously broad right. As understood in many legal systems, it can extend to virtually any action or inaction, ranging from dietary choices to objections to military service, and potentially provide protection against the application of a state's laws in respect of that action or inaction. To understand the proper limits of this right, it is necessary to inquire into its conceptual foundations.

The book shows that protection of liberty of conscience is warranted because of its importance to the exercise and development of the two moral powers of individuals that comprise their moral personality: the power to judge right and justice, and the power to form and pursue a conception of the good. However, some possible limitations for the right relating to the rights of others and the common interest flow from this rationale.

Utilising this theoretical account, the book analyses two case studies at the limits of religious freedom in the law of the UK and USA: pandemic lockdown restrictions on religious gatherings, and non-discrimination laws in their application to same-sex couples.

Liberty of Conscience

Justification and Limits

Guy Baldwin

•HART•
OXFORD • LONDON • NEW YORK • NEW DELHI • SYDNEY

HART PUBLISHING
Bloomsbury Publishing Plc
Kemp House, Chawley Park, Cumnor Hill, Oxford, OX2 9PH, UK
1385 Broadway, New York, NY 10018, USA
Bloomsbury Publishing Ireland Limited, 29 Earlsfort Terrace, Dublin 2, D02 AY28, Ireland

HART PUBLISHING, the Hart/Stag logo, BLOOMSBURY and the Diana logo are trademarks of Bloomsbury Publishing Plc
First published in Great Britain 2026

1

A catalogue record for this book is available from the British Library.

A catalogue record for this book is available from the Library of Congress.

ISBN: HB: 978-1-50998-527-2
ePDF: 978-1-50998-529-6
ePub: 978-1-50998-528-9

Typeset by Lumina Datamatics Ltd

For product safety related questions contact productsafety@bloomsbury.com

To find out more about our authors and books visit www.hartpublishing.co.uk. Here you will find extracts, author information, details of forthcoming events and the option to sign up for our newsletters.

For my beloved wife Claire

ACKNOWLEDGEMENTS

This book derives from my PhD studies at Clare College, University of Cambridge, between 2020 and 2024. I was extremely fortunate to be supervised in the PhD project by Professor Alison Young, the Sir David Williams Professor of Public Law, who provided invaluable guidance and feedback throughout the process, as well as kind and generous support for my academic career. In addition, I benefitted greatly from the input of my advisor, Professor Lars Vinx, who commented in detail on Chapters 2, 3 and 4. The Cambridge Faculty of Law was an ideal environment in which to work on this project. I am profoundly honoured and humbled that the thesis was awarded a Yorke Prize by the Faculty.

I am very thankful to my final examiners, Professor David Feldman and Dr John Adenitire, for their deep engagement with the thesis and insightful comments on it, as well as to my first-year examiners, Professor Kirsty Hughes and Dr Stephanie Palmer, for theirs.

I also acknowledge the helpful feedback that I received on parts of the book from the participants at presentations at:

- The Centre for Public Law Lunchtime Discussion Group at the University of Cambridge, United Kingdom, on 30 November 2021;
- The Australasian Society of Legal Philosophy Conference at the University of Sydney, Australia, on 14–15 July 2022; and
- The Secularism as a Value Workshop at Princeton University, United States, on 3–4 May 2023 (especially Professor Alan Patten, who responded to the paper).

Some material in this book is drawn from the following open access articles:

- G Baldwin, 'The Coronavirus Pandemic and Religious Freedom: Judicial Decisions in the United States and United Kingdom' (2021) 26 *Judicial Review* 297;
- G Baldwin, 'Rawls and Animal Moral Personality' (2023) 13 *Animals* 1238;
- G Baldwin, 'Religious Freedom under the Australian Constitution: Is Proportionality the Answer?' (2023) 3 *Australian Journal of Law and Religion* 20; and
- G Baldwin, 'Positive Obligations to Protect the Population under Human Rights Law' (2025) 30 *Judicial Review* 232.

My studies at Cambridge were supported by a Cambridge Australia Poynton International Scholarship from Cambridge Australia Scholarships and the Cambridge Trust. I am immensely grateful for the scholarship.

My friends at Cambridge – especially Dr Aradhya Sethia, Dr Forest Yu, Dr Ori Pomson, Dr Vandita Khanna, Dr Fabian Eichberger, Dr Tim Cochrane, Dr Ranjini Nair and Dr Alex Allen-Franks – made my time there rich and memorable.

At the University of Manchester Law Department where I have worked as a Lecturer in Public Law and Human Rights since 2023, I have greatly appreciated the guidance and friendship of my colleagues, especially Dr Luke Graham, Professor Robert Thomas, Professor Javier García Oliva, Dr Rachael Ntongho, Dr Shiling Xiao, Dr Emma Nyhan, Dr Emma Scali, Dr Ashley Hannay, Dr Petra Larsen and Dr Fiona Brimblecombe.

Kodak and Fuji provided canine companionship and sometimes let me work on the book.

I owe my mother, Jenny, gratitude for love and kindness spanning nearly four decades.

This book is dedicated to Claire. Marrying you was the best thing to ever happen to me.

CONTENTS

Acknowledgements ... *vi*
Table of Cases ... *xi*
Table of Legislation ... *xvi*

1. Introduction ... 1
I. The Book's Argument ... 2
II. The Meaning of Liberty of Conscience ... 4
A. Hohfeldian Description of the Right to Liberty of Conscience ... 5
B. The Nature of Conscientious Belief ... 6
C. Liberty of Conscience Distinguished from Non-Discrimination ... 7
III. Protection of Liberty of Conscience in UK and US Law ... 9
IV. Methods ... 11

2. The Rationale of Liberty of Conscience ... 17
I. Possible Arguments for Liberty of Conscience ... 18
II. A Moral-Personality-Based Account of Liberty of Conscience ... 26
A. Rawls and Moral Personality ... 26
B. Moral Personality and Recognition Respect ... 30
C. Possible Issues with Moral Personality ... 37
III. Some Possible Objections to the Protection of Liberty of Conscience ... 41
A. Conscientious Belief as a Choice? ... 41
B. Protecting Manifestations of Conscientious Belief? ... 43
C. Conscientious Belief as Potentially 'Intolerant'? ... 45
IV. Conclusion ... 47

3. The Limits of Liberty of Conscience ... 49
I. Non-Negligible Burden on Liberty of Conscience ... 51
II. Compatibility with the Basic Liberties of Others ... 54
A. The Nature of Compatibility with the Basic Liberties of Others ... 54
B. Assessing Compatibility with the Basic Liberties of Others ... 57
III. Necessity in the Common Interest ... 62
A. The Nature of Necessity in the Common Interest ... 63
B. Assessing Necessity in the Common Interest ... 67
IV. Conclusion ... 70

4. Liberty of Conscience and Neutrality **71**
I. Disambiguating Neutrality 71
II. Neutrality as Non-Establishment 74
III. Neutrality as No Purpose to Limit Exercise 76
IV. Conclusion 85
5. Coronavirus Pandemic **87**
I. A Basic Liberty of Integrity of the Person 89
II. Key Case Law 94
A. US Case Law 94
B. UK Case Law 97
III. Compatibility Analysis 100
IV. Necessity Analysis 111
V. Conclusion 119
6. Discrimination towards Same-Sex Couples **121**
I. A Basic Liberty of Non-Discrimination 123
A. Nature and Unfairness of Discrimination 124
B. Non-Discrimination as Required by Recognition Respect for Moral Personality 128
C. Other Approaches to Non-Discrimination 132
II. Key Case Law 135
A. US Case Law 136
B. UK Case Law 139
III. Compatibility Analysis 142
IV. Necessity Analysis 152
V. Conclusion 160
7. Conclusion **161**

Bibliography 172
Index 183

TABLE OF CASES

303 Creative LLC v Elenis (2023) 143 S Ct 2298 (Supreme Court of the United States) ... 2, 122, 159
A v United Kingdom (2009) 49 EHRR 29 (European Court of Human Rights) .. 110
Abdulaziz v United Kingdom (1985) 7 EHRR 471 (European Court of Human Rights) ... 125
Adelaide Company of Jehovah's Witnesses v Commonwealth (1943) 67 CLR 116 (High Court of Australia) ... 44–45, 78
Attorney-General (Vic) ex rel Black v Commonwealth (1981) 146 CLR 559 (High Court of Australia) ... 74, 79
Bank Mellat v Her Majesty's Treasury (No 2) [2014] AC 700 (Supreme Court of the United Kingdom) ... 64, 68, 116
Biden v Missouri (2022) 142 S Ct 647 (Supreme Court of the United States) ... 170
Bostock v Clayton County (2020) 140 S Ct 1731 (Supreme Court of the United States) ... 121, 147
Braunfeld v Brown (1961) 366 US 599 (Supreme Court of the United States) ... 44
Brown v Board of Education of Topeka (1954) 347 US 483 (Supreme Court of the United States) ... 131
Bull v Hall [2013] 1 WLR 3741 (Supreme Court of the United Kingdom) ... 2, 122, 126, 135, 139–40, 143, 146–48, 150–52, 155, 159–60, 163, 165
Burwell v Hobby Lobby Stores, Inc (2014) 573 US 682 (Supreme Court of the United States) ... 40, 50, 52
Calvary Chapel Dayton Valley v Sisolak (2020) 140 S Ct 2603 (Supreme Court of the United States) ... 95, 113
Campbell and Cosans v United Kingdom (1982) 4 EHRR 293 (European Court of Human Rights) ... 9
Cannavacciuolo v Italy (2025) 81 EHRR 15 (European Court of Human Rights) ... 104, 106
Cantwell v Connecticut (1940) 310 US 296 (Supreme Court of the United States) ... 10, 44
Carson v Makin (2022) 142 S Ct 1987 (Supreme Court of the United States) ... 84
Casamitjana Costa v League against Cruel Sports [2020] Employment Tribunal ET/3331129/2018 ... 53
Christian Education South Africa v Minister of Education (2000) (4) SA 757 (Constitutional Court of South Africa) ... 44, 165–66
Church of the Lukumi Babalu Aye v City of Hialeah (1993) 508 US 520 (Supreme Court of the United States) ... 10, 61, 71, 73, 77, 83–85, 94, 110, 113–116, 119, 122, 137–138, 154, 162

Church of the New Faith v Commissioner for Pay-roll Tax (Vic) (1983) 154 CLR 120 (High Court of Australia)....53
City of Boerne v Flores (1997) 521 US 507 (Supreme Court of the United States)....10
Collins v Wilcock [1984] 1 WLR 1172 (Divisional Court of the Queen's Bench Division)....93
Communauté Genevoise D'Action Syndicale (CGAS) v Switzerland App no 21881/20 (ECtHR, 27 November 2023)....102
Communauté Genevoise D'Action Syndicale (CGAS) v Switzerland (2024) 78 EHRR 22 (European Court of Human Rights)....102
Conisbee v Crossley Farms Ltd [2019] Employment Tribunal ET/3335357/2018....53
Cruzan v Director, Missouri Department of Health (1990) 497 US 261 (Supreme Court of the United States)....101
Cyprus v Turkey (2002) 35 EHRR 30 (European Court of Human Rights)....130
Dobbs v Jackson Women's Health Organization (2022) 142 S Ct 2228 (Supreme Court of the United States)....101
Does 1–3 v Mills (2021) 142 S Ct 17 (Supreme Court of the United States)....170
Dolan v Secretary of State for Health and Social Care [2020] EWHC 1786 (Administrative Court).... 2, 87, 98
Dolan v Secretary of State for Health and Social Care [2021] WLR 2326 (Court of Appeal Civil Division)....2, 87, 98, 106, 109
Employment Division, Department of Human Resources of Oregon v Smith (1988) 485 US 660 (Supreme Court of the United States)....76
Employment Division, Department of Human Resources of Oregon v Smith (1990) 494 US 872 (Supreme Court of the United States)....2, 10, 44, 68, 71, 76–77, 80–81, 84–85, 94, 100, 110, 113–116, 119, 122, 135, 138, 154, 159, 164–165, 167–170
Everson v Board of Education (1947) 330 US 1 (Supreme Court of the United States)....74
Eweida v United Kingdom (2013) 57 EHRR 8 (European Court of Human Rights)....9, 53
Fenech v Malta App no 19090/20 (ECtHR, 1 March 2022)....102
Fulton v City of Philadelphia (2021) 141 S Ct 1868 (Supreme Court of the United States)....2, 85, 117, 122, 135, 137–139, 143, 147–48, 151–52, 154–56, 158–60, 163, 168–70
Gäfgen v Germany (2011) 52 EHRR 1 (European Court of Human Rights)....89
Gallagher v Crown Kosher Super Market of Massachusetts, Inc (1961) 366 US 617 (Supreme Court of the United States)....44
Gillan v United Kingdom (2010) 50 EHRR 45 (European Court of Human Rights)....93
Gillick v West Norfolk and Wisbech Area Health Authority [1986] AC 112 (United Kingdom House of Lords)....92
GN v Italy App no 43134/05 (ECtHR, 1 December 2009)....102
Grainger plc v Nicholson [2010] ICR 360 (Employment Appeal Tribunal)....53

Griggs v Duke Power Co (1971) 401 US 424 (Supreme Court of the United States)......126
Hamilton v Regents of the University of California (1934) 293 US 245 (Supreme Court of the United States)......10
Ivanova v Bulgaria (2008) 47 EHRR 54 (European Court of Human Rights)......9, 43
In the matter of an application by JR87 [2025] UKSC 40 (Supreme Court of the United Kingdom)......75
Katz v United States (1967) 389 US 347 (Supreme Court of the United States)....93
Kennedy v Bremerton School District (2022) 142 S Ct 2407 (Supreme Court of the United States)......74, 84
Kennedy v Mendoza-Martinez (1963) 372 US 144 (Supreme Court of the United States)......118
Kokkinakis v Greece (1994) 17 EHRR 397 (European Court of Human Rights)......11, 25
Korematsu v United States (1944) 323 US 214 (Supreme Court of the United States)......117
Kosteski v Former Yugoslav Republic of Macedonia (2007) 45 EHRR 31 (European Court of Human Rights)......101
Kruger v Commonwealth (1997) 190 CLR 1 (High Court of Australia)...... 71, 78–82, 84–85
Krygger v Williams (1912) 15 CLR 366 (High Court of Australia)......43, 78
Largent v Texas (1943) 318 US 418 (Supreme Court of the United States)......44
Lautsi v Italy (2010) 50 EHRR 42 (European Court of Human Rights)......75
Le Mailloux v France App no 18108/20 (ECtHR, 3 December 2020)......102
Lee v Ashers Baking Co Ltd [2020] AC 413 (Supreme Court of the United Kingdom)......2, 41, 122, 135, 141, 143–44, 149–52, 155, 157–60, 163
Lee v United Kingdom App no 18860/19 (ECtHR, 6 January 2022) (European Court of Human Rights)......142
Leela Förderkreis EV v Germany (2009) 49 EHRR 5 (European Court of Human Rights)......101
Lemon v Kurtzman (1971) 403 US 602 (Supreme Court of the United States)......74, 171
Lochner v New York (1905) 198 US 45 (Supreme Court of the United States)......14
Lovell v City of Griffin (1938) 303 US 444 (Supreme Court of the United States)......44
Mahmoud v Taylor (2025) 145 S Ct 2332 (Supreme Court of the United States)......85, 170
Masterpiece Cakeshop v Colorado Civil Rights Commission (2018) 138 S Ct 1719 (Supreme Court of the United States)...... 2, 84, 100, 122, 135–37, 142–48, 150–60, 163–65, 169
McCann v United Kingdom (1996) 21 EHRR 97 (European Court of Human Rights)......89

Montgomery v Lanarkshire Health Board [2015] AC 1430 (Supreme Court of the United Kingdom)......93
Mouvement Laïque Québécois v Saguenay [2015] 2 SCR 3 (Supreme Court of Canada)......71
Murdock v Pennsylvania (1943) 319 US 105 (Supreme Court of the United States)......44
National Federation of Independent Business v Department of Labor (2022) 142 S Ct 661 (Supreme Court of the United States)......170
Obergefell v Hodges (2015) 576 US 644 (Supreme Court of the United States)...121
Öneryildiz v Turkey (2005) 41 EHRR 20 (European Court of Human Rights)...... 102, 104
Oyal v Turkey (2010) 51 EHRR 30 (European Court of Human Rights)......102
Pasquinelli v San Marino (2025) 80 EHRR 8 (European Court of Human Rights)......102
Percy v Board of National Mission of the Church of Scotland [2006] 2 AC 28 (United Kingdom House of Lords)......9, 99
Philip v Scottish Ministers 2021 SLT 559 (Outer House of the Court of Session)......
2, 9, 87, 94, 99–103, 105–07, 109–10, 113–19, 162–63, 165, 169–70
Pretty v United Kingdom (2002) 35 EHRR 1 (European Court of Human Rights)......89
Prince v Massachusetts (1944) 321 US 158 (Supreme Court of the United States)......44, 109–110
R (AB) v Secretary of State for Justice [2022] AC 487 (Supreme Court of the United Kingdom)...... 104–05
R (Begum) v Governors of Denbigh High School [2007] 1 AC 100 (United Kingdom House of Lords)......56
R (E) v Governing Body of JFS [2010] 2 AC 728 (Supreme Court of the United Kingdom)......140
R (Elan-Cane) v Secretary of State for the Home Department [2023] AC 559 (Supreme Court of the United Kingdom)
R (Gardner) v Secretary of State for Health and Social Care [2022] PTSR 1338 (Administrative Court)......103–06, 110
R (Hussain) v Secretary of State for Health & Social Care [2020] EWHC 1392 (Admin)......97–98, 106–08, 110, 113–14, 116
R (SC) v Secretary of State for Work and Pensions [2022] AC 223 (Supreme Court of the United Kingdom)......125
R (Steinfeld) v Secretary of State for International Development [2020] AC 1 (Supreme Court of the United Kingdom)......135
R (Ullah) v Special Adjudicator [2004] 2 AC 32 (United Kingdom House of Lords)......104
R (Williamson) v Secretary of State for Education and Employment [2005] 2 AC 246 (United Kingdom House of Lords)......53, 101, 166
Reynolds v United States (1879) 98 US 145 (Supreme Court of the United States)......2, 43–45, 76

Ricci v DeStefano (2009) 557 US 557 (Supreme Court of the United States)......126
Rochin v California (1952) 342 US 165 (Supreme Court of the United States)......101
Roman Catholic Diocese v Cuomo (2020) 141 S Ct 63 (Supreme Court of the United States)........2, 87, 95–96, 107, 109, 112–15, 117–18, 162, 165, 169
SAS v France (2015) 60 EHRR 11 (European Court of Human Rights) 10, 57
Schilder v The Netherlands App no 2158/12 (ECtHR, 16 October 2012)............101
Schloendorff v Society of New York Hospital (1914) 211 NY 125 (Court of Appeals of New York)......101
Schneider v New Jersey (1939) 308 US 147 (Supreme Court of the United States)......44
Sherbert v Verner (1963) 374 US 398 (Supreme Court of the United States)........... 15, 44, 68–69, 76, 168–70
South Bay United Pentecostal Church v Newsom (No 1) (2020) 140 S Ct 1613 (Supreme Court of the United States) 87, 94
South Bay United Pentecostal Church v Newsom (No 2) (2021) 141 S Ct 716 (Supreme Court of the United States) 96
Spînu v Romania App no 29443/20 (ECtHR, 11 October 2022) (European Court of Human Rights)......106
Suraj v Attorney General of Trinidad and Tobago [2023] AC 337 (Judicial Committee of the Privy Council)......105
Syndicat Northcrest v Amselem [2004] 2 SCR 551 (Supreme Court of Canada)...53
Tandon v Newsom (2021) 141 S Ct 1294 (Supreme Court of the United States)......96, 111–12, 119
Terheş v Romania App no 49933/20 (ECtHR, 20 May 2021)......102
Tesco Supermarkets Ltd v Nattrass [1972] AC 153 (United Kingdom House of Lords) 40
Thomas v Review Board of Indiana Employment Security Division (1981) 450 US 707 (Supreme Court of the United States)......52
Union Pacific Railway Co v Botsford (1891) 141 US 250 (Supreme Court of the United States) 100–01
United States v Carolene Products Co (1938) 304 US 144 (Supreme Court of the United States) 64
United States v Seeger (1965) 380 US 163 (Supreme Court of the United States) 53
Verein KlimaSeniorinnen Schweiz v Switzerland (2024) 79 EHRR 1 (European Court of Human Rights)...... 89, 106
Washington v Davis (1976) 426 US 229 (Supreme Court of the United States)..126
Washington v Harper (1990) 494 US 210 (Supreme Court of the United States)......101
Welsh v United States (1970) 398 US 333 (Supreme Court of the United States)......11
Winston v Lee (1985) 470 US 753 (Supreme Court of the United States)............101
Wisconsin v Yoder (1971) 406 US 205 (Supreme Court of the United States)...... 15, 68–69, 85, 168, 170

TABLE OF LEGISLATION

Aboriginals Ordinance 1918 (NT) 78
African Charter of Human and Peoples' Rights 1981 2
American Convention on Human Rights 1969 2
Australian Constitution 1901 .... 74, 78–79
Charter of Fundamental Rights of the European Union 2000 2
Charter of Human Rights and Freedoms 1975 (Quebec Charter) 71
Colorado Anti-Discrimination Act 136
Constitution of Japan 1947 82
Constitution of the Republic of South Africa 1997 166
Constitution of the Republic of Trinidad and Tobago 1976 105
Constitution of the United States 1789 .... 5–6, 8, 10, 13, 43, 61, 73, 76, 79, 84–85, 94, 110–111, 118, 120, 126, 135, 137–138, 143, 151–152, 156–159, 162–163, 168, 171
Civil Rights Act of 1964 .... 8, 121, 126
Civil Rights Act of 1991 126
Equality Act 2010 .... 8, 41, 53, 121, 126–27, 140, 147
Equality Act (Sexual Orientation) Regulations 2007 SI 2007/1263 .... 140, 146
Equality Act (Sexual Orientation) Regulations (Northern Ireland) 2006 SI 2006/439 141
European Convention on Human Rights 1950 .... 2, 6, 9–11, 13, 25, 43, 53, 57, 89, 94, 97–99, 101–07, 110, 118, 120, 125, 130, 135, 140–42, 149, 158–59, 165–166, 169–170
Fair Employment and Treatment (Northern Ireland) Order 1998 SI 1998/3162 (NI 21) 141, 159
Fair Practices Ordinance (Philadelphia) 138–39
Health Protection (Coronavirus, Restrictions) (England) Regulations 2020 SI 2020/250 97–98
Health Protection (Coronavirus) (Restrictions and Requirements) (Local Levels) (Scotland) Amendment (No 11) Regulations 2021 SSI 2021/3 98–99
Human Rights Act 1998 .... 6, 8–9, 13, 135, 142, 159, 162
International Covenant on Civil and Political Rights 1966 2
Marriage (Same Sex Couples) Act 2013 121
Religious Freedom Restoration Act of 1993 .... 8, 10, 52
Religious Land Use and Institutionalized Persons Act of 2000 .... 8, 10

1

Introduction

According to Thomas Jefferson, the 'constitutional freedom of religion' is 'the most inalienable and sacred of all human rights'.[1] But the potentially expansive scope of religious convictions risks making the exercise of that human right controversial. That is because the right is usually taken to offer protection not merely to the holding of particular beliefs, but also to their exercise or manifestation. Such exercise or manifestation may be inconsistent with laws enacted to advance the public interest, or to protect the rights of others. That raises a dilemma: should legal protection for this right be allowed to trump other laws, even if they are in the public interest or protect the rights of others? The project of this book is to explore that dilemma of the justification and limits of liberty of conscience (a term that encompasses, but is not limited to, religious freedom).

In this introduction, I set out the book's argument in Section I. I elaborate on the problem of liberty of conscience inherent in the potential of this right to allow personal belief to trump laws, and summarise the analysis of this problem offered in the book. This book develops from the philosophy of John Rawls,[2] supplemented by some other ideas,[3] an account of liberty of conscience and its limits, before applying it to two illustrative case studies involving the law of the UK and US. In Section II, I discuss the meaning of liberty of conscience. In Section III, I briefly outline the protection of liberty of conscience in the law of the United Kingdom (UK) and United States (US). In Section IV, I explain the methods of the book, which are theoretical and philosophical in the early chapters of the book, and then also doctrinal and comparative in the later chapters.

[1] See SD Smith, 'The Rise and Fall of Religious Freedom in Constitutional Discourse' (1991) 140 *University of Pennsylvania Law Review* 149, 153.

[2] See J Rawls, *A Theory of Justice* (Cambridge, MA: Harvard University Press, 1971); J Rawls, *A Theory of Justice (Revised Edition)* (Cambridge, MA: Harvard University Press, 1999); J Rawls, *Justice as Fairness: A Restatement* (E Kelly ed, Cambridge, MA: Harvard University Press, 2001); J Rawls, *Political Liberalism* (New York: Columbia University Press, 2005). Given the focus on domestic systems, this book does not rely on J Rawls, *The Law of Peoples* (Cambridge, MA: Harvard University Press, 2001).

[3] See especially SL Darwall, 'Two Kinds of Respect' (1977) 88 *Ethics* 36. See also MC Nussbaum, *Liberty of Conscience: In Defense of America's Tradition of Religious Equality* (New York: Basic Books, 2008); J Adenitire, *A General Right to Conscientious Exemption: Beyond Religious Privilege* (Cambridge: Cambridge University Press, 2020).

I. The Book's Argument

Consider two examples, which need not be especially hypothetical to illustrate the challenge that liberty of conscience may pose. In the first example, a deadly pandemic sweeps the globe. Governments scramble to protect their populations from the spread of the virus. Should liberty of conscience mean that places of worship cannot be closed while the crisis rages – regardless of the potential impact on public health of keeping them open?[4] In the second example, same-sex couples achieve legal recognition for their relationships after a long history of discrimination. However, some religious believers do not want to provide services to same-sex weddings, due to their religious convictions, and in potential violation of laws that ban discrimination on the basis of sexual orientation. Does liberty of conscience protect the believers' right to refuse service?[5] These are undoubtedly difficult questions.

Liberty of conscience is widely protected in national constitutions and human rights instruments.[6] However, due to the difficulties with the concept and its potential interaction with other laws, the desirability, and proper scope, of liberty of conscience have long been debated. It is this problem of the desirability and proper scope of the right that I explore in this book. Should liberty of conscience allow each person to become a 'law unto himself', as Scalia J put it in the US Supreme Court decision of *Employment Division v Smith*?[7] I approach the problem from the perspective of both theory and legal doctrine, developing first a normative theoretical framework to understand the rationale for and proper scope of liberty of conscience, before turning to explore some doctrinal case studies – based on the two examples above – of particular interest in understanding the proper limits of this right.

[4] See, eg, *Dolan v Secretary of State for Health and Social Care* [2020] EWHC 1786 (Admin) (Administrative Court); *Roman Catholic Diocese v Cuomo* (2020) 141 S Ct 63 (Supreme Court of the United States); *Dolan v Secretary of State for Health and Social Care* [2021] WLR 2326 (Court of Appeal Civil Division); *Philip v Scottish Ministers* 2021 SLT 559 (Outer House of the Court of Session).

[5] See, eg, *Bull v Hall* [2013] 1 WLR 3741 (Supreme Court of the United Kingdom); *Masterpiece Cakeshop v Colorado Civil Rights Commission* (2018) 138 S Ct 1719 (Supreme Court of the United States); *Lee v Ashers Baking Co Ltd* [2020] AC 413 (Supreme Court of the United Kingdom); *Fulton v City of Philadelphia* (2021) 141 S Ct 1868 (Supreme Court of the United States); *303 Creative LLC v Elenis* (2023) 143 S Ct 2298 (Supreme Court of the United States).

[6] For an overview of protection of religious freedom at the national level in a comparative, empirical study, see FB Cross, *Constitutions and Religious Freedom* (Cambridge: Cambridge University Press, 2015). For protection under international human rights instruments, see, eg, International Covenant on Civil and Political Rights 1966, Art 18; European Convention on Human Rights 1950, Art 9; American Convention on Human Rights 1969, Art 12; African Charter of Human and Peoples' Rights 1981, Art 8; Charter of Fundamental Rights of the European Union 2000, Art 10. For commentary on international law protection, see, eg, C Evans, *Freedom of Religion under the European Convention on Human Rights* (Oxford: Oxford University Press, 2001); PM Taylor, *Freedom of Religion: UN and European Human Rights Law and Practice* (Cambridge: Cambridge University Press, 2005); H Bielefeldt et al, *Freedom of Religion or Belief: An International Law Commentary* (Oxford: Oxford University Press, 2016).

[7] *Employment Division, Department of Human Resources of Oregon v Smith* (1990) 494 US 872, 879. Scalia J was quoting the earlier decision of *Reynolds v United States* (1879) 98 US 145 (Supreme Court of the United States) 166–67. However, although never overruled, that decision did not accurately represent the approach of the US Supreme Court at the time that Scalia J wrote the judgment in *Smith*.

In this book, I defend the protection of liberty of conscience as against a state's laws (that is, what are sometimes called 'exemptions'). Drawing on the ideas of Rawls – in particular, the concepts of moral personality and the basic liberties – as well as the work of other theorists,[8] I suggest in Chapter 2 that the right to liberty of conscience is based on recognition respect for people as moral persons who have the capacity for a conception of the good and for a sense of justice (I explain the concept of recognition respect further below). Protection for liberty of conscience is important for the exercise and development of both of these moral powers. Moreover, legal officials, like anyone else, owe duties of respect to the population that should entail respect for their liberty of conscience, and accordingly this explains why government should accommodate this immunity by granting exemptions from the law when needed.

Notwithstanding the respect which is owed, I argue that the right to liberty of conscience is only one basic liberty among several of equal status. That equality of status results from their similar derivation from the Rawlsian moral powers of a capacity for a conception of the good and for a sense of justice. As a result, liberty of conscience is not absolute. Drawing on Rawls, in Chapter 3 I identify two bases for the defeat of a claim to liberty of conscience: that the exercise of liberty of conscience is incompatible with the basic liberty or liberties of others, in circumstances where the other basic liberty or liberties should be prioritised (*compatibility*), or that limitation of the exercise of liberty of conscience is necessary in the common interest (*necessity*). In contrast, a focus on neutrality, employed by some theorists and courts to assess claims of liberty of conscience, is eschewed in this book, as explained in Chapter 4.

I then turn to apply the theoretical work undertaken in the book to two case studies involving the limits of claims to liberty of conscience. The case studies focus on the law of the US and UK, and mirror the examples given above. One case study concerns the coronavirus pandemic and claims made on the basis of human rights and constitutional law against the enforcement of lockdown restrictions on places of worship. The other case study concerns discrimination towards same-sex couples on the basis of religious belief, in contravention of non-discrimination laws. The framework suggests that the claims to liberty of conscience in these case studies should generally fail on the basis of the rights of others or the common interest; judicial decisions suggesting otherwise fail to reflect the moral position in the theoretical framework.

The book's conclusion draws out three wider implications of the analysis. First, although the potential breadth of liberty of conscience represents the central problem that it raises for legal systems, this breadth also means that claims to liberty of conscience sometimes travel a long way outside the central range of application of the right, which offers a legitimate moral basis for their possible restriction in certain cases. Second, the rights of others are underappreciated in the case law of both the US and, to a lesser extent, the UK as an intuitive basis for limiting claims to

[8] See, eg, Darwall (n 3); Nussbaum, *Liberty of Conscience* (n 3); Adenitire, *A General Right to Conscientious Exemption* (n 3).

liberty of conscience – a deficiency that is highlighted by the framework developed in this book. Third, evaluation of the necessity of a law in the common interest is appropriate as an additional basis for limiting claims to liberty of conscience, though means-end scrutiny is a preferable test of this kind to structured proportionality.

The book has seven chapters. Chapters 2–4 develop my theory of liberty of conscience. Chapter 2 offers a rationale for liberty of conscience that serves as the starting point for the inquiry, drawing primarily on Rawls, who defended liberty of conscience as a basic liberty under his first principle of justice. Chapter 3 further develops this account by identifying the limitations that can apply to claims of liberty of conscience on the basis of the theoretical justification for the right – namely, limitations that are necessary in the common interest or to protect the rights of others. Chapter 4 critically analyses state neutrality to address its omission from the framework established in Chapters 2 and 3. Chapters 5 and 6 consider two case studies. The purpose of the case studies is to understand the limits of claims to liberty of conscience when they intersect with both other rights and the common interest. Chapter 5 explores the case study of restrictions on places of worship during the coronavirus (SARS-CoV-2) pandemic. Chapter 6 analyses the case study of discrimination towards same-sex couples. In both chapters, it is concluded that both the rights of others and the common interest are usually sufficient to defeat a claim to liberty of conscience in the circumstances. In Chapter 7, I conclude the book with some reflections about the analysis and its implications.

II. The Meaning of Liberty of Conscience

Expressed simply, the idea of liberty of conscience is that a person is free to believe conscientious beliefs and to practise, exercise or manifest (terms which I consider to be synonymous with each other) those beliefs. By being free to do so, I mean that the person is not prevented by the state from such belief, practice, exercise or manifestation.[9] In a similar vein to this understanding of liberty of conscience, Rawls offers a helpful definition of the concept in *A Theory of Justice*. He writes that, if we

> consider liberty of conscience as defined by law, then individuals have this basic liberty when they are free to pursue their moral, philosophical, or religious interests without legal restrictions requiring them to engage or not to engage in any particular form of religious or other practice, and when other men have a legal duty not to interfere.[10]

There are two distinct aspects to Rawls's definition: first, there is an absence of legal restrictions by the state (the 'absence of state restrictions aspect'); and second, there is a legal duty on others not to interfere (the 'duty of others aspect').

[9] Although there may be positive obligations on the state in respect of this right in some systems (such as a duty to facilitate religious freedom), I do not address that aspect of liberty of conscience in this book.

[10] Rawls, *A Theory of Justice (Revised Edition)* (n 2) 177.

As Rawls points out, '[a] rather intricate complex of rights and duties characterizes any particular basic liberty. Not only must it be permissible for individuals to do or not to do something, but government and other persons must have a legal duty not to obstruct'.[11] To understand the complex of rights and duties that make up liberty of conscience, it is helpful to consider it in terms of Wesley Newcomb Hohfeld's analysis of the nature of legal rights.[12]

A. Hohfeldian Description of the Right to Liberty of Conscience

In Hohfeld's scheme, there are four kinds of legal positions that may be called 'rights', each of which has a correlative legal position borne by a person.[13] First, there is a legal right (sometimes called a claim-right in the literature), which is correlated to a legal duty owed by a person in respect of that right. Second, there is a legal privilege (sometimes called a liberty, and which constitutes an absence of a legal duty), correlated to an absence of claim-right by a person (a no-right). Third, there is a legal power (an ability to change others' legal relations or one's own), correlated with a person's liability to such change. Fourth, there is a legal immunity (an insusceptibility to a legal power), correlated to a person's legal disability.

Despite the language that will be used throughout this book of 'liberty of conscience' – which is termed a 'basic liberty' by Rawls – liberty of conscience in its absence of state restrictions aspect is not strictly speaking a liberty or privilege in the Hohfeldian sense, because it does not consist merely in the absence of a duty. Certainly, there may be a privilege or liberty consisting in the absence of any conflicting legally imposed duties relating to conscientious belief. However, when we invoke liberty of conscience in law we are primarily referring to a Hohfeldian immunity: an insusceptibility to a legal power or, put in negative terms, the negation of a liability that might otherwise be borne by a person. Specifically, it is an immunity from action by the legislature or the executive government of a state to alter one's legal position in respect of liberty of conscience, for example, by creating a duty inconsistent with one's religious beliefs. Matthew Kramer puts this point as follows:

> Most (though not all) of the entitlements conferred by so-called bills of rights are in fact [Hohfeldian] immunities. For example, the First Amendment to the US Constitution protects various legal liberties by disabling Congress from restricting or removing those

[11] ibid 177–78.

[12] See WN Hohfeld, 'Some Fundamental Legal Conceptions as Applied in Judicial Reasoning' (1913) 23 *Yale Law Journal* 16; WN Hohfeld, 'Fundamental Legal Conceptions as Applied in Judicial Reasoning' (1917) 26 *Yale Law Journal* 710. For commentary and interpretation of Hohfeld's analysis of legal rights, see MH Kramer et al, *A Debate over Rights: Philosophical Enquiries* (Oxford: Oxford University Press 2000); MH Kramer, 'Rights in Legal and Political Philosophy' in GA Caldeira et al (eds), *The Oxford Handbook of Law and Politics* (Oxford: Oxford University Press, 2008).

[13] Hohfeld, 'Fundamental Legal Conceptions as Applied in Judicial Reasoning' (n 12) 710.

> liberties. Under that constitutional amendment, each person in the United States enjoys an immunity vis-à-vis Congress concerning liberties such as freedom of speech, freedom of assembly, free exercise of religion, and so forth.[14]

However, in the duty of others aspect of liberty of conscience that is identified by Rawls, liberty of conscience also entails claim-rights to prevent others from interfering with the right. Moreover, it is possible that there are further immunities associated with these claim-rights to prevent their removal, as Kramer suggests:

> if John has a legal right against being punched in the face by Jim, and if he has no immunities against being divested of that right through countless elementary means (for example, through Jim's looking at him or through Jim's utterance of any word in his presence), then John's right is hollowly nominal rather than genuine.[15]

Although there is no doubt that both aspects are important to liberty of conscience, in this book, I focus on the first of the aspects: the immunity in respect of lawmaking or executive government action (correlated with a state disability).

Accordingly, a claim to liberty of conscience is a claim by a person to immunity for an action or inaction on the basis of that person's beliefs of conscience. For the purposes of the theoretical analysis in this book, a successful claim entails the non-application or non-enforcement of a law that interferes with conscience, rather than a positive duty by the state to facilitate the exercise of liberty of conscience. An action that is sought to be protected might be, for example, attending a place of worship; the term is also taken to include the holding of a belief. An inaction might be a refusal to act – for example, refusing to serve in the military on religious grounds. The term *law* is used broadly to include both legislative and executive measures, such as restrictions (up to and including outright prohibitions) on the action sought to be taken, as well as compulsions to act in particular ways in respect of which the beliefs might instead dictate to the believer *not* to act in that way (inaction).

B. The Nature of Conscientious Belief

This definition raises an issue about the nature of conscientious belief. Although not a key focus of the book, which is primarily addressed to religious rather than secular belief, the theoretical framework that I develop does not distinguish between

[14] Kramer, 'Rights in Legal and Political Philosophy' (n 12) 417. The analysis becomes more complicated in a system like the UK's, where the Human Rights Act 1998 does not invalidate primary legislation that violates human rights; hence, the UK Parliament is not, strictly speaking, 'disabled' from legislating contrary to rights. However, a declaration of incompatibility issued under s 4 of the Human Rights Act 1998 indicates an Act of Parliament's incompatibility with a right in the European Convention on Human Rights (as set out in Sch 1 to the 1998 Act), while s 6 limits the ability of the executive government (and other public authorities) to act incompatibly with Convention rights: see generally A Kavanagh, 'What's So Weak about "Weak-Form Review"? The Case of the UK Human Rights Act 1998' (2015) 13 *International Journal of Constitutional Law* 1008.

[15] ibid.

religious belief and certain kinds of secular beliefs that are similar to it in nature. As John Adenitire puts it, this right 'should be equally available to those who object [to an obligation imposed by law] on the basis of religious and non-religious conscientious beliefs' – in other words, it 'should not be a privilege of religious believers'.[16] As a rough guide to the kinds of secular beliefs that I refer to as falling within the concept of conscientious belief, I adopt Rawls's concept of a comprehensive doctrine. In *Political Liberalism*, Rawls defines a comprehensive doctrine as follows:

> A moral conception is general if it applies to a wide range of subjects, and in the limit to all subjects universally. It is comprehensive when it includes conceptions of what is of value in human life, and ideals of personal character, as well as ideals of friendship and of familial and associational relationships, and much else that is to inform our conduct, and in the limit to our life as a whole. A conception is fully comprehensive if it covers all recognized values and virtues within one rather precisely articulated system; whereas a conception is only partially comprehensive when it comprises a number of, but by no means all, nonpolitical values and virtues and is rather loosely articulated. Many religious and philosophical doctrines aspire to be both general and comprehensive.[17]

As Rawls makes clear, comprehensive doctrines may include both religious and other philosophical doctrines that are not religious in nature. In the same way, my theoretical argument for protecting liberty of conscience will turn out to be the same for both religious belief and certain kinds of non-religious beliefs. Further, I reflect this inclusiveness by referring to the right as liberty of conscience, which I use as a wider term that includes freedom in respect of both religion and other conscientious beliefs. When I seek to be specific about religious freedom only, I use that term, as happens from time to time in the book, but otherwise, I refer to the right as liberty of conscience. Use of the term 'conscience' also aligns my analysis with that of Rawls, who consistently refers to this right as liberty of conscience, as well as others such as Adenitire and Martha Nussbaum.[18]

C. Liberty of Conscience Distinguished from Non-Discrimination

In defining liberty of conscience, it is important to make clear that it is to be distinguished from other legal requirements that also concern religion, including prohibitions of discrimination on the basis of conscientious belief (including religious belief). Tarunabh Khaitan and Jane Norton write that religious freedom

[16] Adenitire, *A General Right to Conscientious Exemption* (n 3) 2–3.

[17] Rawls, *Political Liberalism* (n 2) 13.

[18] See Nussbaum, *Liberty of Conscience* (n 3); Adenitire, *A General Right to Conscientious Exemption* (n 3). In the academic literature, the term 'freedom of religion or belief', usually abbreviated to 'FORB', is often used as well: see, eg, F Raza, 'Limitations to the Right to Religious Freedom: Rethinking Key Approaches' (2020) 9 *Oxford Journal of Law and Religion* 435. Personally, I prefer not to use this term as the language of freedom of 'belief' could be read to imply *forum internum* (even if that is often not what is meant by the term).

and non-discrimination on the basis of religious belief 'are often conflated' but 'the right to freedom of religion and the right against religious discrimination are in fact distinct human rights'.[19] It seems apparent that they are separate rights. As Rawls's own definition of liberty of conscience makes clear, this right does not contain any concept of non-discrimination. (Rawls notes that there may be a duty on private persons under liberty of conscience not to 'obstruct' the exercise of the right, but he makes no suggestion that there is a duty of non-discrimination as part of this.) There are several differences between the rights of liberty of conscience and non-discrimination. The former, in its primary aspect, creates a disability on the part of the state, while the latter a duty owed by private persons in various contexts. In addition to affecting different actors, the two rights are different in nature. Non-discrimination involves a claim-right to particular treatment by others, as distinct from the immunity entailed by liberty of conscience.

This difference is legally obvious as well. In the UK, non-discrimination on the basis of religion or belief is provided for nationally by the Equality Act 2010.[20] In the US, religious discrimination is prohibited by the Civil Rights Act of 1964,[21] as well as similar state and local laws. In contrast, liberty of conscience or religious freedom is provided for by different instruments: the Human Rights Act 1998 in the case of the UK, and the First Amendment to the US Constitution and various statutes, such as the Religious Freedom Restoration Act of 1993 and the Religious Land Use and Institutionalized Persons Act of 2000, and similar State and local laws, in the case of the US.[22] As these are rights primarily affecting different actors, different in nature, and provided for by different legal instruments, it is correct to say they should not be conflated. For an abundance of clarity, this book focuses on liberty of conscience, not the right to non-discrimination on the basis of conscientious or religious belief. Although there may be links between liberty of conscience and non-discrimination on the grounds of religion or belief, the concepts can be analysed separately. The right to non-discrimination on the grounds of religion or belief falls outside the scope of the book.[23]

[19] T Khaitan and JC Norton, 'The Right to Freedom of Religion and the Right against Religious Discrimination: Theoretical Distinctions' (2019) 17 *International Journal of Constitutional Law* 1125, 1125.

[20] Equality Act 2010, ss 4, 10.

[21] Civil Rights Act of 1964 tit VII, addressing employment discrimination.

[22] See Adenitire, *A General Right to Conscientious Exemption* (n 3) 20, 176.

[23] That is not to say that, although these rights are distinct, they cannot share a similar underlying normative foundation. For example, for an argument that both rights are justified by 'the moral right to ethical independence': see I Trispiotis, 'Religious Freedom and Religious Antidiscrimination' (2019) 82 *Modern Law Review* 864, 865. In this book, I offer distinct rationales for non-discrimination and liberty of conscience, though there is a significant overlap: they are both supported, albeit in different ways, by recognition respect for moral personality. Whereas my account of liberty of conscience is set out in Chapter 2, the conceptual basis of non-discrimination is discussed in Chapter 6, primarily in respect of sexual orientation, in order to lay groundwork for the case study involving the interaction of rights to non-discrimination and liberty of conscience. Under the account that is offered, a basic liberty of non-discrimination is supported by recognition respect for the individual, drawing on Benjamin Eidelson's respect-based account: see B Eidelson, *Discrimination and Disrespect* (Oxford: Oxford University Press, 2015).

III. Protection of Liberty of Conscience in UK and US Law

In the UK, liberty of conscience is protected by Article 9 of the European Convention on Human Rights, as incorporated into domestic law by Schedule 1 to the Human Rights Act 1998.[24] (Another possible basis of protection specific to Scotland is the independence of the Church of Scotland, which is said to create a separation between civil and spiritual authority, though the scope of this protection remains unclear.[25]) Article 9(1) of the European Convention provides as follows:

> Everyone has the right to freedom of thought, conscience and religion; this right includes freedom to change his religion or belief and freedom, either alone or in community with others and in public or private, to manifest his religion or belief, in worship, teaching, practice and observance.

The protection of internal belief (*forum internum*) under the European Convention on Human Rights is absolute,[26] but the protection for manifestation of religion or beliefs (*forum externum*) is qualified and can be limited pursuant to Article 9(2).

Article 9(2) provides as follows:

> Freedom to manifest one's religion or beliefs shall be subject only to such limitations as are prescribed by law and are necessary in a democratic society in the interests of public safety, for the protection of public order, health or morals, or for the protection of the rights and freedoms of others.

For a belief to be protected, it must 'attain a certain level of cogency, seriousness, cohesion and importance'.[27] Further, in order to protect the manifestation of a belief, 'the existence of a sufficiently close and direct nexus between the act and the underlying belief must be determined on the facts of each case. In particular, there is no requirement on the applicant to establish that he or she acted in fulfilment of a duty mandated by the religion in question'.[28] A limitation on manifestation

[24] Section 13 of the Human Rights Act 1998 also requires that a court 'must have particular regard to the importance' of Art 9 if its determination of any question arising under the Human Rights Act 'might affect the exercise by a religious organisation (itself or its members collectively) of the Convention right'. As David Feldman points out, '[i]t is not clear what [the provision] means', though 'the same formulation appears in s 12 of the Act in relation to freedom of expression', and it 'seems likely to mean that Article 9 must be very carefully considered and given great weight when interpreting legislation and scrutinizing the legality of administrative action, but not that it should necessarily have greater weight than other Convention rights if they conflict': D Feldman, 'Rights to Life, Physical and Moral Integrity, Freedom of Lifestyle and Religion or Belief' in D Feldman (ed), *English Public Law*, 2nd edn (Oxford: Oxford University Press, 2009) 417.

[25] See generally *Percy v Board of National Mission of the Church of Scotland* [2006] 2 AC 28 (United Kingdom House of Lords). An issue related to this separation arose in a challenge to coronavirus restrictions in Scotland in *Philip* (n 4). As such, it is briefly referred to in Chapter 5.

[26] See *Ivanova v Bulgaria* (2008) 47 EHRR 54 (European Court of Human Rights).

[27] See *Campbell and Cosans v United Kingdom* (1982) 4 EHRR 293 (European Court of Human Rights) [36].

[28] See *Eweida v United Kingdom* (2013) 57 EHRR 8 (European Court of Human Rights) [82].

of religion or beliefs must meet three requirements: it must be prescribed by law; it must have a legitimate aim from among those listed in Article 9(2) (or at least linked to them[29]); and it must be necessary in a democratic society for that aim (a requirement that has been interpreted as requiring an assessment of proportionality).

In US law, liberty of conscience is protected under the US Constitution by the First Amendment. It relevantly provides as follows: 'Congress shall make no law respecting an establishment of religion, or prohibiting the free exercise thereof'. These two clauses are known as the Establishment Clause and the Free Exercise Clause respectively (and together, as the Religion Clauses). In addition to the federal constitutional protection (which also applies at State level due to incorporation through the Due Process Clause of the Fourteenth Amendment[30]), there are protections for religious freedom in many State constitutions.[31] There is also, as noted above, additional statutory protection for religious freedom, through the Religious Freedom Restoration Act and the Religious Land Use and Institutionalized Persons Act at the federal level,[32] and similar State level Religious Freedom Restoration Acts.[33] The test under the First Amendment is different from that of the European Court: courts inquire into whether the law burdening religious exercise is neutral and of general applicability.[34] If it is, then it is constitutionally valid. If it is not, then the law must survive strict scrutiny by being shown to be narrowly tailored to a compelling state interest.[35]

[29] See *SAS v France* (2015) 60 EHRR 11 (European Court of Human Rights) [113].

[30] See *Hamilton v Regents of the University of California* (1934) 293 US 245 (Supreme Court of the United States); *Cantwell v Connecticut* (1940) 310 US 296 (Supreme Court of the United States).

[31] See PB Linton, 'Religious Freedom Claims and Defenses under State Constitutions' (2013) 7 *University of St Thomas Journal of Law and Public Policy* 103.

[32] The Religious Freedom Restoration Act was enacted to provide broader protection to religious freedom than under the First Amendment, after the interpretation of the Free Exercise Clause of that Amendment was narrowed by the US Supreme Court in *Employment Division v Smith* (n 7). Subsequently, the Religious Land Use and Institutionalized Persons Act, which imposes certain religious-freedom-related conditions in respect of prisoners and land use upon the receipt of federal funding by other levels of government, was enacted after the US Supreme Court struck down the Religious Freedom Restoration Act in its application to State and local governments in *City of Boerne v Flores* (1997) 521 US 507 (Supreme Court of the United States). For further background on this legislation, see generally D Laycock, 'The Religious Freedom Restoration Act' [1993] *Brigham Young University Law Review* 221; MA Hamilton, 'Federalism and the Public Good: The True Story behind the Religious Land Use and Institutionalized Persons Act' (2003) 78 *Indiana Law* Journal 311.

[33] See D Bridge, 'Religious Freedom or Libertarianism: What Explains State Enactments of Religious Freedom Restoration Act Laws?' (2014) 56 *Journal of Church and State* 347.

[34] See *Employment Division v Smith* (n 7). The merits of this test, focusing on its neutrality aspect, are considered in some detail in Chapter 4 below.

[35] *Church of the Lukumi Babalu Aye v City of Hialeah* (1993) 508 US 520 (Supreme Court of the United States) 546–47. Some wrinkles have been added to this test by recent case law, addressed in Chapters 4 and 7. In addition to these protections, the US Supreme Court's doctrine of 'church autonomy', addressing the 'autonomous management of a religious organization's internal affairs', may be a further source of protection for religious freedom, though it is not addressed in this book: see generally D Laycock, 'Church Autonomy Revisited' (2009) 7 *Georgetown Journal of Law and Public Policy* 253, 254.

A significant potential difference between the UK and US law concerns the protection of secular beliefs. As the European Court of Human Rights explained in *Kokkinakis v Greece*, Article 9's protection extends to secular beliefs: it is,

> in its religious dimension, one of the most vital elements that go to make up the identity of believers and their conception of life, but it is also a precious asset for atheists, agnostics, sceptics and the unconcerned. The pluralism indissociable from a democratic society, which has been dearly won over the centuries, depends on it.[36]

The US protections are usually interpreted as extending only to the protection of religious belief,[37] however that is not a consensus view, and Adenitire for example argues that they should be interpreted as applying to secular beliefs as well (following the reasoning of the decision of the US Supreme Court in case of *Welsh v United States*, in which a statutory conscientious objection provision in compulsory military service legislation was interpreted as extending to non-religious objections).[38]

IV. Methods

The book adopts two distinct methods. In Chapters 2–4, the analysis is primarily theoretical and philosophical. It draws on, in substantial part, philosophical and secondary legal analysis of liberty of conscience, as well as case law. In the ongoing debate about whether human rights require any kind of philosophical foundation, as opposed to it being sufficient that they are a political reality,[39] I do seek to establish such a foundation in relation to liberty of conscience, despite the difficulties inherent to such projects. Relying on human rights as a political achievement without offering theoretical arguments to defend that achievement carries the risk of reversal, particularly if opponents of the protection of particular (or all) human rights do offer such arguments, and manage to persuade others to agree with them.

In this book, I focus on the law of the UK and US. However, in the course of the analysis about the theoretical foundations of the right to liberty of conscience (Chapters 2, 3 and 4), I also make reference to the constitutions and judicial decisions of various other jurisdictions, in order to explore the theoretical issues in an appropriately informed way. Since these examples are only used to illustrate possible approaches and considerations, not to establish any wider conclusions about, say, the frequency of adoption of particular legal practices at a global level,

[36] *Kokkinakis v Greece* (1994) 17 EHRR 397 (European Court of Human Rights) [31].

[37] See, eg, KA Brady, *The Distinctiveness of Religion in American Law: Rethinking Religion Clause Jurisprudence* (Cambridge: Cambridge University Press, 2015).

[38] Adenitire, *A General Right to Conscientious Exemption* (n 3) Ch 3. See *Welsh v United States* (1970) 398 US 333 (Supreme Court of the United States).

[39] See generally the debate in R Cruft et al (eds), *Philosophical Foundations of Human Rights* (Oxford: Oxford University Press, 2015). See also R Rorty, 'Human Rights, Rationality, and Sentimentality' (1998) 318 *Headline Series* 116.

I do not consider that it is necessary to confine myself to any particular jurisdictions in these chapters.

In the case studies of Chapters 5 and 6 in which there is comparative and doctrinal analysis, I am stricter with research methods and restrict myself to the case law of the US and UK as comparator systems. In recent years there has been a discussion of methods in comparative constitutional law, pioneered by scholars such as Ran Hirschl, who has placed an emphasis on explaining and justifying the choice of comparator jurisdictions, at least when certain general conclusions are sought to be drawn.[40] Hirschl identifies what he calls a 'World Series' syndrome of comparative constitutional law, which he defines as

> the pretense that insights based on the constitutional experience of a small set of 'usual suspect' settings – all prosperous, stable constitutional democracies of the 'global north' – are truly representative of the wide variety of constitutional experiences worldwide, and constitute a 'gold standard' for understanding and assessing it. The question here is this: how truly 'comparative' or generalizable is a body of knowledge that seldom draws on or refers to the constitutional experience, law, and institutions of the global south? What are we to make of supposedly universal insights that are constructed by focusing mainly (and often solely) on a very small fraction of the world's constitutions?[41]

It seems correct that some care is required with generalising based on small numbers of comparator jurisdictions. Although overly general claims are to be avoided in the absence of suitably broad studies, what can safely be done even in comparisons of small numbers of jurisdictions is to identify potential tendencies, possibilities, or (in the view of the author) normatively desirable practices. Moreover, although I consider that a desire to emulate the research methods of the social sciences can sometimes be misplaced in this field, and indeed contrary to the legal method, it works well for this project at least to carefully select the jurisdictions in the case studies in Chapters 5 and 6. These jurisdictions are similar enough to make comparison feasible – both common law systems with rights protection that experienced the coronavirus pandemic and have had issues relating to discrimination towards same-sex couples – but are different enough to make comparison worthwhile.

The comparison between the two jurisdictions of the UK and US is functionalist, in the sense that although the approach to human rights protection differs between the two systems, there are legal provisions that play a comparable role in their respective systems, and this similar function can be compared. As Ralf Michaels explains it, functionalist comparative law

> focuses not on rules alone but on their effects, not on doctrinal structures and arguments alone but on the consequences they bring about. Therefore, its objects are often

[40] See R Hirschl, *Comparative Matters: The Renaissance of Comparative Constitutional Law* (Oxford: Oxford University Press, 2014) Chs 5, 6.

[41] ibid 192–93.

judicial decisions as responses to real life situations, and legal systems are compared by considering their various judicial responses to similar situations.[42]

In a similar way, Vicki Jackson describes this approach as follows:

> Perhaps the dominant method of comparative analysis, in constitutional law, as in other fields of law, is functionalist. The scholar may identify an institution that exists in multiple constitutional systems and explore its function(s); or the scholar may identify one or more functions performed by constitutions or constitutional institutions or doctrines in some societies, and analyze whether in fact the constitutional institution or doctrine believed to perform a valid function does so, or may analyze whether and how that function is performed elsewhere.[43]

The function that is addressed in this book, across jurisdictions, is the protection of liberty of conscience. As has been outlined above, in the US, this right is protected at the federal level by the Free Exercise Clause of the First Amendment to the US Constitution, as well as by some statutes, which are not considered in the book. In the UK, the most relevant source of protection is Article 9 of the European Convention on Human Rights, as incorporated into Schedule 1 to the Human Rights Act 1998. Although these instruments do not work in exactly the same way – in particular, courts have the power to strike down primary legislation under the US Constitution but not under the UK Human Rights Act – they are nonetheless broadly comparable, as they perform the same function within their respective systems.

The analysis in Chapters 5 and 6 is not purely doctrinal and comparative, and retains a theoretical dimension, because I apply the theoretical framework established earlier in the book, and in particular in Chapter 3, in order to understand and analyse the two case studies. In that sense the book project is interdisciplinary as philosophical and theoretical analysis informing the preferable moral position in respect of the right to liberty of conscience is applied to assess the legal position. However, I also seek to engage in sound legal doctrinal analysis in these chapters, and to assess judicial reasoning against the legal standards adopted in the US and UK, while critiquing these standards against the moral position reflected in the framework. The framework's concepts of compatibility and necessity are used to guide the analysis, but do not operate to the exclusion of doctrinal legal analysis.

It might be asked: why is the moral position relevant, and does this indicate (perhaps implicitly) an anti-positivist commitment?[44] In placing an emphasis on moral rights, I do not make any commitment as to whether law needs to reflect the

[42] R Michaels, 'The Functional Method of Comparative Law' in M Reimann and R Zimmerman (eds), *The Oxford Handbook of Comparative Law*, 2nd edn (Oxford: Oxford University Press, 2019) 347–48.

[43] VC Jackson, 'Comparative Constitutional Law: Methodologies' in M Rosenfeld and A Sajó (eds), *The Oxford Handbook of Comparative Constitutional Law* (Oxford: Oxford University Press, 2012) 62–63.

[44] See generally H Dindjer, 'The New Legal Anti-Positivism' (2020) 26 *Legal Theory* 181. For the contours of this long-running debate in legal theory, see R Dworkin, *Law's Empire* (Cambridge, MA: Harvard University Press, 1986); MH Kramer, *In Defense of Legal Positivism: Law without Trimmings* (Oxford: Oxford University Press, 2003); HLA Hart, *The Concept of Law*, 3rd edn (Oxford: Oxford University Press, 2012); R Dworkin, *Justice for Hedgehogs* (Cambridge, MA: Harvard University Press, 2013).

moral position in order to be valid law. I explore the moral position on the basis that the legal position should generally follow the moral position as a matter of legal policy. Law is open to possible criticism when it fails to reflect morality, and positivism is in no way inconsistent with such criticism; even if morally unsound law remains law, it does not mean that we should hold our tongues about it. In particular, I consider that the findings and reasoning of the US Supreme Court in some recent cases prove questionable when studied with the framework, while the decisions of the UK Supreme Court fare better.

In formulating a general theoretical approach, Chapters 2, 3 and 4 of the book may face the possible objection that they are insensitive to cultural differences. Although the framework operates as a kind of ideal position that is analytically useful as a starting point, I do not exclude the possibility that cultural issues might modify matters in respect of any particular legal system. In relation to the case studies in Chapters 5 and 6, it assists the comparison that the US and UK are not wildly dissimilar systems, although there are obviously some differences, including in legal and constitutional culture.[45] The similarities between them help to enable comparative analysis to take place, while the differences help to bring issues in each system into focus.

Further, although I focus on the criterion of moral personality (specifically, the exercise and development of the moral powers) in establishing the theoretical basis for basic liberties, this does not imply the view that there has to be only one basis for human rights. I acknowledge that it is possible that the liberties that we regard as basic may be justified on different bases. For example, John Tasioulas suggests that the right not to be tortured need not be justified by the fact that torture would impair agency, but rather may be explained on a more direct and intuitive basis.[46] Although the possibility of other moral bases for human rights is acknowledged, the basic liberties that I focus on in this book can in fact be justified by reference to the moral powers.

Finally, in approaching the US case law, I am aware of the possible objection that due to concerns about its politicisation (including a famously ideologically-driven appointments process) and excesses of judicial creativity on both ends of the political spectrum, dating back at least to *Lochner v New York* in 1905,[47] the US Supreme Court is not a court,[48] or, expressed more cautiously, at least not a

[45] On the relevance of context in comparative constitutional analysis, see M Tushnet, 'Some Reflections on Method in Comparative Constitutional Law' in S Choudhry (ed), *The Migration of Constitutional Ideas* (Cambridge: Cambridge University Press, 2007). See also D Kenny, 'Examining Constitutional Culture: Assisted Suicide in Ireland and Canada' (2022) 17 *Journal of Comparative Law* 85; J García Oliva and H Hall, *Constitutional Culture, Independence, and Rights: Insights from Quebec, Scotland, and Catalonia* (Toronto: University of Toronto Press, 2023).

[46] J Tasioulas, 'Human Rights, Universality and the Values of Personhood: Retracting Griffin's Steps' (2002) 10 *European Journal of Philosophy* 79, 93. See also MH Kramer, *Torture and Moral Integrity: A Philosophical Enquiry* (Oxford: Oxford University Press, 2014).

[47] (1905) 198 US 45 (Supreme Court of the United States).

[48] See, eg, B Leiter, 'Constitutional Law, Moral Judgment, and the Supreme Court as Super-Legislature' (2015) 66 *Hastings Law Journal* 1601; EJ Segall, *Supreme Myths: Why the Supreme Court Is Not a Court and Its Justices Are Not Judges* (Westport, CT: Praeger, 2012).

well-functioning one according to the usual norms of a court. However, by taking the US Supreme Court seriously, we can better understand the problems with some of its decisions. Moreover, as will be seen, some of the US Supreme Court's earlier decisions on religious freedom, especially from the 1960s to the 1980s, do reflect a more principled and reasonable approach to the issue of liberty of conscience that could conceivably be rediscovered.[49]

[49] See, eg, *Sherbert v Verner* (1963) 374 US 398 (Supreme Court of the United States); *Wisconsin v Yoder* (1972) 406 US 205 (Supreme Court of the United States).

2

The Rationale of Liberty of Conscience

Liberty of conscience has long been a contentious idea. In the past, it was often thought socially harmonious for the members of a society to share the same beliefs, eschewing the diversity of belief permitted by liberty of conscience.[1] For example, John Cotton, an influential religious leader in seventeenth century Massachusetts, 'wrote copiously in defense of religious persecution, arguing that it was necessary for civil order'.[2] In pluralistic societies, freedom of belief is more likely to be widely accepted, but people may still take issue with liberty of conscience when it extends to the protection of the manifestation of a belief. This contentiousness seems only to be increasing as claims to liberty of conscience on the basis of religious belief clash with various social policies, ranging from public health measures during the coronavirus pandemic to the rights of same-sex couples to non-discrimination.[3]

The focus of this chapter is on the justification for liberty of conscience. Nelson Tebbe observes that

> [s]ome skeptics … argue that a convincing theory of religious freedom is impossible. After all, a central aim of such theories is to account for particular outcomes in a way that makes sense across a range of cases. But deep discontinuities frustrate that effort, and necessarily so. According to these thinkers, then, no theory of religious freedom is attainable.[4] (emphasis removed)

I do not share the view of the sceptics. Indeed, I consider that Rawls came close to offering a satisfactory account of liberty of conscience decades ago, and his explanation requires only some further refinement, supplementation and development in order to serve as a basis for understanding why states should protect liberty of conscience.[5]

[1] See the discussion of historical approaches to liberty of conscience in MC Nussbaum, *Liberty of Conscience: In Defense of America's Tradition of Religious Equality* (New York: Basic Books, 2008) Ch 2.

[2] ibid 38. Nussbaum describes how, in the context of early colonial North America, others opposed religious persecution, such as Roger Williams.

[3] See, eg, G Baldwin, 'The Coronavirus Pandemic and Religious Freedom: Judicial Decisions in the United States and United Kingdom' (2021) 26 *Judicial Review* 297.

[4] N Tebbe, *Religious Freedom in an Egalitarian Age* (Cambridge, MA: Harvard University Press, 2017) 37.

[5] Although I draw on some Rawlsian ideas, such as moral personality and the basic liberties, I do not make recourse to others, such as public reason, overlapping consensus and reflective equilibrium, in order to understand liberty of conscience. For an analysis of the potential relevance of public reason to religious freedom questions, see M Hunter-Henin, *Why Religious Freedom Matters for Democracy: Comparative Reflections from Britain and France for a Democratic 'Vivre Ensemble'* (Oxford: Hart Publishing, 2020) Ch 4. As noted below, I also do not make use of the original position or veil of ignorance, which are not necessary for my approach.

The account set out in this chapter and Chapters 3 and 4 can, I contend, be usefully addressed to a range of possible cases, as I seek to do in Chapters 5 and 6 of the book.

Drawing on Rawls's concept of the moral powers, I argue that recognition respect for moral personality entails protection for liberty of conscience. This notion of moral personality is an under-explored potential basis for a rationale for liberty of conscience: it is a thinner concept than some accounts of autonomy (perhaps the most commonly deployed normative basis for the right),[6] and the account also differs from those that invoke, for example, state neutrality[7] or group rights[8] as the basis for protecting liberty of conscience. Some possible objections to this understanding of the need to protect liberty of conscience – that it protects what is merely a 'choice', that it extends to potentially disruptive manifestations of belief, and that religion may be 'intolerant' – are considered and rejected.

The chapter is structured as follows. In Section I, I consider some possible arguments for liberty of conscience in order to explain their shortcomings. In Section II, I outline an argument for the protection of liberty of conscience utilising the concepts of moral personality and recognition respect. The concept of moral personality involves being able to pursue the exercise and development of certain moral powers. I argue that moral personality remains a compelling notion even without relying on the social contract aspect of Rawls's theory. In Section III, I consider some possible objections to the protection of liberty of conscience. Section IV concludes the chapter.

I. Possible Arguments for Liberty of Conscience

Perhaps the most common argument for liberty of conscience is autonomy.[9] However, autonomy-based accounts have an obvious difficulty, since, as Michael Sandel points out, 'not all religious beliefs can be redescribed without loss as "the product of free and voluntary choice by the faithful"'.[10] Similarly, John Locke observes in *A Letter Concerning Toleration* that 'it is absurd that things should be enjoined by laws which are not in men's power to perform', and 'to believe

[6] See, eg, JC Norton, *Freedom of Religious Organizations* (Oxford: Oxford University Press, 2016) 14–15; K Greenawalt, *Religion and the Constitution: Free Exercise and Fairness* (Princeton, NJ: Princeton University Press, 2006) 3–4; T Khaitan and JC Norton, 'The Right to Freedom of Religion and the Right against Religious Discrimination: Theoretical Distinctions' (2019) 17 *International Journal of Constitutional Law* 1125, 1139–40; MJ Sandel, 'Religious Liberty – Freedom of Conscience or Freedom of Choice?' [1989] *Utah Law Review* 597, 611.

[7] See, eg, J Adenitire, *A General Right to Conscientious Exemption: Beyond Religious Privilege* (Cambridge: Cambridge University Press, 2020) Ch 1.

[8] See, eg, R Moon, 'Conscience in the Image of Religion' in J Adenitire (ed), *Religious Beliefs and Conscientious Exemptions in a Liberal State* (Oxford: Hart Publishing, 2019).

[9] Related to this are self-determination-based accounts: see, eg, A Patten, 'Religious Exemptions and Fairness' in C Laborde and A Bardon (eds), *Religion in Liberal Political Philosophy* (Oxford: Oxford University Press, 2017) 207–209.

[10] Sandel (n 6) 610.

this or that to be true, does not depend upon our will'.[11] In a related vein, Farrah Ahmed criticises autonomy-based justifications for religious freedom on the basis that religious choices may not meet the standard expected of autonomous choice under many understandings of autonomy. Ahmed explains that 'autonomy generally refers to the ideal of controlling, creating, authoring or shaping one's own life'.[12] She argues that

> while autonomy is an attractive rationale [for religious freedom], it does not count in favour of the full range of protection currently offered by the right in liberal states. This is because there are tensions between autonomy on one hand, and religious belief, practice and proselytism on the other. … The first tension stems from the resistance of some religious beliefs to revision. The second stems from the manipulative nature of some modes of religious proselytism. … [A]s a result of these tensions, the legal protection offered to religious freedom does not always enhance, and may even diminish, autonomy. Therefore autonomy on its own does not support or count in favour of the protection currently offered to religious beliefs, practices and proselytism by the right to religious freedom. In particular, autonomy cannot support the protection currently offered to some religious beliefs which are resistant to revision, and to certain types of manipulative proselytism.[13]

Likewise, David Feldman describes the tension that may exist between autonomy and religious freedom as stemming from the hierarchical nature of organised religion, the tendency for people to adopt their family's religion, the sometimes-manipulative methods of proselytism, and the difficulties involved with leaving religious groups:

> The most successful religions tend to be organized hierarchically, with a system in which authoritative rule-makers set the parameters of permissible beliefs and practices, and enforce them by imposing discipline on their followers. This compromises the quality of autonomy which is at the heart of classical human rights. To this extent, freedom of religion is often at odds with freedom of belief: allying one's self to an organized religion involves surrendering one's freedom of belief to the whim or judgement of the religious authorities. … The fact that those who adhere to religious groups have limited autonomy in matters of belief might not particularly matter if everyone under a religious authority had subjected himself or herself voluntarily to it. However, a person forced to accept a religion because his or her parents follow it may never be given the opportunity to experience opportunities for free thought and belief. … Even the apparently free acceptance of a religion by a convert may be questionable, if the conversion was the result of persuasion and proselytism (which may often shade into emotional bullying) rather than personal investigation, free thought, and free choice. Where a religion allows people to depart from its beliefs or to leave a religious group without penalty, they can at least change their religious adherence in the exercise of their freedom (although it may take immense courage and lead to serious social disadvantages),

[11] J Locke, *First Letter Concerning Toleration* (William Popple tr, 1689) 30.

[12] F Ahmed, 'The Autonomy Rationale for Religious Freedom' (2017) 80 *Modern Law Review* 238, 239.

[13] ibid.

> but some religious groups actively seek to prevent people from exercising that freedom, or inflict social damage on those who succeed in exercising it.[14]

Due to these considerations, it is difficult to square religious belief with the notion of autonomous choice – indeed, religious belief may in fact be thought sometimes to impair such autonomous choice. This may be a particular problem for reliance on 'thicker' conceptions of autonomy, such as that espoused by Joseph Raz; Raz's understanding of autonomy has conditions of sufficient mental abilities (including rationality), adequate options, and independence from others.[15] (Although it might be suggested that 'thinner' understandings of autonomy can justify liberty of conscience, such thinner accounts of autonomy may be open to objection about whether they have moral value if they are shorn of Raz's conditions.) As will be developed below, the account in this book does not rely on autonomy. Rather, I suggest that religious and other conscientious belief can be useful for the exercise and development of Rawls's moral powers in a way that justifies the protection of liberty of conscience even if such belief is not a matter of autonomous choice.

Other accounts identify the value of toleration in protecting the peace of the community. For example, Locke observes that whereas anyone can persuade and 'draw [others] into truth', the magistrate can 'compel with the sword'; but religious belief has to be 'thoroughly believed', rather than compelled.[16] Moreover, compulsion in this context can sow a 'seed of discord and war' and 'endless hatreds, rapines, and slaughters'.[17] Locke adds that '[i]n private domestic affairs, in the management of estates, in the conservation of bodily health, every man may consider what suits his own convenience and follow what course he likes best', and the same applies to religious belief.[18] Calling for a duty of toleration, he claims that, in addition to refraining from violence and persecution of different faiths, a religious leader

> is obliged also to admonish his hearers of the duties of peace and goodwill towards all men, as well towards the erroneous as the orthodox; towards those that differ from them in faith and worship as well as towards those that agree with them therein. And he ought industriously to exhort all men, whether private persons or magistrates (if any such there be in his church), to charity, meekness, and toleration, and diligently endeavour to ally and temper all that heat and unreasonable averseness of mind which either any man's fiery zeal for his own sect or the craft of others has kindled against dissenters.[19]

Although Locke is undoubtedly correct that problems may often ensue from failing to tolerate other faiths, it is at least theoretically possible that highly efficient state repression could suppress religious minorities without violence ensuing. Locke is right that such coercion is unlikely to lead to genuine belief, but a tyrant

[14] D Feldman, 'Public Law and Freedom of Religion: General Conclusions' (2005) 17 *European Review of Public Law* 735, 739–41.

[15] See J Raz, *The Morality of Freedom* (Oxford: Oxford University Press, 1986) 372–73.

[16] Locke (n 11) 8.

[17] ibid 15.

[18] ibid 16.

[19] ibid 15–16.

may not be perturbed by that fact. This possibility points to the limitations of an account that focuses on the peace of the community. Further, Nussbaum objects to the language of 'toleration', which is used in Locke's account as well as others, as 'too grudging and weak'.[20] The term toleration does tend to imply that one is being somewhat put upon by the presence of differing conscientious beliefs but nonetheless one is forbearing from interfering with them. As will be discussed further below, the language of respect, which will be employed in the account developed in this chapter, seems to take people's conscientious beliefs more seriously, without necessarily implying any agreement with the beliefs.

Another approach to liberty of conscience focuses on a possible obligation of the state to be neutral. For example, Adenitire describes the existence of a 'limited duty of non-interference by the state in the individual moral responsibility to choose one conception of a good life over another', which he terms 'neutral pluralism'.[21] Thus, he contends that when the state imposes a 'barrier' to pursuing a particular way of life, it violates the duty of neutral pluralism because 'the state makes certain ways of life less accessible and thereby incentivizes individuals to choose other conceptions of a good life'.[22] As a result, Adenitire says that the state is required to remain neutral among these conceptions and 'grant an exemption to alleviate the barrier it has created'.[23] He argues for this duty from the existence of 'ethical pluralism', that is, the notion that 'there are various ways to live a good life and that, by implication, there are various legitimate conceptions of what the good life is'.[24]

Although Adenitire's account is sophisticated, the concept of state neutrality is open to challenges as to its workability – some scholars express the view that it is not a viable basis on which a state can function.[25] This is especially true of

[20] Nussbaum, *Liberty of Conscience* (n 1) 24. See also J Adenitire, 'Conscientious Exemptions: From Toleration to Neutrality; From Neutrality to Respect' (2017) 6 *Oxford Journal of Law and Religion* 268.

[21] Adenitire, *A General Right to Conscientious Exemption* (n 7) 12.

[22] ibid.

[23] ibid.

[24] ibid 11.

[25] See, eg, MH Kramer, *Liberalism with Excellence* (Oxford: Oxford University Press, 2017). See also G Baldwin, 'Review of *A General Right to Conscientious Exemption: Beyond Religious Privilege*. By John Adenitire' (2022) 81 *Cambridge Law Journal* 430; Y Nehushtan, 'Review of Adenitire, John, *A General Right to Conscientious Exemption: Beyond Religious Privilege*' (2022) 85 *Modern Law Review* 1097. Nehushtan, as one example, explains his view of the difficulty with the concept of state neutrality as follows: 'When the state enacts laws, especially laws that are likely to be objected to on conscientious grounds, the state must make value judgments about conflicting conceptions of the good and about many aspects of its citizens' lives. Many of these judgments reflect moral choices and preferences of one set of values over another. Such is the case, for example, regarding legal decisions about the mere existence of income tax and its rate; the existence of national health insurance and its extent; privatisation; abortions; euthanasia; criminalising hate speech; polygamy; anti-discrimination laws; privacy laws; sexual harassment laws; same-sex marriage laws; subsidising primary and higher education; subsidising cultural institutions and so on. Almost any legal or political decision regarding these issues is in fact a moral decision, at least in part. In order to make these decisions, the state must embrace some values and reject others, or accord greater weight to some values and less weight to others. Almost any meaningful political or legal decision distributes rights, duties, benefits, responsibilities, and goods. Therefore, all states must make moral decisions about how to apply a chosen version of distributive justice – and justify that chosen version': ibid 1098–99.

neutrality of effect, the kind of neutrality which Adenitire appears to invoke, given that virtually every state action can be expected to have uneven effects across the population, including differential effects on conscientious beliefs. Neutrality of justification of the state's actions, although perhaps more feasible to imagine as a guiding principle for state regulation, has been convincingly challenged by Kramer on the basis that there may be some fields of regulation, such as abortion, on which the state cannot be neutral as any stance it adopts constitutes a moral position.[26] (Although state neutrality is often associated with Rawls, in fact Rawls did not support this idea for day-to-day governance.[27])

A further possible basis of challenge to Adenitire's account of the normative foundations of liberty of conscience concerns its limits. Adenitire accepts that the state can limit the manifestation of conscientious beliefs if it is in the public interest to do so or to protect the rights of others, and proposes that such limitations can be assessed through the proportionality principle.[28] Although this focus on the public interest and the rights of others aligns to a significant extent with the approach that I will be presenting in Chapter 3, there may be some degree of tension in the underlying rationale offered by Adenitire. Specifically, if the state is under a duty of neutral pluralism, it may not be altogether clear why these limitations pertaining to the rights of others and the public interest do not constitute violations of that duty. Thus, although I do not rule out the possibility that neutrality could in some form provide a possible normative basis for the protection of liberty of conscience, due to these issues I consider it to be less attractive than the approach advanced in this book.

The rationales for liberty of conscience discussed so far focus on the individual, or the position of the state relative to the individual. In contrast, Richard Moon focuses on group rights, stating that:

> I am inclined to think that the justification for accommodation (and the treatment of religious practices as a matter of cultural identity) rests on a practical concern about the status of religious groups, and not on the principled protection of the liberty or integrity of individual conscience. Accommodation should be made to avoid the marginalisation of such groups within the larger community. Or more positively, accommodation should be made for the practices of different religious groups, because these groups are a source of identity and meaning for their members.[29]

On this view, liberty of conscience is justified because of the desirability of enabling pluralism, particularly given the risk of marginalisation of religious groups

[26] Kramer, *Liberalism with Excellence* (n 25) Ch 3. The difficulties with both of these forms of neutrality have been extensively considered in the philosophical literature. For a middle ground approach to neutrality, see A Patten, *Equal Recognition: The Moral Foundations of Minority Rights* (Princeton, NJ: Princeton University Press, 2014) Ch 4.

[27] See J Rawls, *Political Liberalism* (New York: Columbia University Press, 2005) 137, 230.

[28] ibid 268–77.

[29] Moon (n 8) 81. Group-based approaches to liberty of conscience may also conceivably lead to the conclusion that non-minority religious groups should not receive accommodations. For an example of this argument, see P Gowder, 'Why Majority Religions Should Not Be Accommodated' (2023) 108 *Iowa Law Review* 2153.

without it. However, although it might be possible to imagine a society in which conferring group rights is necessary to address serious social problems, a group-based approach has some readily apparent drawbacks that mean that it cannot be considered an appealing option for explaining liberty of conscience. There is, first of all, a practical difficulty with determining group membership. Who decides? If it is the state, then there may be a difference of opinion between the state and members of a religious community. If it is the leaders of a religious community, then they would exercise significant power in determining the rights of their members, even though their position might potentially be unelected and unaccountable.

A group-based approach also cannot address the position of those whose membership of the group may be unclear – such as a heretic, an outcast, or a gadfly who challenges the leadership of the community. As Paul Billingham points out, there are usually 'dissenters' in, or at the margins of, religious groups.[30] Is such a person to lose her rights to liberty of conscience on account of uncertain group membership? All of that is assuming that there is a group to begin with. This account cannot address the possibility of conscientious beliefs held by only a few, or even only one person. It seems to mean that if beliefs are held by small numbers, or indeed only one person, and the adherents accordingly do not constitute a group, they would not be eligible for protection. Finally, there may be a risk of tribalism and the enshrinement of social division to an approach to liberty of conscience that seeks to justify rights on a group rather than an individual basis. By carving society up and putting these divisions on a legal basis, such an approach may push people further apart.

Some other possible accounts seek to point to special features of religion, as distinct from non-religious belief, to justify liberty of conscience, but it has proved difficult to identify unique features of religion that are morally valuable. Nussbaum argues that 'a special respect' belongs to 'search[ing] for life's ultimate meaning', a seeming reference to religion.[31] She thus contends that society needs to 'respect the space required by any activity that has the general shape of searching for the ultimate meaning of life'.[32] However, whether religion is the only body of thought that searches for life's ultimate meaning may be doubted, as other fields, including philosophy, might be thought to do this. Indeed, Nussbaum herself speaks of 'mitigat[ing] the unfairness to nonreligious searchers as much as we possibly can, by extending the account of religion as far as we can, compatibly with administrability', so she evidently favours some extension of liberty of conscience beyond religion.[33]

Timothy Macklem claims that 'the moral foundation of freedom of religion is to be found in the value that the practice of faith, understood as a mode of belief

[30] P Billingham, 'Exemptions for Religious Groups and the Problem of Internal Dissent' in Adenitire, *Religious Beliefs and Conscientious Exemptions* (n 8) 53.

[31] Nussbaum, *Liberty of Conscience* (n 1) 19.

[32] ibid 169.

[33] ibid 173.

distinct from reason, contributes to human well-being'.[34] Faith 'exists as a type of rival to reason', constituting 'a commitment to that which cannot be established by reason, or to that which can be established by reason but is not believed for reason's sake'.[35] According to Macklem, it enables 'beliefs in matters that are for some people inaccessible on the basis of reason', which 'can be vital to the achievement of well-being in certain dimensions of life'.[36] This emphasis on faith seems to be intended to mean that non-religious belief would not be entitled to protection.[37] However, even assuming that faith has value (a matter that is open to dispute), it is not entirely clear why matters of faith are indeed limited to religious belief, and non-religious beliefs cannot be held on faith.[38]

On the other side of the debate, Brian Leiter claims that there is no 'apparent moral reason' to protect religious more than non-religious belief, and 'no one has been able to articulate a credible *principled* argument for tolerating religion *qua* religion'.[39] Thus, although he says that one good argument for protecting liberty of conscience generally is that '*being able to choose what to believe and how to live* … makes for a better life', this argument applies both to religious belief and non-religious belief.[40] Similarly, Christopher Eisgruber and Lawrence Sager, making an argument based on equality, contend in the US context that 'we have no constitutional reason to treat religion as deserving special benefits or as subject to special disabilities'.[41] Adenitire says that legal protection should apply to both religious and non-religious conscientious belief because the neutral pluralism of the state extends to both.[42] Charles Taylor and Jocelyn Maclure argue that religious belief is within the set of 'beliefs and commitments [that] allow people to structure their moral identity', being 'meaning-giving beliefs and commitments'.[43]

[34] T Macklem, 'Faith as a Secular Value' (2000) 45 *McGill Law Journal* 1, 4.

[35] ibid 33.

[36] ibid 48–49.

[37] ibid 54–55.

[38] There are too many approaches seeking to identify the specialness of religion for it to be possible to canvass all of them. However, I will refer to a couple more. One is John Finnis's argument that religion is 'the practical expression of, or response to, truths': JM Finnis, 'Does Free Exercise of Religion Deserve Constitutional Mention?' (2009) 54 *American Journal of Jurisprudence* 41, 56. However, valuing religion as true would seem to persuade only the religious (and, potentially, lead to disputes between religions as to their competing claims to truth). Another approach is that of John Corvino, who focuses on the injustice suffered by religious minorities as justifying treating religion as special: see J Corvino, 'Is Religion Special? Exemptions, Conscience and the Culture Wars' in Adenitire, *Religious Beliefs and Conscientious Exemptions* (n 8). However, as will be discussed in the context of non-discrimination in Chapter 6, it may be doubted whether accounts that hinge on contingent considerations about historical injustice (even if the relevant claims are adequately substantiated) can sustain general norms. That is equally true of liberty of conscience.

[39] B Leiter, *Why Tolerate Religion?* (Princeton, NJ: Princeton University Press 2013) 7, 63.

[40] ibid 17–18.

[41] CL Eisgruber and LG Sager, *Religious Freedom and the Constitution* (Cambridge, MA: Harvard University Press, 2010) 52.

[42] Adenitire, *A General Right to Conscientious Exemption* (n 7) 11–12, 18.

[43] J Maclure and C Taylor, *Secularism and Freedom of Conscience* (Jane Marie Todd tr, Cambridge, MA: Harvard University Press, 2011) 76–77.

The account that I develop in the remainder of this chapter, which is based in part on Rawls's work on moral personality, seeks to avoid the difficulties set out above. Unlike an autonomy-based account, Ahmed's critique does not apply. As will be seen, liberty of conscience is important to the development and exercise of the Rawlsian moral powers – a capacity for a conception of the good and a capacity for a sense of justice – because those moral powers can be developed and exercised in the light of a comprehensive doctrine. That importance is so even if the adoption of a comprehensive doctrine is not on the basis of an autonomous choice. Moreover, in drawing on the concept of respect, rather than toleration, it avoids Nussbaum's concern that toleration may be too grudging a concept; further, it does not hinge on Locke's concern that religious repression may cause social discord.

The account also does not depend on the contested concept of state neutrality. (In Chapter 4, I return to consider another sense of neutrality – neutrality as no purpose to limit exercise, a concept employed by the US Supreme Court – and raise doubts about its utility as a test for liberty of conscience. This sense of neutrality is different from the sense discussed in this chapter.) The analysis that I offer also does not rest on group rights, an approach that may pose significant practical challenges and unattractive social consequences. As will be seen, the approach is an individualistic one, and therefore offers protection to conscientious beliefs irrespective of whether they can be proved to be held by a group. Although, from an evidentiary perspective, it may be easier in court to establish the existence of a belief shared with others, this is not, at least, a conceptual requirement. Finally, the account does not rely on there being anything unique about religious, as opposed to secular, belief.

Indeed, the justification for liberty of conscience that will be advanced here on the basis of recognition respect for moral personality does not confer any special status on religious belief as distinct from secular belief. Rawls, in the context of his own defence of liberty of conscience, refers to the holding of 'comprehensive doctrines', whether religious, philosophical or moral.[44] Secular belief of certain kinds, as much as religious belief, may inform the exercise and development of the moral powers as kinds of comprehensive doctrines. That is not to say that including secular belief within the scope of liberty of conscience is entirely without practical difficulty. It may be enough to observe that group-based beliefs that can be more readily substantiated as a belief system through evidence may prove easier to protect as a practical matter in adjudicative processes than purely individual beliefs. However, these difficulties are at risk of being overstated, as courts applying the European Convention on Human Rights successfully protect secular beliefs under Article 9.[45]

[44] Rawls, *Political Liberalism* (n 27) 36–37. However, for a view that special treatment of religion is compatible with Rawlsian thought, see A Koppelman, 'A Rawlsian Defence of Special Treatment for Religion' in C Laborde and A Bardon (eds), *Religion in Liberal Political Philosophy* (Oxford: Oxford University Press, 2017).

[45] See, eg, *Kokkinakis v Greece* (1994) 17 EHRR 397 (European Court of Human Rights) [31].

II. A Moral-Personality-Based Account of Liberty of Conscience

In this section, I turn to outline the moral-personality-based account of liberty of conscience that is employed in the remainder of this book. I first describe the significance of moral personality to Rawls's theory of justice,[46] before pairing this concept with recognition respect to explain why the state, through its legal officials, should protect liberty of conscience, and lastly discussing some difficulties with moral personality as the basis for equality in Rawls's work, and why the current account can evade these difficulties.

A. Rawls and Moral Personality

The 'primary subject' of justice in Rawls's theory is the 'basic structure of society, or more exactly, the way in which the major social institutions distribute fundamental rights and duties and determine the division of advantages from social cooperation'.[47] The question that Rawls poses is: 'viewing society as a fair system of cooperation between citizens regarded as free and equal, what principles of justice are most appropriate to specify basic rights and liberties, and to regulate social and economic inequalities in citizens' prospects over a complete life?'[48] As a thought experiment to answer this question, Rawls develops the concept of the 'veil of ignorance', which applies in an 'original position' in which the basic structure of society is to be decided by representatives of its citizens. Behind the veil,

> the parties are not allowed to know the social positions or the particular comprehensive doctrines of the persons they represent. They also do not know persons' race and ethnic group, sex, or various native endowments such as strength and intelligence, all within the normal range.[49]

So veiled in this original position, Rawls contends that the parties would adopt two principles of justice. The first principle is that '[e]ach person has the same indefeasible claim to a fully adequate scheme of equal basic liberties, which scheme is compatible with the same scheme of liberties for all'.[50] This is sometimes called the 'liberty principle'. The second principle is that '[s]ocial and economic inequalities

[46] See J Rawls, *A Theory of Justice* (Cambridge, MA: Harvard University Press, 1971); J Rawls, *A Theory of Justice (Revised Edition)* (Cambridge, MA: Harvard University Press, 1999). For background on, and analysis of, Rawls's theory, see T Pogge, *Realizing Rawls* (Ithaca, NY: Cornell University Press, 1989); S Freeman, *Rawls* (Abingdon: Routledge, 2007); K Forrester, *In the Shadow of Justice: Postwar Liberalism and the Remaking of Political Philosophy* (Princeton, NJ: Princeton University Press 2019).

[47] Rawls, *A Theory of Justice* (n 46) 7.

[48] J Rawls, *Justice as Fairness: A Restatement* (E Kelly ed, Cambridge, MA: Harvard University Press, 2001) 41.

[49] ibid 15. See similarly Rawls, *A Theory of Justice* (n 46) 137.

[50] Rawls, *Justice as Fairness: A Restatement* (n 48) 42.

are to satisfy two conditions: first, they are to be attached to offices and positions open to all under conditions of fair equality of opportunity; and second, they are to be to the greatest benefit of the least-advantaged members of society'.[51] (These conditions in the second principle are known as 'fair equality of opportunity' and the 'difference principle' respectively.) The basic liberties said to be protected by the first principle have varied across Rawls's works, but in his final statement in *Justice as Fairness: A Restatement*, published in 2001, they appear to be: freedom of thought and liberty of conscience; political liberties such as the right to vote and participate in politics, freedom of speech and freedom of association; the rights and liberties specified by the liberty and integrity (physical and psychological) of the person; and the rights and liberties covered by the rule of law.[52]

In the original 1971 version of *A Theory of Justice*, Rawls presents an argument for the protection of basic liberties, as part of the first principle of justice, by reference to the irrationality of 'gambling' with those basic liberties in the original position, when the parties are behind the veil of ignorance.[53] Being ignorant of personal attributes, the parties would be careful to protect their rights. In a later formulation of this argument 30 years later, Rawls explains it as follows:

> given the capacity of those [that the parties in the original position] represent to be free and equal persons and fully cooperating members of society over a complete life, those persons would never put their basic rights and liberties in jeopardy so long as there was a readily available and satisfactory alternative. … Their responsibility as trustees for citizens so regarded does not allow them to gamble with the basic rights and liberties of those citizens.[54]

As discussed in Chapter 1, Rawls considers that people have liberty of conscience

> when they are free to pursue their moral, philosophical, or religious interests without legal restrictions requiring them to engage or not to engage in any particular form of religious or other practice, and when other men have a legal duty not to interfere.[55]

He points to the ignorance of the parties about whether they represent persons who belong to a majority or minority religion – and therefore their ignorance as to the likelihood of its violation – as underpinning a particular concern to secure this liberty. Rawls explains the choice made by the representatives as follows:

> They cannot take chances with their liberty by permitting the dominant religious or moral doctrine to persecute or to suppress others if it wishes. Even granting (what may

[51] ibid.

[52] ibid 44 (listing most of these), 169 (also mentioning freedom of speech). For an earlier statement, see Rawls, *A Theory of Justice* (n 46) 61 ('The basic liberties of citizens are, roughly speaking, political liberty (the right to vote and to be eligible for public office) together with freedom of speech and assembly; liberty of conscience and freedom of thought; freedom of the person along with the right to hold (personal) property; and freedom from arbitrary arrest and seizure as defined by the concept of the rule of law').

[53] Rawls, *A Theory of Justice* (n 46) 207.

[54] Rawls, *Justice as Fairness: A Restatement* (n 48) 102.

[55] Rawls, *A Theory of Justice (Revised Edition)* (n 46) 177.

> be questioned) that it is more probable than not that one will turn out to belong to the majority (if a majority exists), to gamble in this way would show that one did not take one's religious or moral convictions seriously, or highly value the liberty to examine one's beliefs.[56]

However, there may be too much breadth to this argument. Behind the veil of ignorance, it might be that the representatives would be rather anxious to protect a great many rights – indeed, they would be *obliged* to do so if they were to rationally protect the interests of those that they represent. Let us suppose that the representatives begin to debate whether to guarantee a right to a car. A right to a car may seem, outside the veil of ignorance, to be a very strange inclusion as a basic liberty. But, being ignorant of the social position of those that they represent, the logic of Rawls's argument suggests that the representatives would be particularly anxious to secure a right to a car because they have no way of knowing whether those that they represent would be able to afford a car. They may also not know where those that they represent live. In the city, a car might not be that useful. But if the citizens they represented lived in a rural or regional area, having a car would be very valuable indeed.

Put in Rawlsian terms, were the parties to 'gamble' over whether the parties have a car, they would show that they did not take seriously the usefulness and convenience of owning a car (which are considerable). Therefore, so the reasoning goes, the representatives would quite possibly adopt the position that there should, indeed, be a basic liberty of owning a car. The same reasoning could play out in countless other scenarios in which the ignorance of the representatives about the social position of those that they represent leads them to secure all their interests. What this seems to demonstrate is that, behind the veil of ignorance, the representatives, following Rawls's reasoning, would demonstrate a tendency to equalise conditions between citizens, because they are ignorant of the circumstances of those that they represent. In the absence of any particular limiting *criteria* by which the basic liberties are to be identified by the representatives, the list could become almost endless.

Fortunately, Rawls in his later writing applies a criterion for the selection of basic liberties, which may resolve this concern that, absent guidance, the representatives would enshrine a great many basic liberties that are not truly important enough to merit inclusion in the basic structure. The criterion that Rawls focuses on is the concept of moral personality, being the idea that certain 'moral powers' are necessary for 'being counted a full and equal member of society in questions of political justice'.[57] Rawls contends that there are two moral powers. One is the capacity for a sense of justice and the other is the capacity for a conception of the good.[58] Moral persons have the capacity for these moral powers – whether

[56] ibid 181. See also Rawls, *Justice as Fairness: A Restatement* (n 48) 104–105; Rawls, *A Theory of Justice* (n 46) 206–207.

[57] Rawls, *Political Liberalism* (n 27) 302.

[58] Rawls, *A Theory of Justice (Revised Edition)* (n 46) 442.

or not exercised – and so are entitled to equal justice.[59] I will briefly outline how Rawls has described the moral powers before turning to address why liberty of conscience is important to them.

In *A Theory of Justice*, Rawls explains the moral power of a capacity for a conception of the good as involving a 'rational plan of life'.[60] In *Political Liberalism*, the moral power is defined as 'the capacity to form, to revise, and rationally to pursue' a conception of the good, being 'a conception of what we regard for us as a worthwhile human life', which normally consists of a 'determinate scheme of final ends and aims, and of desires that certain persons and associations, as objects of attachments and loyalties, should flourish'.[61] In *Justice as Fairness: A Restatement*, Rawls describes such a conception as 'an ordered family of final ends and aims which specifies a person's conception of what is of value in human life or, alternatively, of what is regarded as a fully worthwhile life'; he adds that the elements of such a conception are 'normally set within, and interpreted by, certain comprehensive religious, philosophical, or moral doctrines'.[62]

In *A Theory of Justice*, Rawls defines the moral power of a capacity for a sense of justice as 'a normally effective desire to apply and to act upon the principles of justice, at least to a certain minimum degree'.[63] In *Political Liberalism*, he refers to it as 'the capacity to understand, to apply, and normally to be moved by an effective desire to act from (and not merely in accordance with) the principles of justice as the fair terms of social cooperation'.[64] In *Justice as Fairness: A Restatement*, he describes it in similar terms as 'the capacity to understand, to apply, and to act from (and not merely in accordance with) the principles of political justice that specify the fair terms of social cooperation'.[65]

This notion of moral personality is intuitive: we would understandably consider that people should be able to pursue a conception of the good and judge justice as part of being free and equal. It acknowledges something fundamental about personhood to say that people should be able to develop and pursue their own vision of their lives and their own sense of right and wrong. The point is similar to Leiter's encapsulation of an argument for liberty of conscience as the idea that 'being able to choose what to believe and how to live … makes for a better life' (emphasis removed).[66] However, there are necessarily limits to this idea that people should be able to develop and pursue a vision of their lives and their own sense of right and wrong. Some may develop a vision of their lives that involves harming others or polluting the environment, and a sense of right and wrong that is skewed, and may resent being told that they must live otherwise. Therefore, although Rawls's

[59] ibid 442, 445–46.
[60] ibid 442.
[61] Rawls, *Political Liberalism* (n 27) 302.
[62] Rawls, *Justice as Fairness: A Restatement* (n 48) 18–19.
[63] Rawls, *A Theory of Justice (Revised Edition)* (n 46) 442.
[64] Rawls, *Political Liberalism* (n 27) 302.
[65] Rawls, *Justice as Fairness: A Restatement* (n 48) 18–19.
[66] Leiter (n 39) 17–18.

argument for moral personality is compelling, the question of the limits to the exercise and development of the moral powers will be taken up in Chapter 3.

Rawls explains his list of basic liberties by reference to what is required to enable free and equal citizens 'adequately to develop and fully exercise' the two moral powers.[67] Political liberties, freedom of speech and freedom of assembly are 'necessary for the development and exercise of citizens' sense of justice and are required if citizens are to make rational judgments in the adoption of just political aims and in the pursuit of effective social policies'.[68] Liberty of conscience and freedom of association are

> necessary for the development and exercise of citizens' capacity for a conception of the good: that is, the capacity to form, to revise and rationally to pursue what one views as worthwhile in human life, as understood in the light of a (fully or partially) comprehensive religious, philosophical, or moral doctrine.[69]

Rawls also identifies some 'remaining and supporting basic liberties' that 'are necessary if the other basic liberties are to be properly guaranteed', being liberty and integrity (physical and psychological) of the person and the rights and liberties covered by the rule of law.[70] Other rights, such as owning a car, would not have the required connection with the moral powers, and accordingly would not be eligible for inclusion.

In Rawls's account, the significance of a liberty being 'basic' is that it has lexical priority over the second principle of justice (as well as, for example, laws outside the basic structure of society). The concept of the 'basicness' of certain liberties seems comprehensible, since it is common in various systems of government for certain rights and liberties to be protected in constitutional or human rights instruments in a way that prevails over other laws, and indeed other rights not so protected. For the purposes of the account of liberty of conscience offered in this book, I consider that a 'basic liberty' is simply a right of some kind that is to be protected in a superior way. Depending on the system, that might mean that the right should be constitutionally enshrined, or it might mean that it should be protected in ordinary legislation that grants courts the power to declare the incompatibility of other legislation with the protection of those basic rights. The exact method of protection is less important than the priority status.

B. Moral Personality and Recognition Respect

My account relies on Rawls's notion of moral personality, but I do not utilise Rawls's veil of ignorance or original position, or a social contract approach generally.

[67] Rawls, *Justice as Fairness: A Restatement* (n 48) 88.
[68] ibid 112–13, 169.
[69] ibid 113, 169.
[70] ibid 112–13.

Instead, I seek to show that consideration of Rawlsian moral personality can justify the protection of liberty of conscience on grounds independent of the original position and veil of ignorance. I argue by reference to the notion of recognition respect that people should be able to develop and exercise their moral powers (out of acknowledgement of their moral personality). The restriction of liberty of conscience is inconsistent with this development and exercise of the moral powers, and accordingly the state, as an aspect of the recognition respect owed to its population as moral persons, needs to guarantee liberty of conscience, subject to what will be said in Chapter 3 about the possibility of certain limitations on the liberty. This approach avoids any objections that may be made to social contract theory, though it remains liable to any possible objections to moral personality.

In putting forward a respect-based account of liberty of conscience, I rely on Darwall's famous distinction between 'appraisal respect' and 'recognition respect'. According to Darwall, 'appraisal respect' is respect that 'consists in a positive appraisal of a person, or his qualities'.[71] It is:

> an attitude of positive appraisal of a person either judged as a person or as engaged in some more specific pursuit. In the first case, the appropriate grounds are features of the person's character: dispositions to act for particular reasons or a higher-level disposition to act for the best reasons. In the second case, though features of character do not exhaust the appropriate grounds for appraisal respect, some such character traits will be relevant … Also, the other features which constitute the appropriate excellences of the pursuit must be related to traits of character in the way specified. In both cases, the positive appraisal of the person, and of his traits, must be categorical. It cannot depend on the fact that the person, because of his traits, serves an interest or purpose of one's own.[72]

In contrast, 'recognition respect' is 'a disposition to weigh appropriately some feature or fact in one's deliberations. … Thus to have recognition respect for persons is to give proper weight to the fact that they are persons'.[73] As a moral attitude, recognition respect entails that 'some fact or feature is an appropriate object of respect if inappropriate consideration or weighing of that fact or feature would result in behavior that is morally wrong'.[74] Thus, '[t]o have recognition respect for someone as a person is to give appropriate weight to the fact that he or she is a person by being willing to constrain one's behavior in ways required by that fact'.[75] It is 'identical with recognition respect for the moral requirements that are placed on one by the existence of other persons'.[76]

If we accept Rawls's account of moral personality, then it seems to follow that we owe each other recognition respect as moral persons (persons who have the

[71] SL Darwall, 'Two Kinds of Respect' (1977) 88 *Ethics* 36, 39.
[72] ibid 44–45.
[73] ibid 39.
[74] ibid 40.
[75] ibid 45.
[76] ibid.

potential of developing and exercising the moral powers).[77] The concept of recognition respect therefore supplies a connection, explaining the basis on which people owe moral duties to each other flowing from their moral personality. Although the duty entailed by recognition respect attaches to people generally, I focus on the position of legal officials. Legal officials are not, on this view, in a different position from members of society generally. They, too, owe recognition respect, and the laws should therefore demonstrate the respect of the legal officials and lawmakers.

On this basis, the state should protect the liberty of conscience of the population. Denial of liberty of conscience inhibits the exercise and development of the moral powers, and accordingly protecting liberty of conscience is implied by recognition respect for moral personality. As Rawls says, liberty of conscience is important to the moral power of formulating and pursuing a conception of the good, which can be informed by comprehensive doctrines, religious or otherwise. Samuel Freeman puts it, summarising Rawls's view, as that liberty of conscience is 'needed to come to an informed decision about the moral, philosophical, and religious principles that provide authoritative guidance' for forming and pursuing a conception of the good.[78] However, arguably comprehensive doctrines also inform judging right and justice, so liberty of conscience is important to this moral power as well. Both moral powers support the protection of liberty of conscience.

This account evades Ahmed's concerns about autonomy-based rationales for liberty of conscience in two ways.[79] First, the Rawlsian moral powers, including the moral power of forming, revising and pursuing a conception of the good, are thinner than some accounts of autonomy, and may not require the high standards for decision-making that Ahmed identifies as potentially inconsistent with religious belief. However, I consider that exercise and development of the moral powers remain morally valuable activities irrespective of the omission of Razian requirements,[80] because they relate to basic aspects of personhood. Second, even if religious belief may not itself always entail autonomous choice, it remains useful to the exercise of the moral powers. Religious or philosophical ideas may serve as an important aspect of how people consider the morally right course of action; they may equally prove important to formulating a plan of life pursuant to a conception of the good. This usefulness *to* the exercise and development of the moral powers is a separate point from whether religious belief is *itself* an exercise of autonomy.

For clarity, this account does not suggest that recognition respect is owed to moral persons only when or if they have actually managed to develop or

[77] Although Rawls makes reference to the relevance of these moral powers to certain 'fundamental cases', this concept is not relied upon for present purposes.

[78] Freeman (n 46) 56.

[79] See Ahmed (n 12).

[80] See Raz (n 15).

exercise the moral powers. Rather, the recognition respect relates to people's *potential* to develop and exercise the moral powers. Rawls makes this much clear, stating that

> the minimal requirements defining moral personality refer to a capacity and not a realization of it. A being that has this capacity, whether or not it is yet developed, is to receive the full protection of the principles of justice. Since infants and children are thought to have basic rights (normally exercised on their behalf by parents and guardians), this interpretation of the requisite conditions seems necessary to match our considered judgments. Moreover, regarding the potentiality as sufficient accords with the hypothetical nature of the original position, and with the idea that as far as possible the choice of principles should not be influenced by arbitrary contingencies.[81]

Further, if one adopted the position that recognition respect for moral persons is required only where the powers have been developed and exercised, the argument for liberty of conscience would be self-defeating, as a state could deny liberty of conscience, impairing the exercise and development of the moral powers in its population, and thereby absolve itself of any duties arising from recognition respect of the moral personality of the population. It therefore makes sense that recognition respect for moral persons is owed on the basis of the potential for the exercise and development of the moral powers, not on the basis of such exercise and development having already occurred.

A further ambiguity might arise in respect of whether the required 'respect' means that a person's beliefs, including religious beliefs, must necessarily be respected. It does not mean that, since what is required is recognition respect for the person, not the beliefs. The position of requiring respect for people, rather than beliefs, is similar to Nussbaum's analysis of liberty of conscience, pursuant to which

> the argument for religious liberty and equality in the tradition begins from a special respect for the faculty in human beings with which they search for life's ultimate meaning. This faculty was held to be present in all human beings in such a way as to make human beings equal: anyone who has it (and all humans do) is worthy of boundless respect, and that respect should be equally given to high and low, male and female, to members of the religions one likes and also to members of religions one hates. Conscience is precious, worthy of respect, but it is also vulnerable, capable of being wounded and imprisoned. The tradition argues that conscience, on that account, needs a protected space around it within which people can pursue their search for life's meaning (or not pursue it, if they choose). Government should guarantee that protected space.[82]

Leiter criticises Nussbaum's account of liberty of conscience as part of his argument that religious belief should not be given any special protection over non-religious belief. He distinguishes two concepts of respect, 'affirmative' and

[81] Rawls, *A Theory of Justice (Revised Edition)* (n 46) 445–46.
[82] Nussbaum, *Liberty of Conscience* (n 1) 19.

'minimal'; the latter, he says, corresponds to Darwall's 'recognition respect', while the former resembles his 'appraisal respect'.[83] Leiter says that although

> Nussbaum has defended an account of the moral foundations of the law of religious liberty as based on a principle of 'equal respect for conscience' … the minimal concept of respect does not, at least with regard to religion, move us far beyond the moral ideal of toleration, and that only if religion warrants the affirmative concept of respect would we have reason to think our law of religious liberty should answer to a more demanding moral standard.[84]

Leiter goes on to ask:

> Has one discharged all one's moral obligations of respect toward the religious beliefs and practices of a person if one tolerates them? Only an argument that morality demands more by way of our attitudes and practices toward religion would support a negative answer.[85]

It is true, as has been discussed previously, that Nussbaum considers that speaking of religious 'tolerance', rather than respect, 'seems too grudging and weak'.[86] Indeed, to describe 'tolerance' as 'grudging and weak' seems correct, since in the philosophical literature, tolerance is often taken to refer to a person having an objection to something, and believing they have the power to act on that objection, but deciding not to act – that is, tolerance is about restraint or forbearance in the face of something objectionable.[87]

However, Leiter's analysis seems to evince confusion as to what the object of the required respect is. Nussbaum is not calling for 'respect toward the religious beliefs and practices of a person', as Leiter seems to consider.[88] Rather, Nussbaum argues that it is necessary to respect the *person*. As she makes clear, '[r]espect for fellow citizens does not mean saying or believing that their religious views are correct, or even that all religions are valid routes to the understanding of life'; it 'means respecting them as human beings with their own choices to make in religious matters, and a right to make those choices freely'.[89] She clarifies that '*people* are respected as equals, but actions that threaten the rights of others may still be reasonably opposed, and opinions that teach the political inequality of others, while they will not be suppressed, will still be at a disadvantage in the community'.[90]

[83] Leiter (n 39) 68–69.
[84] ibid 69.
[85] ibid 72.
[86] Nussbaum, *Liberty of Conscience* (n 1) 24.
[87] See, eg, AJ Cohen, 'What Toleration Is' (2004) 115 *Ethics* 68. See also J Habermas, 'Religious Tolerance: The Pacemaker for Cultural Rights' (2004) 79 *Philosophy* 5; M Minow, 'Tolerance in an Age of Terror' (2007) 16 *Southern California Interdisciplinary Law Journal* 453; S Fredman, 'Tolerating the Intolerant: Religious Freedom, Complicity, and the Right to Equality' (2020) 9 *Oxford Journal of Law and Religion* 305.
[88] Leiter (n 39) 72.
[89] Nussbaum, *Liberty of Conscience* (n 1) 23.
[90] ibid 24.

Feldman makes a similar point that it is *people*, not beliefs, that can be said to warrant respect:

> Why should one respect all confessions and beliefs? In a European society, one must start by assuming that a good society values human autonomy and dignity and the equal treatment of all its members, and that the organization of society and its main institutions should be settled by way of a democratic process. If we take those beliefs seriously, it would be illogical and counter-productive to respect confessions and beliefs which do not accord a similar primacy to those basic values and to democracy, unless 'respect' has a meaning so thin as to be more or less meaningless. One may respect the people who hold views inconsistent with autonomy, dignity and democracy, but one should not sympathise with their confessions and beliefs. The only sensible and appropriate attitude to those is one of mingled fear and opposition. Respect for the confessions and beliefs, if it is appropriate at all, must be limited to allowing people to hold the views, but not allowing them to do anything to put them into practice. The manifestation of such confessions and beliefs must be strictly controlled to protect the fundamental values of society.[91]

This account, too, calls for respect for moral persons, and protection of liberty of conscience as a consequence of that, rather than respect for beliefs that people hold. On this account, it is acceptable to show disrespect for beliefs and to criticise them without hesitation when appropriate. The distinction is apparent from an example of a person, named Robert, who is granted liberty of conscience and develops and exercises his moral powers, only to come up with a religious belief to the effect that God supports slavery and wants society to condone it. Although recognition respect for Robert's personhood requires facilitation of the development and exercise of his moral powers, it does not mean that the beliefs he comes up with need to be themselves respected in the sense of thought of positively (appraisal respect). To the contrary, they should be condemned. Thus, although Robert should be allowed to hold the belief – he need not be, for example, forcibly re-educated – if he attempted to put his views into practice (or, on one view, even merely to express them), he would harm the rights of others, as will be discussed in detail in Chapter 3. Contempt for Robert's pro-slavery religious beliefs would be entirely apposite, and so would denial by the state of any attempt by Robert to implement his beliefs in practice.

Although there are similarities between them, this account differs from Nussbaum's in some respects. For one, it does not limit the scope of liberty of conscience to the 'search for life's ultimate meaning',[92] a vague expression, alluding to religious belief, which may exclude the exercise of conscience in important areas of relevance to the Rawlsian moral powers, such as judging rightness and wrongness (which does not necessarily relate to life's ultimate meaning), or formulating a conception of the good that does not rise to the level of being an assessment of life's ultimate meaning. This account also does not depend on characterising conscientious belief as a 'choice', a point which will be addressed further below.

[91] Feldman, 'Public Law and Freedom of Religion' (n 14) 742.
[92] Nussbaum, *Liberty of Conscience* (n 1) 19.

On the analysis offered here, what matters is that liberty of conscience is valuable to the exercise and development of the moral powers, not whether conscientious belief is truly a choice.

One concern with this account might relate to whether the exercise and development of the moral powers will *always* require the protection of liberty of conscience. At least in theory, the moral powers could develop and be exercised even where there is no liberty of conscience. For example, consider Mary who lives in a state where her religion is banned. Mary chooses to go to live in a small hut in the mountains, away from the eyes of the state (or indeed of anyone else), and therefore is able to practise her religion without interference (as this religion happens not to require any communal worship). In this situation, even though the state is limiting liberty of conscience, there is no practical impairment of the exercise and development of the moral powers in this respect because of the steps taken by Mary to seclude herself. Thus, it may be possible in theory to develop and exercise the moral powers in the absence of liberty of conscience, and even under severe restrictions. Such development and exercise of the moral powers may also depend on questions of Mary's psychological fortitude. For example, Jason Brennan objects to using Rawlsian moral powers as a basis for determining basic liberties because, according to him, it would mean that 'people's rights are contingent on empirical issues concerning developmental psychology'.[93]

In response to such concerns, I would elaborate on a point of nuance in the account, and define carefully the relationship that is required between the protection of liberty of conscience and the exercise and development of the moral powers. In my account, what needs to be shown is merely a *sufficient tendency* of the protection of liberty of conscience to facilitate the exercise and development of the moral powers, and thus to give effect to recognition respect for moral persons. It is not necessary to demonstrate that in every instance restriction of liberty of conscience actually succeeds in impairing the exercise and development of the moral powers. This relationship of sufficient tendency is also broad enough to avoid Brennan's concern that it would hinge on psychological happenstance. Just as we would not require the absolute certainty of a house being robbed in order to take the step of locking one's door, so it cannot be said that an absolute certainty of impairment of exercise and development of the moral powers is required in order for there to be a need to guard against actions that may tend to have that result.

In relying on the relevance of liberty of conscience to the moral powers, this account bears some resemblance to that of Cécile Laborde, as set out in *Liberalism's Religion*, which similarly stresses liberties that are 'essential to the exercise of … core moral powers: notably, [the] capacity to formulate and live by their own ethical commitments and projects'.[94] However, despite this overlap, I do not follow

[93] J Brennan, 'Against the Moral Powers Test of Basic Liberty' (2020) 28 *European Journal of Philosophy* 492, 503.

[94] C Laborde, *Liberalism's Religion* (Cambridge, MA: Harvard University Press 2017) 147. See also I Trispiotis, 'Religious Freedom and Religious Antidiscrimination' (2019) 82 *Modern Law Review* 864.

Laborde's suggestion that, because liberty of conscience merits protection in order to facilitate the exercise of the moral powers, it is therefore desirable to '*disaggregate* religion into a plurality of different interpretive dimensions', because '[e]ach facet of religion raises its own set of normative questions'.[95] As the argument above indicates, it is possible to describe liberty of conscience as a single right even if it is supported by reference to multiple Rawlsian moral powers. Moreover, given that the right is a single one in many legal systems, there is a practical difficulty, even if not necessarily a conceptual one, with 'disaggregating' it in the way suggested.[96]

To summarise my argument, then, moral persons – those with the capacity to develop and exercise the moral powers – are owed recognition respect. There is a sufficient tendency for the restriction of liberty of conscience to result in the impairment of this development and exercise of the moral powers (albeit that it may be possible to find exceptional cases where the exercise and development of the moral powers can occur even when liberty of conscience is restricted). For these reasons, it is necessary to protect liberty of conscience. Because recognition respect is owed not merely by other citizens but also by the legislators and legal officials of a society, liberty of conscience should be protected by the state through its laws. (Although there is no doubt that there are moral duties owed by others in society, as recognised by Rawls in the second aspect of his definition of liberty of conscience, these are not the focus of the present account.) However, as will be discussed in Chapter 3, this account also implies the existence of some possible limitations on liberty of conscience, which is not, on this rationale, an absolute right.

C. Possible Issues with Moral Personality

Before turning to consider some possible challenges to the protection of liberty of conscience in the way proposed above, I will first assay some potential issues with the concept of moral personality employed as the foundation for this account. To do so, it is necessary to provide some wider context about the role of the moral powers. Moral personality plays a significant role in Rawls's theory as the basis of equality between free and equal persons. Rawls describes 'the basis of equality' as 'the features of human beings in virtue of which they are to be treated in accordance with the principles of justice'.[97] As we have seen, moral persons are 'capable of having (and are assumed to have) a conception of their good (as expressed by a rational plan of life)' and 'capable of having (and are assumed to acquire) a sense of justice, a normally effective desire to apply and to act upon the principles of justice,

[95] Laborde (n 94) 2. For an argument that religious freedom can be adequately protected by other rights, such as the rights to freedom of expression and freedom of association, see JW Nickel, 'Who Needs Freedom of Religion?' (2005) 76 *University of Colorado Law Review* 941. However, such an approach 'arguably weakens the protection of freedom of religion': F Raza, 'Limitations to the Right to Religious Freedom: Rethinking Key Approaches' (2020) 9 *Oxford Journal of Law and Religion* 435, 439.

[96] See Hunter-Henin, *Why Religious Freedom Matters for Democracy* (n 5) 86.

[97] Rawls, *A Theory of Justice (Revised Edition)* (n 46) 441.

at least to a certain minimum degree'.[98] Thus, 'equal justice is owed to those who have the capacity to take in and to act in accordance with the public understanding of the initial situation'.[99]

As noted above, moral personality refers to a *capacity*, not its *realisation*; a being that has the required capacity, whether or not it is developed, receives 'full protection' under the theory of justice.[100] Moreover, it is a 'range property', similar to how 'the property of being in the interior of the unit circle is a range property of points in the plane', because all points inside the circle have the property of being in the interior and they have the property equally.[101] In the same way, 'provided the minimum for moral personality is satisfied, a person is owed all the guarantees of justice'.[102] One difficulty that confronts moral personality as a concept is therefore how this extends to so-called 'marginal cases' – humans who may lack the capacities required because they are severely disabled or unwell.

In this regard, Rawls emphasises that what is required for moral personality is the potential to exercise and develop the moral powers 'that is ordinarily realized in due course'.[103] Thus, infants and children are included, as are those who have lost their capacity temporarily. However, it could be objected that Rawls does not account for the moral status of those humans whose incapacity may be permanent or lifelong. He observes that the problem of 'those more or less permanently deprived of moral personality may present a difficulty' but declines to examine it.[104] One possible approach may be to accept that some 'scattered' humans, as Rawls puts it,[105] do not meet the threshold. There is ongoing philosophical debate about questions of moral equality.[106]

[98] ibid 442.
[99] ibid.
[100] ibid 445–46.
[101] ibid 444.
[102] ibid 443.
[103] ibid 442.
[104] ibid 446.
[105] ibid 443.
[106] See generally G Cupit, 'The Basis of Equality' (2000) 75 *Philosophy* 105; I Carter, 'Respect and the Basis of Equality' (2011) 121 *Ethics* 538; U Steinhoff (ed), *Do All Persons Have Equal Moral Worth? On 'Basic Equality' and Equal Respect and Concern* (Oxford: Oxford University Press, 2014); G Sher, *Equality for Inegalitarians* (Cambridge: Cambridge University Press, 2014); T Parr and A Slavny, 'Rescuing Basic Equality' (2019) 100 *Pacific Philosophical Quarterly* 837; S Husi, 'Why We (Almost Certainly) Are Not Moral Equals' (2017) 21 *Journal of Ethics* 375; F Zuolo, 'Misadventures of Sentience: Animals and the Basis of Equality' (2019) 9 *Animals* 1044; Z Miklosi, 'The Problem of Equal Moral Status' (2022) 21 *Politics, Philosophy & Economics* 372; G Floris, 'Contingency, Arbitrariness, and the Basis of Moral Equality' (2023) 36 *Ratio* 224. For my part, I am not sure that Rawls's omission of the 'marginal cases' is as serious a problem as it may seem. The issue may not be an insuperable barrier to the concept of moral personality as the basis for equal moral status because it might be addressed with an adjustment to Rawls's formulation, for example by considering the potential of a human in hypothetical ideal circumstances, free of disability or illness. On this view, even a severely disabled or ill person who cannot exercise or develop the moral powers is a moral person because of the ability of that person to exercise or develop the moral powers in ideal circumstances, albeit that such circumstances cannot be realised with present medical technology.

In the present book, it is not necessary to take a position on the debate over egalitarianism and the basis for equality within Rawls's theory, or within political and moral philosophy generally. That is because I do not rely on moral personality as a range property for my own account, and nor does my account proceed from an assumption of equal moral status between individuals (whether or not such an assumption would be correct). Rather, the claims that I make are much narrower: the exercise and development of the moral powers are morally valuable activities; on this basis, recognition of moral personality is a moral duty arising from recognition respect; and protection of liberty of conscience is an aspect of this recognition respect because it facilitates the exercise and development of the moral powers. That is so regardless of whether moral personality can be viewed as a binary or as a matter of degree (scalar): liberty of conscience remains useful to the moral powers either way.

As such, possible concerns, which I have discussed elsewhere,[107] about whether moral personality can extend to non-human animals (hereafter, 'animals') do not count against the account here. Rawls himself did not regard animals as being able to possess moral personality, and explains his view of the position of animals in a key passage:

> Last of all, we should recall here the limits of a theory of justice. Not only are many aspects of morality left aside, but no account is given of right conduct in regard to animals and the rest of nature. A conception of justice is but one part of a moral view. While I have not maintained that the capacity for a sense of justice is necessary in order to be owed the duties of justice, it does seem that we are not required to give strict justice anyway to creatures lacking this capacity. But it does not follow that there are no requirements at all in regard to them, nor in our relations with the natural order. Certainly it is wrong to be cruel to animals and the destruction of a whole species can be a great evil. The capacity for feelings of pleasure and pain and for the forms of life of which animals are capable clearly imposes duties of compassion and humanity in their case. I shall not attempt to explain these considered beliefs. They are outside the scope of the theory of justice, and it does not seem possible to extend the contract doctrine so as to include them in a natural way.[108]

In short, then, Rawls does not accept that animals are capable of a sense of justice, and therefore we are not required to give 'strict' justice to creatures lacking this capacity. However, Rawls's position that animals are not entitled to 'strict' justice raises questions. How do we square this with his view that cruelty towards animals or the destruction of an entire species would be wrong? Presumably, these may be moral duties, but not duties of justice or at least not of 'strict' justice. This position is open, of course, to objection that animals might conceivably be owed justice on the basis of their sentience or consciousness,[109]

[107] G Baldwin, 'Rawls and Animal Moral Personality' (2023) 13 *Animals* 1238.

[108] Rawls, *A Theory of Justice (Revised Edition)* (n 46) 448.

[109] See, eg, S Donaldson and W Kymlicka, *Zoopolis: A Political Theory of Animal Rights* (Oxford: Oxford University Press, 2011); A Cochrane, *Sentientist Politics: A Theory of Global Inter-Species Justice* (Oxford: Oxford University Press, 2018).

or experience of pain and pleasure,[110] without it being necessary to demonstrate that they themselves have a sense of justice. For Rawls, it seems that such matters might suffice to demonstrate that animals are due moral consideration, but not justice (or 'strict' justice).

In other words, as Ruth Abbey puts it, Rawls 'makes it clear that humans have duties to animals that derive not from the considerations of justice, but from those of morality'.[111] Rawls's position therefore does not seem to preclude animal welfare laws or even animals holding non-basic liberties – legislators can presumably grant animals welfare protections or rights even if this is not compelled by the principles of justice, but merely considerations of morality. Indeed, animal welfare laws have been introduced in many jurisdictions. From one perspective, animals may already have 'simple' rights under these welfare laws.[112] Legislators might even choose to confer 'fundamental' rights on animals. Such conferrals of rights may take place on the basis of the sentience of animals or other considerations.

However, finding that animals are not entitled to justice may mean that they enjoy lesser protection. Nonetheless, even if Rawls's own treatment of moral personality does prove to be under-inclusive in omitting any duties of justice to animals, that does not affect the rationale advanced here: it remains morally valuable to facilitate the exercise and development of the moral powers in humans. In this book, it will not be necessary to assess the moral status of animals. It is my view that many animals have some degree of moral personality, and some sophisticated animals might meet the threshold that Rawls sets. The case of animals exposes difficulties with drawing a line and may render the concept of a range property problematic, but that does not affect the usefulness of moral personality in this book, because I do not need to draw such lines in this account of liberty of conscience.[113]

[110] See, eg, P Singer, *Animal Liberation*, rvsd edn (London: Bodley Head 2015); P Singer, *Animal Liberation Now* (London: Bodley Head, 2023).

[111] R Abbey, 'Rawlsian Resources for Animal Ethics' (2007) 12 *Ethics and the Environment* 1, 6.

[112] S Stucki, 'Towards a Theory of Legal Animal Rights: Simple and Fundamental Rights' (2020) 40 *Oxford Journal of Legal Studies* 533.

[113] A further issue concerns the religious freedom of 'collectivities' that might be unable to exercise the moral powers, though their members can: see JC Norton, *Freedom of Religious Organizations* (Oxford: Oxford University Press, 2016). The issue may be less controversial in the case of, for example, a church, but difficulties particularly arise when rights to liberty of conscience are said to extend to commercial corporations: see F Cranmer, 'Can Secular Non-Natural Persons Be Said to Have a "Conscience"?' in Adenitire, *Religious Beliefs and Conscientious Exemptions* (n 8); WE Lee, 'The Conscience of Corporations and the Right Not to Speak' (2019) 43 *Harvard Journal of Law & Public Policy* 155. Certainly, corporations can possess interests and therefore, under the interest theory, can be recognised as legal persons and rights holders, as they usually are in legal systems: see MH Kramer, 'Getting Rights Right' in MH Kramer (ed), *Rights, Wrongs and Responsibilities* (London: Palgrave Macmillan, 2001). However, they lack a 'mind' of their own: see, eg, *Tesco Supermarkets Ltd v Nattrass* [1972] AC 153 (United Kingdom House of Lords); *cf Burwell v Hobby Lobby Stores, Inc* (2014) 573 US 682 (Supreme Court of the United States). It is not necessary to resolve this issue for present purposes, so it is left beyond the scope of the book.

III. Some Possible Objections to the Protection of Liberty of Conscience

I will now consider three possible objections to the protection of liberty of conscience along the lines proposed in the account above: first, that because conscientious belief, religious or otherwise, is viewed by some as a 'choice', liberty of conscience should not receive protection, or it should receive a reduced degree of protection; second, that external manifestations of conscientious belief can be disruptive socially or to the legal order and thus should not be protected within the scope of liberty of conscience; and third, that religious belief can be 'intolerant' of others, and therefore liberty of conscience does not merit protection. In the result, none of these objections prove to be persuasive, and it is concluded that it is necessary to protect liberty of conscience in the way proposed in this chapter.

A. Conscientious Belief as a Choice?

I have mentioned above that it may be problematic to describe conscientious belief as a choice, though at least one significant account describes liberty of conscience as involving the making of a choice.[114] However, the claim that it is a choice, if it may be accepted, seems to raise the issue: why protect a person's choice? For example, Kenneth Norrie criticises the UK Supreme Court's decision in *Lee v Ashers Baking Co Ltd*,[115] which concerned the refusal of a baker to sell a cake with a message endorsing same-sex marriage and found that that refusal did not constitute discrimination on the basis of a protected characteristic, for treating protected characteristics under the Equality Act 2010 as of equal weight, when (he claims) religious belief is a choice while sexual orientation is not. Norrie writes as follows:

> There is an unfortunate undercurrent throughout the Supreme Court's decision in *Ashers Baking Co Ltd v Lee*: that all protected characteristics are of equal weight ... But they are not all equally worthy of protection. Some characteristics are in need of more protection than others because of a long history of discrimination; some characteristics demand more protection because they are immutable (race, for example, and sexual orientation); others are chosen but not necessarily based on rational choice (political beliefs, religious beliefs). Opinions can change but skin colour cannot.[116]

An argument in opposition to liberty of conscience might therefore be formulated as follows: liberty of conscience does not merit protection (or merits lesser protection) because it protects a choice, unlike other rights (such as non-discrimination) that do not protect the making of a choice. However, what this argument overlooks is that because of the character of moral persons, liberty of

[114] Nussbaum, *Liberty of Conscience* (n 1) 23.
[115] [2020] AC 413 (Supreme Court of the United Kingdom).
[116] KM Norrie, '*Lee v Ashers Baking Co Ltd*' (2019) 1 *Juridical Review* 88, 95.

conscience specifically merits protection because it assists people to pursue their conception of the good and judge rightness and wrongness. Such an understanding of why liberty of conscience should be protected applies irrespective of whether that belief is a choice. If it is indeed a choice, then it is a choice that is important and valuable to the exercise and development of the moral powers.

However, as discussed above, it is far from clear that conscientious belief is a choice, and it does not follow from the character of such belief as mutable that it is necessarily a choice. Conscientious belief might be difficult to change, particularly if it is linked to one's upbringing or group or cultural identity. It might also be possible to think of conscience as, in a sense, compelling beliefs rather than those beliefs being freely chosen. For example, one might believe or not believe in God without a conscious decision-making process. Conscience may, in this regard, be a question what we are *persuaded of*, not what we *choose to believe*: as Locke observes astutely, 'to believe this or that to be true does not depend upon our will'.[117] Whether Norrie is correct to characterise conscientious belief as a 'choice' might depend on what is meant by 'choice' and how much it suggests a kind of freely made choice.

A separate problem with Norrie's observation is that the 'immutability' of certain personal attributes is not a sound justification for a norm of non-discrimination. That is because even if one could change, for example, one's skin colour, discrimination on the basis of skin colour would not cease to be wrongful. It is therefore apparent that the wrongfulness of discrimination is not based on the immutability of certain attributes, despite the frequency of references to immutability in this context.[118] In a compelling account, Benjamin Eidelson instead traces the basis for the wrongfulness of certain types of discrimination to the failure to respect the individual.[119] Eidelson's account parallels the argument here for respect for moral personality as underpinning liberty of conscience; respect for people, in differing forms, underpins both the norms of non-discrimination and liberty of conscience. (This will be addressed further in my analysis of non-discrimination in Chapter 6.)

What seems to be motivating Norrie's concern about the 'mutability' of religious belief – and how this differs from the 'immutability' of sexual orientation – is the possibility of clashes between rights to liberty of conscience and non-discrimination, and it is indeed true that such clashes have become a regular occurrence, particularly in relation to the issue of discrimination on the grounds of sexual orientation. However, to the extent that there may be such clashes, there are approaches to adjudicating clashes that seek to construe the two rights conformably with one another without drawing a distinction based on the mutability or immutability of attributes. This issue is taken up in Chapter 3 in addressing the

[117] Locke (n 11) 30.

[118] See C McCrudden, *Litigating Religions: An Essay on Human Rights, Courts, and Beliefs* (Oxford: Oxford University Press, 2018) 78–79.

[119] See B Eidelson, *Discrimination and Disrespect* (Oxford: Oxford University Press, 2015).

limits of rights of conscience in relation to the compatibility of such rights with the rights of others, and in the case study analysis in Chapter 6. In short, it is not necessary to create a hierarchy of rights that elevates non-discrimination over liberty of conscience in order to respond to legitimate concerns about the potential breadth of liberty of conscience as a right.

B. Protecting Manifestations of Conscientious Belief?

A further concern relates to whether to protect only internal belief (*forum internum*), and not external manifestations of belief (*forum externum*), given the risk to the legal certainty and social stability potentially entailed in protecting external manifestations of belief that clash with the law. Under the case law of the European Court of Human Rights, internal belief is given superior protection, because protection of it is absolute,[120] while protection of manifestations of belief is qualified, and can be limited on various bases under Article 9(2) of the European Convention on Human Rights. However, another possible approach is *only* to protect internal belief. Waite CJ of the US Supreme Court in the decision of *Reynolds v United States* in 1879, relating to polygamy, drew a distinction between 'practices', which were said not to be protected by the Free Exercise Clause of the First Amendment to the US Constitution, and 'belief', which was protected.[121] Waite CJ explained his position as follows:

> [T]he only question which remains is whether those who make polygamy a part of their religion are excepted from the operation of the statute. If they are, then those who do not make polygamy a part of their religious belief may be found guilty and punished, while those who do, must be acquitted and go free. This would be introducing a new element into criminal law. Laws are made for the government of actions, and while they cannot interfere with mere religious belief and opinions, they may with practices. Suppose one believed that human sacrifices were a necessary part of religious worship; would it be seriously contended that the civil government under which he lived could not interfere to prevent a sacrifice? Or if a wife religiously believed it was her duty to burn herself upon the funeral pile of her dead husband; would it be beyond the power of the civil government to prevent her carrying her belief into practice?
>
> So here, as a law of the organization of society under the exclusive dominion of the United States, it is provided that plural marriages shall not be allowed. Can a man excuse his practices to the contrary because of his religious belief?
>
> To permit this would be to make the professed doctrines of religious belief superior to the law of the land, and, in effect, to permit every citizen to become a law unto himself. Government could exist only in name under such circumstances.[122]

[120] See *Ivanova v Bulgaria* (2008) 47 EHRR 54 (European Court of Human Rights).

[121] *Reynolds v United States* (1879) 98 US 145 (Supreme Court of the United States) 166. See similarly *Krygger v Williams* (1912) 15 CLR 366 (High Court of Australia).

[122] *Reynolds v United States* (n 121) 166–67.

However, the 'belief' approach set forth in *Reynolds* is plainly inadequate because it does not amount to giving any real protection to liberty of conscience. As Nussbaum correctly says, 'if these guarantees of liberty of religion … are to have any meaning at all, they must mean that these liberties are upheld against legislative judgments, at least in some instances'.[123] In this context, what is often called an 'exemption' is simply when a manifestation of belief clashes with a law and the belief is accommodated in priority over the law. Due to its undue narrowness, the approach of the US Supreme Court in *Reynolds* fell out of favour, beginning with cases concerning Jehovah's Witnesses in the 1930s,[124] and culminating in a statement of a much broader understanding of free exercise in *Sherbert v Verner*.[125] The current US approach adopted in *Employment Division v Smith*,[126] although putatively narrower than *Sherbert*, is not restricted to *forum internum*.

This analysis is reinforced by the observation that people do not develop and pursue their conceptions of the good and of rightness and wrongness – pertaining to each of the Rawlsian moral powers – in a purely internal way, but rather do so in the wider world. So much was cogently explained by Sachs J of the Constitutional Court of South Africa in *Christian Education South Africa v Minister of Education*, who said that

> religion is not always merely a matter of private individual conscience or communal sectarian practice. Certain religious sects do turn their back on the world, but many major religions regard it as part of their spiritual vocation to be active in the broader society. Not only do they proselytise through the media and in the public square, religious bodies play a large part in public life, through schools, hospitals and poverty relief. They command ethical behaviour from their members and bear witness to the exercise of power by state and private agencies; they promote music, art and theatre; they provide halls for community activities, and conduct a great variety of social activities for their members and the general public. They are part of the fabric of public life, and constitute active elements of the diverse and pluralistic nation contemplated by the Constitution. Religion is not just a question of belief or doctrine. It is part of a way of life, of a people's temper and culture.[127]

In a similar way, Latham CJ of the High Court of Australia, in the 1943 decision of *Adelaide Company of Jehovah's Witnesses Inc v Commonwealth*, critiqued the approach of the US Supreme Court in *Reynolds* as frustrating the object of religious freedom protections:

[123] Nussbaum, *Liberty of Conscience* (n 1) 210.

[124] *Lovell v City of Griffin* (1938) 303 US 444 (Supreme Court of the United States); *Schneider v New Jersey* (1939) 308 US 147 (Supreme Court of the United States); *Cantwell v Connecticut* (1940) 310 US 296 (Supreme Court of the United States); *Murdock v Pennsylvania* (1943) 319 US 105 (Supreme Court of the United States); *Largent v Texas* (1943) 318 US 418 (Supreme Court of the United States); *Prince v Massachusetts* (1944) 321 US 158 (Supreme Court of the United States); *Braunfeld v Brown* (1961) 366 US 599 (Supreme Court of the United States); *Gallagher v Crown Kosher Super Market of Massachusetts, Inc* (1961) 366 US 617 (Supreme Court of the United States).

[125] (1963) 374 US 398 (Supreme Court of the United States).

[126] (1990) 494 US 872 (Supreme Court of the United States).

[127] (2000) (4) SA 757 (Constitutional Court of South Africa) [33].

> There are obvious difficulties in the principle laid down in [*Reynolds*]. When the suggestion that religious beliefs should be superior to the law of the land is rejected as a matter of course, it may well be asked whether the very object of the constitutional protection of religious freedom is not to prevent the law of the land from interfering with either the holding of religious beliefs, or bona fide conduct in pursuance of such beliefs.[128]

Although it is clearly necessary to protect external manifestations of conscientious belief in order to protect liberty of conscience in a meaningful way, and thereby demonstrate recognition respect for free and equal persons as bearers of moral personality, that is not to say that concerns, such as those expressed by Waite CJ, about legal certainty and social stability in allowing exemptions to laws are without basis. These concerns can be overstated, and given the close supervision of courts, it might sometimes be implausible to suggest that claims to liberty of conscience will create 'anarchy', as Ian Leigh notes.[129] Nonetheless, there is still a legitimate point to be made given the potentially vast array of bases on which laws may be objected to in respect of conscientious belief. What I suggest is that it is possible to address the point by limiting liberty of conscience through the concept of necessity in the common interest, addressed in Chapter 3; this offers a way that claims to liberty of conscience may be overridden in order to address wider social considerations.

C. Conscientious Belief as Potentially 'Intolerant'?

Yossi Nehushtan challenges the position that religious beliefs should be accommodated with exemptions because, on the basis of both empirical and conceptual arguments, he contends that 'there is a special, strong link between religion and intolerance and … on the whole, religious people are more likely to be intolerant than non-religious ones', such that, as he expresses it at one point, religion is 'inherently intolerant'.[130] Thus, Nehushtan argues that the 'religiosity of claims for accommodation or exemption should be a relevant reason within the balance of reasons, and … it should normally be a reason for refusing to accommodate religion or to grant an exemption'.[131] Nehushtan defines the 'truly intolerant person' as 'one who unjustly infringes the autonomy of others or unjustly harms or offends others, because he has a negative view about the other's values, way of life, identity and so on', where 'autonomy is unjustly infringed, and harm or offence unjustly

[128] *Adelaide Company of Jehovah's Witnesses Inc v Commonwealth* (1943) 67 CLR 116 (High Court of Australia), 129. For background on this case, see PT Babie, '*Adelaide Company of Jehovah's Witnesses v Commonwealth*: Balancing Free Exercise and Public Order' in R Barker et al (eds), *Law and Religion in the Commonwealth: The Evolution of Case Law* (Oxford: Hart Publishing, 2022).

[129] I Leigh, 'The Courts and Conscience Claims' in Adenitire, *Religious Beliefs and Conscientious Exemptions* (n 8) 109.

[130] Y Nehushtan, *Intolerant Religion in a Tolerant-Liberal Democracy* (Oxford: Hart Publishing, 2015) 94, 200.

[131] ibid 198.

caused when it is not done in accordance with a perfectionist-liberal perception of the harm principle'.[132]

Adenitire criticises Nehushtan's empirical evidence, which is concentrated on North America, as not 'proving Nehushtan's claim that religious beliefs necessarily lead to intolerance/prejudice', but rather merely that 'certain religious attitudes may lead to certain kinds of intolerance/prejudice'.[133] Adenitire is correct, but even assuming *arguendo* that Nehushtan's claim about the intolerance of religion is true, this is not a basis on which to deny the importance of protecting liberty of conscience (including as it applies to religious belief). That is because of the distinction drawn in the discussion of respect between recognition respect for moral persons and appraisal respect for their beliefs. It is possible to accord individuals the required recognition respect while being sharply critical of the beliefs that they end up holding through this process, if those beliefs are intolerant of others. It does not follow from the recognition respect for persons that appraisal respect for their beliefs is warranted. Equally, it does not follow from the criticism that may appropriately be directed at intolerant beliefs due to the absence of appraisal respect for those beliefs that it is necessary to deny individuals recognition respect as moral persons, which would be entailed by Nehushtan's position. However, what may be necessary, consistent with the analysis in Chapter 3, is to prohibit certain action (including potentially expressive activity) that results from beliefs.

A further difficulty with Nehushtan's argument is factual, in that it seems unlikely that it is correct to single out religious belief as uniquely intolerant. As the history of the twentieth century demonstrates, secular belief may be equally intolerant, if not more so. Many of the most heinous wrongs of the twentieth century were committed in the name of intolerant secular ideology; the revolutionary fervour of those possessed by a secular creed may equal, or exceed, religious fervour. In truth, any kind of belief can be intolerant and religion is not unique in this regard. Nehushtan concedes as much, writing that '[i]t is indeed true that there are non-religious ideologies, beliefs or views that are also intolerant, yet the nature of the link between these ideologies and intolerance differs from that between religion and intolerance'.[134] However, this seems beside the point, as it should not matter whether secular belief and religious belief are not intolerant in precisely the same way or for precisely the same reason if they may both be intolerant in Nehushtan's sense of the word. Given that religious belief is not unique in its potential for intolerance, Nehushtan's argument against accommodating liberty of conscience specifically in respect of religious belief loses force.

As Nehushtan implicitly accepts in his definition of intolerance, which is directed at actions, the mere holding of beliefs by individuals is arguably not a matter for a state to concern itself with. Rather, the problem arises when

[132] ibid 96.
[133] Adenitire, *A General Right to Conscientious Exemption* (n 7) 266–67.
[134] Nehushtan (n 130) 94.

intolerance manifests in the public sphere or in relations with others, resulting, for example, in interference with the rights of others, such as the right to non-discrimination. Although the question of whether and how to regulate hate speech is controversial,[135] similar issues might arise in the context of freedom of expression in addressing hate speech, since in that situation, too, private belief only becomes harmful to others when it results in action (such as statements made to others, and particularly statements made in the public sphere). Accordingly, it is doubtful whether any 'intolerance' associated with religion matters except when it results in some kind of action that harms others. In that circumstance, the possibility of limitations on the right of liberty of conscience becomes relevant. This analysis resembles that of Rawls, who writes as follows:

> Suppose that, in some way or other, an intolerant sect comes to exist within a well-ordered society accepting the two principles of justice. How are the citizens of this society to act in regard to it? Now certainly they should not suppress it simply because the members of the intolerant sect could not complain were they to do so. Rather, since a just constitution exists, all citizens have a natural duty of justice to uphold it. We are not released from this duty whenever others are disposed to act unjustly. A more stringent condition is required: there must be some considerable risks to our own legitimate interests. Thus just citizens should strive to preserve the constitution with all its equal liberties as long as liberty itself and their own freedom are not in danger. They can properly force the intolerant to respect the liberty of others, since a person can be required to respect the rights established by principles that he would acknowledge in the original position. But when the constitution itself is secure, there is no reason to deny freedom to the intolerant.[136]

IV. Conclusion

In this chapter, I have outlined an argument for the protection of liberty of conscience by reference to Rawls's account of moral personality, together with Darwall's notion of recognition respect. The argument is distinct from, and avoids some of the difficulties with, others in the literature. The argument stems from recognition respect for free and equal persons as moral persons, with the potential to exercise and develop the moral powers; this duty of respect extends to the state, in the form of its legislators and legal officials. Restriction of liberty of conscience has a sufficient tendency to impair the exercise and development of the moral powers, and therefore, as part of this recognition respect for free and equal persons as moral persons, the state needs to guarantee liberty of conscience.

In addition to discussing some potential issues with moral personality as a concept, three possible counterarguments to the protection of liberty of conscience

[135] See, eg, J Waldron, *The Harm in Hate Speech* (Cambridge, MA: Harvard University Press, 2012).
[136] Rawls, *A Theory of Justice (Revised Edition)* (n 46) 192.

have been considered: the idea that belief is a choice; the risk to the legal order entailed by protecting external manifestations of belief; and the problem of intolerant beliefs. I have sought to show that the argument for liberty of conscience presented in this chapter, based on recognition respect for moral personality, can address these possible objections. The further implications of this argument for liberty of conscience will be explored further in the next two chapters.

3

The Limits of Liberty of Conscience

In Chapter 2, I argued that respect for moral personality necessitates accommodation by the state of liberty of conscience as a basic liberty. However, as will be explored below, limitations to this accommodation are also implied by the concept of respect for moral personality, because the exercise and development of the moral powers require the existence of some other rights and, moreover, a functioning society within which such exercise and development can occur. Accordingly, this chapter will develop an evaluative framework for claims to liberty of conscience that is based on respect for moral personality. The purpose of this framework is to evaluate the merits of claims to liberty of conscience, with an emphasis on their interaction with the rights of others. It is convenient to summarise the proposed framework at the outset. The framework considers two questions in evaluating a claim to liberty of conscience that is made against the enforcement of a law:

1. Does the action (or inaction) for which protection is sought against a law on the basis of liberty of conscience entail interference with the basic liberties of others (*compatibility*)?
2. Is the law against which protection is sought on the basis of liberty of conscience necessary in the common interest (*necessity*)?

If the activity for which protection is sought on the basis of liberty of conscience entails interference with a basic liberty of another person, an attempt is made to reconcile the two basic liberties. The central range of application, a concept drawn from Rawls's discussion of the basic liberties, is determined by reference to the importance of the freedom under consideration to the exercise and development of the moral powers, in order to seek to construe the two basic liberties conformably with one another. Further, necessity reflects the notion that the basic liberties are not absolute and may be limited for the common interest (for example, in public order and security), providing a kind of override of them. It addresses the issue of where a limitation of basic liberties that occurs for reasons other than intersection with other basic liberties should be allowed, and provides that such a limitation should happen only where strictly necessary in the common interest.

This account of how to limit liberty of conscience – by reference to the rights of others and to the common interest – has similarities to that advanced by other scholars. For example, Adenitire points to the public interest and the rights of others as the basis for possible limitation of the right, assessed through proportionality analysis.[1] For her part, Nussbaum contends 'that we ought to respect the space required by any activity that has the general shape of searching for the ultimate meaning of life, except when that search violates the rights of others or comes up against some compelling state interest'.[2] Tebbe claims that 'officials should lift government burdens on religious citizens only when that does not harm others'.[3] Specifically, he argues that 'accommodations that impose an undue hardship on others will be prohibited by this principle'.[4] Robert Wintemute points to considerations of direct and indirect harm to others, and cost.[5] Douglas NeJaime and Reva Siegel refer to major social goals as well as material or 'dignitary' harms to others as bases for the limitation of religious freedom.[6] Farrah Raza cites harms to others' autonomy.[7]

Nor is the idea of concern for the common interest or the rights of others altogether missing from the case law, though – as will be discussed in later chapters – there are important cases, especially in the US but also in the UK, in which the rights of others are not sufficiently acknowledged. Nonetheless, there has been some awareness, at least in dicta, about this point. For example, Kennedy J wrote in a concurring opinion in *Burwell v Hobby Lobby Stores, Inc* that

> [a]mong the reasons the United States is so open, so tolerant, and so free is that no person may be restricted or demeaned by government in exercising his or her religion. Yet neither may that same exercise unduly restrict other persons, such as employees, in protecting their own interests, interests the law deems compelling.[8]

Although similar to some others, the account that I offer of the limits of liberty of conscience is tailored to the particular moral-personality-based rationale for liberty of conscience offered in Chapter 2 of the book. The main points of distinction between my account and others are that I propose to delimit the right to liberty of conscience at a definitional stage by construing it conformably with the rights of others, prior to subjecting it to any balancing analysis; and that subsequent balancing analysis is tied to the 'common interest', not, say, to *any* major social or public goal or cost.

[1] J Adenitire, *A General Right to Conscientious Exemption: Beyond Religious Privilege* (Cambridge: Cambridge University Press, 2020) 227, 268–77. As will be explained below, I do not assess compatibility with the rights of others through proportionality analysis, though balancing may play a role in assessing necessity in the common interest.

[2] MC Nussbaum, *Liberty of Conscience: In Defense of America's Tradition of Religious Equality* (New York: Basic Books, 2008) 169.

[3] N Tebbe, *Religious Freedom in an Egalitarian Age* (Cambridge, MA: Harvard University Press, 2017) 52.

[4] ibid 66.

[5] R Wintemute, 'Accommodating Religious Beliefs: Harm, Clothing or Symbols, and Refusals to Serve Others' (2014) 77 *Modern Law Review* 223, 228–29.

[6] D NeJaime and R Siegel, 'Conscience Wars in Transnational Perspective: Religious Liberty, Third-Party Harm, and Pluralism' in S Mancini and M Rosenfeld (eds), *The Conscience Wars: Rethinking the Balance between Religion, Identity, and Equality* (Cambridge: Cambridge University Press, 2018) 200.

[7] F Raza, 'Limitations to the Right to Religious Freedom: Rethinking Key Approaches' (2020) 9 *Oxford Journal of Law and Religion* 435, 457–62.

[8] *Burwell v Hobby Lobby Stores, Inc* (2014) 573 US 682 (Supreme Court of the United States) 739.

The present chapter is structured in four parts. In Section I, I briefly consider a threshold question: a requirement for a claim to liberty of conscience that there is a non-negligible burden on liberty of conscience. In Section II, I explore the concept of compatibility with the rights of others as one possible basis for rejecting a claim to liberty of conscience. For example, a liberty of conscience claim will be defeated on the framework's approach if it clashes with another basic liberty in circumstances where the liberty of conscience claim is outside the central range of application while the other basic liberty would be affected within its central range. In Section III, I outline the concept of necessity in the common interest as serving as another possible basis for rejecting a claim to liberty of conscience, since the common interest serves as a premise for the effective exercise and development of the moral powers. Section IV concludes the chapter.

I. Non-Negligible Burden on Liberty of Conscience

The threshold requirement for a liberty of conscience claim is a burden on the holding or manifestation of a sincere conscientious belief where the burden is not *de minimis*. A truly negligible burden might not be thought to count for the purposes of establishing a claim to liberty of conscience.[9] For example, the road rules might limit a car to travelling at 70km per hour down a particular street. Perhaps this speed limitation causes a particular church attendee to become five minutes late for a service. Thus, although there might be viewed as being some slight burden on the manifestation of religious beliefs resulting from the imposition of road rules, this burden is clearly of a very trivial character. In addition, the burden is easily mitigated against by planning travel to the church in a way that factors in the road speed limit. To cross the initial threshold for a legitimate claim to liberty of conscience, there must be a sufficiently meaningful interference by the state with liberty of conscience.

Should a non-negligible burden on *any* conscientious belief count, or is it necessary to distinguish between different kinds of beliefs? It is possible to conceive of a government that wishes to refuse recognition to 'problematic' religious beliefs. It is often thought that cults may be distinguished from religions, though what are called cults are sometimes characterised as 'new religions'.[10] The defect of the approach by this government is that such matters are in the eye of the beholder, and there is no particular reason to have faith in the wisdom of state officials to correctly assess the matter. The state may reject a belief as out of step with

[9] See generally GM Girgis, 'What Is a "Substantial Burden" on Religion under RFRA and the First Amendment?' (2020) 97 *Washington University Law Review* 1755; EH Wang, 'To Prohibit Free Exercise: A Proposal for Judging Substantial Burdens on Religion' (2023) 72 *Emory Law Journal* 723.

[10] See generally DE Cowan and DG Bromley, *Cults and New Religions: A Brief History*, 2nd edn (Chichester: Wiley, 2015); E Baffelli, 'Fear and the Construction of Minority Religions in Japan' (2023) 51 *Religion, State & Society* 223.

its conceptions of morality, and be wrong, much as antebellum governments in the American South were wrong to permit slavery, and abolitionists were correct in their private moral views to oppose it. Any doctrine of liberty of conscience that purports to evaluate religious beliefs to exclude those that are deemed 'problematic' is likely to be excessively confident in the ability of the state, or the state's adjudicators, to correctly judge private morality. As Rawls puts it in *A Theory of Justice*,

> no particular interpretation of religious truth can be acknowledged as binding upon citizens generally; nor can it be agreed that there should be one authority with the right to settle questions of theological doctrine. Each person must insist upon an equal right to decide what his religious obligations are.[11]

Even if a state happens to be correct that a religious doctrine is morally flawed, it might be overstepping its bounds to seek to impose that view. It could evince what Kramer has called, in his discussion of edificatory perfectionism, a 'quidnunc' mentality for the state to interfere in this way with private beliefs.[12] Such concerns were evident in the US Supreme Court majority's analysis in *Hobby Lobby*, decided under the federal Religious Freedom Restoration Act.[13] Where the Secretary of Health and Human Services challenged a religious objection to mandating contraceptive coverage in employer-provided health care on the basis that 'providing the coverage would not itself result in the destruction of an embryo; that would occur only if an employee chose to take advantage of the coverage',[14] the Court declined to evaluate the religious objection in that way. The Court's opinion stated that the argument 'addresses a very different question that the federal courts have no business addressing (whether the religious belief asserted in a [Religious Freedom Restoration Act] case is reasonable)', and tells the plaintiffs that 'their beliefs are flawed'.[15] Rather than consider the 'plausibility' of a religious claim, it was only appropriate to determine that it reflected 'an honest conviction'.[16] In other words, only the sincerity of a belief is required.

In seeking to establish criteria for belief, there is a risk that they will be over- or under-inclusive. Attempts to rule in or out religious or non-religious beliefs from legal protection on the basis of threshold requirements – for example, on the

[11] J Rawls, *A Theory of Justice* (Cambridge, MA: Harvard University Press, 1971) 217; J Rawls, *A Theory of Justice (Revised Edition)* (Cambridge, MA: Harvard University Press, 1999) 191.

[12] MH Kramer, *Liberalism with Excellence* (Oxford: Oxford University Press, 2017) Ch 6.

[13] *Burwell v Hobby Lobby Stores Inc* (n 8).

[14] ibid 723.

[15] ibid 724.

[16] ibid 724–25. See also *Thomas v Review Board of Indiana Employment Security Division* (1981) 450 US 707 (Supreme Court of the United States). For doubts about this kind of approach, see P Jones, 'Conscientious Claims, Ill-Founded Belief and Religious Exemption' in J Adenitire (ed), *Religious Beliefs and Conscientious Exemptions in a Liberal State* (Oxford: Hart Publishing, 2019); SJ Levine, 'The Supreme Court's Hands-Off Approach to Religious Questions in the Era of Covid-19 and Beyond' (2022) 24 *Journal of Constitutional Law* 276.

basis of whether they are 'cogent, serious, cohesive or important'[17] – sometimes seem to evince caprice, with decisions of the Employment Tribunal that veganism, but not vegetarianism, should be eligible for protection as falling within the protected characteristic of philosophical belief under the Equality Act 2010 serving as a salient example.[18] Further, a vexed philosophical issue that I do not propose to address is the meaning or definition of religion.[19] Scholars and lawyers have long debated the nature of religion, but in the final analysis there is a lack of settled philosophical or legal criteria for assessing which beliefs are religious.[20] This book addresses, in its two case studies, some very clear examples of religious belief so it is not necessary to delve into such matters. It is also unwise to assess in an overly stringent fashion the connection between the belief held and the manifestation sought to be protected, as the European Court of Human Rights implicitly recognised in *Eweida v United Kingdom*,[21] by setting forth a general test of 'sufficiently close and direct nexus' between the belief and manifestation. Under the moral framework, the question remains one of the closeness of the connection between belief and manifestation, not one of categorising the manifestation to determine whether it is or should be protected.

Accordingly, as a threshold requirement for any claim to liberty of conscience, it is likely to be necessary that the beliefs are sincerely held, that they do in fact have a sufficient connection with the action (or inaction) sought to be protected, and that there is a non-negligible burden on the action (or inaction) in question. Rather than purporting to judge a conscientious belief, it is better to judge the claims made on the basis of belief for protection from the laws of the state. To raise once again the example of a 'cult', the state may be well advised not to seek immediately to suppress a new religion, but if its members begin committing or planning criminal acts, it obviously needs to intervene to protect others and the public order. Religious belief cannot be a licence to act however one wishes, contrary to the interests of the community and of others. But at the same time, it can be injurious to prevent a person from engaging in religious practice, or to compel a person to act contrary to sincerely held religious beliefs. How do we distinguish

[17] See *R (Williamson) v Secretary of State for Education and Employment* [2005] 2 AC 246, [21] (United Kingdom House of Lords). See also the principles set out to govern philosophical belief as a protected characteristic in *Grainger plc v Nicholson* [2010] ICR 360 (Employment Appeal Tribunal).

[18] See *Conisbee v Crossley Farms Ltd* [2019] Employment Tribunal ET/3335357/2018; *Casamitjana Costa v League against Cruel Sports* [2020] Employment Tribunal ET/3331129/2018.

[19] See, eg, George C Freeman III, 'The Misguided Search for the Constitutional Definition of "Religion"' (1983) 71 *Georgetown Law Journal* 1519; JL Neo, 'Definitional Imbroglios: A Critique of the Definition of Religion and Essential Practice Tests in Religious Freedom Adjudication' (2018) 16 *International Journal of Constitutional Law* 574.

[20] Courts have sometimes attempted definitions, or indicia: see, eg, *United States v Seeger* (1965) 380 US 163 (Supreme Court of the United States); *Church of the New Faith v Commissioner for Pay-roll Tax (Vic)* (1983) 154 CLR 120 (High Court of Australia); *Syndicat Northcrest v Amselem* [2004] 2 SCR 551 (Supreme Court of Canada). The case law under the European Convention on Human Rights avoids this difficulty by protecting secular belief, making it unnecessary to determine whether a belief is religious.

[21] (2013) 57 EHRR 8 (European Court of Human Rights) [82]. See also A Su, 'Judging Religious Sincerity' (2016) 5 *Oxford Journal of Law and Religion* 28.

between claims to liberty of conscience that should be accommodated by the state and those that should not? As will be seen, to assess whether such accommodation should be provided, the framework focuses on questions of compatibility with the basic liberties of others and necessity in the common interest.

II. Compatibility with the Basic Liberties of Others

I turn now to the potential interaction of a claim to liberty of conscience with the basic liberties of others. This is an intuitive basis on which to limit liberty of conscience. As Locke puts it, '[t]he sum of all we drive at is that every man may enjoy the same rights that are granted to others'.[22] John Stuart Mill also argues that 'the only purpose for which power can be rightfully exercised over any member of a civilised community, against his will, is to prevent harm to others'.[23] If respect for moral personality necessitates the protection of liberty of conscience, limitations to this protection are also implied by the concept of respect for moral personality, because the exercise and development of the moral powers necessitate the protection of various other rights as well. Since respect for moral personality does imply other rights, it cannot be that these are necessarily overcome by liberty of conscience. At the same time, it is not necessarily the case that other rights always overcome liberty of conscience. This issue, which it is convenient to term *compatibility*, addresses the situation in which the action (or inaction) for which protection is sought on the basis of conscience entails interference with the basic liberties of others.

A. The Nature of Compatibility with the Basic Liberties of Others

This limitation to liberty of conscience draws from Rawls on the need for reciprocal compatibility between basic liberties within the first principle of justice.[24] Rawls does not regard liberty of conscience as absolute: basic liberties may 'conflict in particular cases and their claims must be adjusted to fit into one coherent scheme of liberties'.[25] Thus, 'a basic liberty can be limited or denied … for the sake of one or more other basic liberties'.[26] However, '[t]he aim is to make these adjustments in such a way that at least the more significant liberties involved in the adequate development and

[22] J Locke, *First Letter Concerning Toleration* (William Popple tr, 1689) 39.
[23] JS Mill, *On Liberty*, 4th edn (London: Longmans, Green, Reader and Dyer, 1869) 22.
[24] J Rawls, *Political Liberalism* (New York: Columbia University Press, 2005) 297.
[25] J Rawls, *Justice as Fairness: A Restatement* (E Kelly ed, Cambridge, MA: Harvard University Press, 2001) 104–105.
[26] ibid 111.

full exercise of the moral powers … are normally compatible'[27] – 'at least within their central range of application'.[28] That is to say, Rawls is describing a definitional approach to resolving clashes of rights in which the rights are defined in a way as not to conflict, rather than a balancing one in which the clash is acknowledged and the two rights weighed against each other. Although there may sometimes not be so much difference in practice as opposed to in theory, that approach is sounder as it correctly captures the deontological nature of a rights claim.

It is the 'central range of application' of a basic liberty – in essence, its core – that Rawls says requires particular protection within the first principle of justice.[29] The 'central range' depends on the closeness of the connection between a liberty and the development and exercise of the moral powers. Thus, he says that

> a liberty is more or less significant depending on whether it is more or less essentially involved in, or is a more or less necessary institutional means to protect, the full and informed exercise of the moral powers in one (or both) of the two fundamental cases [that is, (1) judging the justice of the basic structure of society and its social policies, and (2) forming and revising and rationally pursuing their conceptions of the good]. The more significant liberties mark out the central range of application of a particular basic liberty; and in cases of conflict we look for a way to accommodate the more significant liberties within the central range of each.[30]

Putting to one side the concept of fundamental cases, which is not used in this book, the concept of the central range of application is nonetheless a useful one that captures that certain aspects of a basic liberty may be more closely connected to the exercise and development of the moral powers than other aspects. The criterion for the central range of application is the purpose of the basic liberties, being the development and exercise of the moral powers. The role of the central range of application appears particularly salient in the case of liberty of conscience because it is potentially a very broad basic liberty: beliefs, including religious beliefs, can extend to anything. They can mandate or prohibit virtually any form of action or inaction, depending on the beliefs in question, some of which may not be as closely connected to the exercise and development of the moral powers. Additionally, due to its breadth, liberty of conscience is unusually well positioned to intrude on the rights of others.

In setting out this approach, it is important to distinguish it from other possible approaches that also address the concept of the 'core' of liberty of conscience. For example, Raza describes how

> [s]ome courts and decision makers adjudicating on religious disputes have, either explicitly or implicitly, adopted an approach to limitations that rests on whether a belief in question is a 'core' belief. If the practice in question is considered to be central to that

[27] ibid 104–105.
[28] Rawls, *Political Liberalism* (n 24) 297.
[29] ibid.
[30] Rawls, *Justice as Fairness: A Restatement* (n 25) 113.

> faith, then there is a stronger reason to not limit it. Whereas, if the practice is not a core aspect of the faith, then limiting it is justifiable in principle.[31]

As has been noted, the central range of application of a basic liberty, including liberty of conscience, is assessed by reference to proximity to the development and exercise of the moral powers. It is not assessed, in the case of liberty of conscience, by reference to how important a given activity is according to the beliefs of a particular religion, a matter that may be difficult to determine.

This approach also does not hinge on whether there are 'alternatives' to the activity that is sought to be protected. Raza outlines a focus on alternatives as

> justif[ying] the non-accommodation of a religious practice in cases where viable alternatives are available to the individual or group making the claim. For example, religious adherents are free to choose a job that fits their religious needs rather than burdening employers with requests for accommodation.[32]

However, as she correctly points out, the 'choice of alternatives' approach sets the bar too low for justifying limitations. This is because many religious practices would fail to be accommodated as they could be too easily considered as voluntary so that conflicts could be resolved by, for instance, simply 'getting another job'. Such an approach can place an undue burden on religious believers.[33] Although the possibility of an obvious, effective workaround may be relevant to the nature of the burden on liberty of conscience (a matter addressed, for example, in the case study in Chapter 5), in the moral framework in this book the burden is not *negated* by the existence of alternatives.

Rawls explains that the central range of liberty of conscience 'includes the freedom and integrity of the internal life of religious associations and the liberty of persons to determine their religious affiliations in social conditions that are free'.[34] This is unlikely to be a complete statement of the central range of liberty of conscience, but it is indicative at least of what Rawls considered to be at the core

[31] Raza (n 7) 448. As Raza explains, there are some significant difficulties with an approach that distinguishes between 'core' and 'non-core' religious practices. She describes them as follows: 'Applying an approach to limitations that relies on a distinction between "core" and "non-core" religious beliefs is problematic for three reasons. First, an assessment of what the obligations of a particular religion are, can lead courts to making "thick" evaluations about religious beliefs and potentially draw them into irresolvable theological debates. Second, if religious beliefs are to be limited on the basis of whether they are "core" or not, it is unclear how courts would apply the same test in cases concerning secular and other ethical beliefs. What would constitute "core" beliefs in such categories of cases? It would be difficult, if not impossible, to determine what is not a "requirement" and "obligation" of a particular ethical worldview. For example, whilst it might be clear that for vegetarians not consuming animal products is a core aspect of the belief system, it is difficult to determine what constitutes a "core" belief of other philosophical beliefs such as environmentalism, etc. Third, it is increasingly difficult to legitimately identify the key tenets of a particular faith given the increase in different interpretations of any religion in "a secular age". Thus, the argument that "non-core" or non-mandatory religious practices should attract a lower level of protection potentially limits the protection of the right to FORB': ibid 450.

[32] ibid 450. For a UK case that dealt with a related issue, see *R (Begum) v Governors of Denbigh High School* [2007] 1 AC 100 (United Kingdom House of Lords).

[33] Raza (n 7) 454.

[34] Rawls, *Political Liberalism* (n 24) 341.

of that basic liberty, at least in respect of religious beliefs. Some complexity may also arise in discerning the nature of the central range of application of liberty of conscience in respect of secular beliefs. It may well be a secular belief does not always involve an 'association' with others as readily as might a religious belief. For example, in the case of veganism, vegans do not often gather with others under the umbrella of a particular organisation, such that the internal life of an association is as relevant to the central range of application as it might be for many religious beliefs. What this suggests is that the central range of application for liberty of conscience may depend on the nature of a belief and what is proximate to the development and exercise of the moral powers. For veganism, it may well be that the non-consumption of animal products constitutes the central range of application, since this issue informs a judgement of right and wrong.

Because compatibility analysis depends on reconciling those liberties that are classified as basic, it is different from some other approaches to the 'rights of others' that cast the net for other possible rights a good deal wider. For example, the European Court of Human Rights considers the rights of others as including rights well beyond those protected in the European Convention on Human Rights, even concluding, in *SAS v France*, that the rights of others to 'live together' could be a valid basis for limiting religious manifestation, despite the fact that there is no such express right in the European Convention.[35] Ian Leigh and Andrew Hambler propose a different approach of a 'reversibility test', that is: 'the Court should ask itself whether if the state were to give priority to the less favoured right … would another disappointed person have an admissible Convention claim?'[36] That is essentially the approach under compatibility in the moral framework in this book, since due to the character of liberty of conscience as a basic liberty, it can only be limited on this ground by another basic liberty.

B. Assessing Compatibility with the Basic Liberties of Others

Which other rights are selected as 'basic' liberties is a key question in assessing compatibility with the basic liberties of others. In other words, compatibility implies a hierarchy of liberties, separating 'basic' liberties from 'non-basic' liberties and giving priority to those liberties that are regarded as basic.[37] Although it seems

[35] *SAS v France* (2015) 60 EHRR 11 (European Court of Human Rights).

[36] I Leigh and A Hambler, 'Religious Symbols, Conscience, and the Rights of Others' (2014) 3 *Oxford Journal of Law and Religion* 2, 15.

[37] Laborde also distinguishes between those liberties essential to the moral powers and what she calls 'ordinary freedoms': 'Such liberties paradigmatically (but not exclusively) concern core areas of intimate, expressive activity, such as religion, sexuality, family, and friendship. These liberties have ethical salience because they are closely connected to individuals' basic moral powers and their ability to make "strong evaluations" about how to lead their lives. Other liberties are not so tightly connected to basic moral powers: let us call them ordinary freedoms. The freedom to pursue leisure preferences, the freedom to wear this or that form of dress, the freedom to move unimpeded by traffic regulations, are not as tightly connected to integrity, and therefore not as salient': C Laborde, *Liberalism's Religion* (Cambridge, MA: Harvard University Press, 2017) 147. In this book, I adopt a broadly similar distinction to Laborde's in separating basic and non-basic liberties, using as a criterion the closeness of their connection with the Rawlsian moral powers.

inevitable that there will be more or less important liberties, with those particularly necessary for the exercise and development of the moral powers and thus implied by respect for moral personality assuming the status of 'basic', the question of which liberties are 'basic' becomes critical to assessing conflicts of rights, since a basic liberty would prevail over a non-basic one. The list of basic liberties that Rawls identifies is open to debate, particularly on the omission of socioeconomic rights,[38] as well as other possible rights such as privacy.[39] In Chapters 5 and 6, I consider the status of two particular potential basic liberties (integrity of the person and non-discrimination) that are of relevance to the clashes of rights examined in the second half of this book.

Although liberty of conscience is a potentially broad basic liberty, other basic liberties can also intrude on one another, and the adjudication of these disputes would fall to be decided on the same principles of compatibility using the central range of application, itself determined by the exercise and development of the moral powers. Rawls gives the example of political speech that is 'an incitement to the imminent and lawless use of force' and says this would 'no longer [be] protected as a basic liberty'.[40] Although the reasoning behind this conclusion is not explained, the reason for this lack of protection may be that the political speech would be incompatible with the right to physical integrity of the person of others against whom the force is incited. Though freedom of speech is accepted by Rawls as a basic liberty, incitement to violence seems unlikely to fall within its central range as being particularly necessary for the exercise and development of the moral powers. However, the integrity of the person is threatened within its central range by this incitement, since any serious violence would impair the exercise and development of the moral powers.

That is not to say that the concept of a central range of application will always resolve clashes between basic liberties, since there may be clashes in which both basic liberties are within the central range of application, or outside it. Perhaps we can adjust Rawls's example so that both basic liberties are implicated within the central range of application: the speaker was calling for people to vote in order to end the corruption of certain public officials, a matter clearly within the central range of application of freedom of speech, but the crowd became overexcited and stormed the house of a corrupt public official living nearby, and engaged in non-life threatening physical violence that invaded the central range of application of the

[38] See Rawls, *Justice as Fairness: A Restatement* (n 25) 177. See also RG Peffer, 'Towards a More Adequate Rawlsian Theory of Social Justice' (2017) 75 *Pacific Philosophical Quarterly* 251; WA Edmundson, *John Rawls: Reticent Socialist* (Cambridge: Cambridge University Press, 2017); *cf* J Tomasi, *Free Market Fairness* (Princeton, NJ: Princeton University Press, 2012). For further analysis, see S Freeman, *Rawls* (Abingdon: Routledge, 2007) 59–64; J von Platz, 'Are Economic Liberties Basic Rights?' (2013) 13 *Politics, Philosophy & Economics* 23.

[39] For background on rights to privacy, see generally D Feldman, 'Secrecy, Dignity, or Autonomy? Views of Privacy as a Civil Liberty' (1994) 47 *Current Legal Problems* 41; K Hughes, 'A Behavioural Understanding of Privacy and Its Implications for Privacy Law' (2012) 75 *Modern Law Review* 806; K Hughes, 'The Public Figure Doctrine and the Right to Privacy' (2019) 78 *Cambridge Law Journal* 70.

[40] Rawls, *Justice as Fairness: A Restatement* (n 25) 113–14.

bodily integrity of those they attacked. This presents a difficulty for the framework, since the basic liberties appear to be clashing within their central ranges but, as it turns out, it is a difficulty that can be resolved by reference to considering causation in the interaction of the rights. Where the exercise of one right has some impact on another right, but that impact is of a minor or incidental nature, it seems doubtful whether this raises a compatibility issue.

In other words, we need to acknowledge the possibility that a connection between the exercise of one right and the interference with another is excessively remote. Ronald Dworkin observes that '[w]hen lawyers say that rights may be limited to protect other rights, or to prevent catastrophe, they have in mind cases in which cause and effect are relatively clear, like the familiar example of a man falsely crying "Fire!" in a crowded theatre'.[41] He argues that there would need to be a 'clear and substantial risk that [a person's] speech will do great damage to the person or property of others and no other means of preventing this are at hand'.[42] Though the 'clear and substantial risk' formulation may perhaps be too stringent, it is at least apparent that there needs to be a sufficiently real connection between the exercise of one right and the interference with another for there to be a compatibility issue.

If the connection between the exercise of one right and the interference with another is excessively remote, then it may be doubted whether there is really a clash at all. Viewing such situations as clashes – and thereby construing the interaction of rights under compatibility too broadly – might be used to justify excessive limitations of rights. As Dworkin asks rhetorically:

> Shall we say that some rights to protection are so important that the Government is justified in doing all it can to maintain them? Shall we therefore say that the Government may abridge the rights of others to act when their acts might simply increase the risk, by however slight or speculative a margin, that some person's right to life or property will be violated?[43]

Such issues of causation – when the causal relationship between the exercise of a right and the interference with another right is close enough to be sufficient for the purposes of compatibility – are relevant to the case studies in Chapters 5 and 6.

Although the speech example above may be resolved on the basis of causation, it remains possible to conceive of clashes between two basic liberties within their central ranges for which there are no causation issues. Perhaps one member of the mob that descended on the home of a certain public official became separated from the others. He happened upon an entirely innocent houseguest of the official, and wrongly associating him with the corruption that so exercised the mob, attacked the houseguest armed with a knife. However, the houseguest is not incapable of protecting himself, and, after a desperate fight, he killed his assailant in self-defence. In that example there is a direct clash between one person's right

[41] R Dworkin, *Taking Rights Seriously* (London: Bloomsbury, 2013) 243–44.
[42] ibid 245.
[43] ibid 244–45.

to physical integrity of the person (that of the assailant who is killed) and another person's right to physical integrity of the person (that of the houseguest acting in self-defence against a potentially lethal attack). Given the serious violence entailed in the example, the clash might be thought to relate to the central range of the basic liberties of both persons.

Unfortunately, Rawls is silent on how to resolve a clash between two basic liberties each within their central ranges. He expresses an expectation that the basic liberties 'can be made compatible with one another, at least within their central range of application',[44] so he may not have contemplated the possibility of a clash at the level of central ranges, or at least he does not address that possibility (nor does he address a clash of basic liberties both outside their central range). However, one solution that can be adopted for the purposes of the moral framework in this book is to assess the two basic liberties by reference to the criterion of the development and exercise of the moral powers, and determine which is more important. In the example of self-defence, the basic liberty of integrity of the person of the assailant (in its central range) would be less important than the basic liberty of integrity of the person of the victim of the attack defending himself or herself (in its central range), because, in initiating an unjustified attack, the assailant has not acted in any real sense to develop or exercise the moral powers.

Since, following Rawls, the approach at the compatibility stage is definitional – that is, delimiting the scope of differing rights that would otherwise clash – to refer to this as balancing would be inapposite. The concept of balancing implies consequentialist reasoning, while the issue here is the scope of the right as a matter of deontology. Kramer explains that

> the precisification of the contours of a deontological right is not an exercise in balancing. It is not an effort to curtail or adjust the contours of the right in order to accommodate other desiderata. Rather, it is an effort to specify more precisely the sorts of circumstances in which the factors that account for the all-or-nothing operativeness of the right are present, and the sorts of circumstances in which those factors are absent.[45]

In contrast, the necessity stage of the framework, addressed in the next section below, is consequentialist, as it is analogous to a kind of override of the deontological position expressed by the compatibility stage.

This analysis of compatibility does not rely on the concept of human dignity, despite the popularity of the concept.[46] Human dignity is often ambiguous, or

[44] Rawls, *Political Liberalism* (n 24) 297.

[45] MH Kramer, 'Looking Back and Looking Ahead: Replies to the Contributors' in M McBride and VAJ Kurki (eds), *Without Trimmings: The Legal, Moral, and Political Philosophy of Matthew Kramer* (Oxford: Oxford University Press, 2022) 489. On issues with consequentialist reasoning, see, eg, S Smilansky, 'Should We Sacrifice the Utilitarians First?' (2020) 70 *Philosophical Quarterly* 281.

[46] See, eg, RN Fasel, 'The Old "New" Dignitarianism' (2019) 25 *Res Publica* 531, 531. For discussion of issues with reliance on 'dignity' as a concept in case law of the European Court of Human Rights and Supreme Court of Canada, see L Sirota and G Baldwin, 'Can States Throw Away the Key? Critiquing Human Rights Law Approaches to Whole Life Sentences' [2026] 3 *European Human Rights Law Review* 340.

assigned a broad meaning, and as a result it is doubtful whether it helps in rights analysis. Jacob Weinrib suggests that dignity should not be applied as a concept 'directly to constitutional disputes', but rather used as 'a theory of modern constitutional practice [that] explicates and justifies the inner logic of … doctrines'.[47] Christopher McCrudden points out that

> dignity can often function as a placeholder, accepting that there is no actual or possible agreed articulation of its content. Indeed, some may wish to avoid any too-critical analysis of the concept, preferring to advert to the core mystery of the person, an intuition that reveals the ethical demands for respect.[48]

Indeed, it seems that to discover the content of dignity, it may help to look elsewhere, at other moral principles, such as the moral principles established in this framework. Rawls expresses a similar view, writing as follows:

> I believe … that while the principles of justice will be effective only if men have a sense of justice and do therefore respect one another, the notion of respect or of the inherent worth of persons is not a suitable basis for arriving at these principles. It is precisely these ideas that call for interpretation. The situation is analogous to that of benevolence: without the principles of right and justice, the aims of benevolence and the requirements of respect are both undefined; they presuppose these principles already independently derived. Once the conception of justice is on hand, however, the ideas of respect and of human dignity can be given a more definite meaning.[49]

A further issue with implications for the assessment of compatibility is who can be a right holder. The salience of this issue is apparent from the US Supreme Court case of *Church of the Lukumi Babalu Aye v City of Hialeah*.[50] In that case, the animal sacrifice practices of the Santeria religion were found to have been targeted by prohibitions in local ordinances, which were found to be unconstitutional under the Free Exercise Clause of the First Amendment. The US Supreme Court's analysis did not spend even a sentence contemplating any clash between the rights of the believers in the religion and the rights of animals who were being killed, because US constitutional law did not recognise the latter rights to begin

[47] J Weinrib, *Dimensions of Dignity: The Theory and Practice of Modern Constitutional Law* (Cambridge: Cambridge University Press, 2016) 21–22.

[48] C McCrudden, 'In Pursuit of Human Dignity: An Introduction to Current Debates' in C McCrudden (ed), *Understanding Human Dignity* (Oxford: Oxford University Press, 2013) 11. McCrudden nonetheless suggests that dignity (which he defines as 'intrinsic worth') can be used for 'commensurability to be identified between the values to be balanced in situations where there is an apparent clash of the rights protected': C McCrudden, *Litigating Religions: An Essay on Human Rights, Courts, and Beliefs* (Oxford: Oxford University Press, 2018) 131, 144. The difficulty is that since McCrudden seems to consider that in a clash of rights, dignity underpins rights on both sides of the dispute, and the concept of 'intrinsic worth' is so general and unspecific, it is not clear how dignity aids the analysis. 'Intrinsic worth' would point in both directions, and due to its breadth, is unlikely to supply guidance on how to resolve a clash. In contrast, compatibility analysis as set out in this chapter is more viable, as the concept of the exercise and development of the moral powers is specific, and exercises of rights can be compared in terms of how much they promote these activities.

[49] Rawls, *A Theory of Justice* (n 11) 586; Rawls, *A Theory of Justice (Revised Edition)* (n 11) 513.

[50] (1993) 508 US 520 (Supreme Court of the United States).

with. The rights of animals are a complex matter and, for present purposes, this issue does not need to be resolved. However, as discussed in Chapter 2, if at least some animals may have basic liberties, then those basic liberties may be relevant for compatibility analysis. (Even if they do not, however, their interests could be protected through necessity analysis.)

In approaching compatibility, it bears stressing that the framework is not concerned with constitutional design – it does not make any commitments as to which institution should be responsible for the assessment of these types of questions in respect of liberty of conscience within a particular political system. It is possible to conceive of a range of possible approaches to the assessment of these considerations; the framework is not tied to any particular model of constitutionalism. Jeremy Waldron, for example, advocates that rather than human rights being finally assessed by judges, these matters should be left to the legislature.[51] Alison Young argues that democratic dialogue as a model has normative advantages compared with legal constitutionalism or political constitutionalism.[52] The framework does not imply judicial supremacy as the only possible means of assessing the scope of liberty of conscience, and it is possible for such matters to be determined by branches other than the judiciary, or for the determination by the judiciary to be not necessarily the 'final word' in a dialogue between branches. However, the framework does suggest that there should be a meaningful form of rights protection that is undertaken by the state to assess these matters.

III. Necessity in the Common Interest

A further possible limitation on liberty of conscience (and other possible basic liberties) is the necessity in the common interest of the interference with that basic liberty. In addition to implying that accommodation of liberty of conscience needs to be construed conformably with other rights, respect for moral personality also suggests that the broader social welfare should serve as a basis, at least in some circumstances, for limiting rights where this is necessary in the common interest, as a kind of override of the right. The basis for this limitation of a basic liberty is that moral persons would not be able to exercise and develop their moral powers in circumstances where society as a whole is dysfunctional, because, for example, there is a lack of public order or security.

[51] See J Waldron, 'The Core of the Case against Judicial Review' (2006) 115 *Yale Law Journal* 1346. See also L Vinx, *Hans Kelsen's Pure Theory of Law: Legality and Legitimacy* (Oxford: Oxford University Press, 2007); KE Whittington, *Political Foundations of Judicial Supremacy: The Presidency, the Supreme Court, and Constitutional Leadership in US History* (Princeton, NJ: Princeton University Press, 2009); JK Greene, *How Rights Went Wrong: Why Our Obsession with Rights Is Tearing America Apart* (Boston, MA: Houghton Mifflin Harcourt, 2021).

[52] AL Young, *Democratic Dialogue and the Constitution* (Oxford: Oxford University Press, 2017) 31, 305. See also AL Young, *Parliamentary Sovereignty and the Human Rights Act* (Oxford: Oxford University Press, 2009).

A. The Nature of Necessity in the Common Interest

The second question posed by the framework is therefore necessity in the common interest of the law against which the claim of conscience is made. Necessity takes account of a criticism commonly made of theories of rights, such as Rawls's, that liberty can come at a cost to society in general, or to particular individuals in society. Writing in response to the original edition of *A Theory of Justice*, Hart criticises Rawls for insufficiently appreciating these potential costs of enshrining basic liberties. He says that

> Rawls fails to recognise sufficiently that a weighing of advantage and disadvantage must always be required to determine whether the general distribution of any specific liberty is in a man's interest, since the exercise of that liberty by others may outweigh the advantages to him of his own exercise of it. A rather startling sign that this is ignored appears in Rawls's remark that 'from the standpoint of the original position, it is rational' for men to want as large a share as possible of liberty, since 'they are not compelled to accept more if they do not wish to, nor does a person suffer from a greater liberty.' This I find misleading because it seems to miss the vital point that, whatever advantage for any individual there may be in the exercise of some liberty taken in itself, this may be outweighed by the disadvantages for him involved in the general distribution of that liberty in the society of which he is a member.[53]

Nonetheless, it is plain that Rawls does accept the need for at least some regulation of the basic liberties beyond ensuring their compatibility with each other, though it is true that he gives the first principle of justice lexical priority over the second principle. Thus, although basic liberties 'cannot be denied to certain social groups on the grounds that their having these liberties may enable them to block policies needed for economic efficiency and growth'[54] or 'for a greater public good understood as a greater net sum of social and economic advantages for society as a whole',[55] Rawls acknowledges in *A Theory of Justice* that '[l]iberty of conscience is limited … by the common interest in public order and security' because 'the disruption of these conditions is a danger for the liberty of all'.[56] Liberty of conscience is 'subject to reasonable regulations';[57] in his discussion of civil disobedience, Rawls observes that although '[t]here is a temptation to say that the law must always respect the dictates of conscience … this cannot be right'.[58] In *Justice as Fairness: A Restatement*, Rawls gives an example that seems to envisage the state overriding religious preferences on education, saying it would be possible for the state to require that

[53] HLA Hart, 'Rawls on Liberty and Its Priority' (1973) 40 *University of Chicago Law Review* 534, 550–51.

[54] Rawls, *Political Liberalism* (n 24) 294–95.

[55] Rawls, *Justice as Fairness: A Restatement* (n 25) 111.

[56] Rawls, *A Theory of Justice* (n 11) 212–13; Rawls, *A Theory of Justice (Revised Edition)* (n 11) 186–87.

[57] Rawls, *A Theory of Justice* (n 11) 244–45; Rawls, *A Theory of Justice (Revised Edition)* (n 11) 215–16. See also Rawls, *Political Liberalism* (n 24) 341.

[58] Rawls, *A Theory of Justice* (n 11) 370; Rawls, *A Theory of Justice (Revised Edition)* (n 11) 325.

> children's education include such things as knowledge of their constitutional and civic rights, so that, for example, they know that liberty of conscience exists in their society and that apostasy is not a legal crime, all this to ensure that their continued religious membership when they come of age is not based simply on ignorance of their basic rights or fear of punishment for offenses that are only considered offenses within their religious sect.[59]

Thus, in addition to implying that accommodation of liberty of conscience needs to be construed conformably with other basic liberties, in my account respect for moral personality suggests that the broader social welfare should serve as a basis for limiting the basic liberties where this is necessary in the common interest. Moral persons would not be able to exercise and develop their moral powers in circumstances where society as a whole is dysfunctional. The inquiry into whether to accommodate a claim of conscience cannot stop at the point of construing the basic liberties in a way that ensures that they are compatible, but must continue on to an evaluation of the claim in the light of the common interest, because it is possible to conceive of religious activities for which protection may be sought that harm the common interest of society.

At the necessity stage of the framework proposed in this book, we ask: is the state limitation of the action (or inaction) necessary in the common interest (*necessity*)? There are two operative terms to consider: 'necessary' and 'common interest'. Neither will be defined very narrowly. Implicit in talk of compromise of a basic liberty being 'necessary' is some kind of assessment of the end being pursued and the means used to pursue it. Rawls adverts to differences in means of limitation of a basic liberty by discussing the difference between its regulation and restriction.[60] Moreover, as Rawls makes plain, mere economic arguments are unlikely to gain much traction in such an analysis: a basic liberty must not be limited merely for convenience or financial reasons.[61] This makes sense, as we would not accept that basic liberties should be overridden for an end that does not truly reflect what is in the common interest. The assessment here might be addressed with approaches like strict and intermediate scrutiny in the US constitutional law context[62] and proportionality in European and other jurisdictions[63] (though I will address proportionality critically below).

By 'common interest', what I mean is interests shared by everyone (or, perhaps, generally everyone, and in that sense, at least everyone who is affected). Rawls

[59] Rawls, *Justice as Fairness: A Restatement* (n 25) 156.
[60] ibid 111–12.
[61] ibid 111.
[62] See *United States v Carolene Products Co* (1938) 304 US 144 (Supreme Court of the United States).
[63] See *Bank Mellat v Her Majesty's Treasury (No 2)* [2014] AC 700 (Supreme Court of the United Kingdom) [74]. See also G Baldwin, 'Freedom of Religion under the Australian Constitution: Is Proportionality the Answer?' (2023) 3 *Australian Journal of Law and Religion* 20; G Baldwin, 'A Chance to Close the Proportionality Chapter in Australian Constitutional Law?' (*AUSPUBLAW*, 17 November 2023) www.auspublaw.org/blog/2023/11/a-chance-to-close-the-proportionality-chapter-in-australian-constitutional-law.

identifies measures such as the maintenance of public order, public health, security, safety and national defence as lying in the common interest in this way.[64] It is plain from Rawls's account that the common interest is not some kind of aggregation of individual interests in a utilitarian sense, but rather an interest common to members of a society. Rawls addresses the common interest in *A Theory of Justice*, explaining that

> there are matters which concern the interests of everyone and in regard to which distributive effects are immaterial or irrelevant. In these cases the principle of the common interest can be applied. According to this principle institutions are ranked by how effectively they guarantee the conditions necessary for all equally to further their aims, or by how efficiently they advance shared ends that will similarly benefit everyone. Thus reasonable regulations to maintain public order and security, or efficient measures for public health and safety, promote the common interest in this sense. So do collective efforts for national defense in a just war. It may be suggested that maintaining public health and safety or achieving victory in a just war have distributive effects: the rich benefit more than the poor since they have more to lose. But if social and economic inequalities are just, these effects may be left aside and the principle of the common interest applied. The standpoint of equal citizenship is the appropriate one.[65]

To draw an analogy with moral philosophy, necessity resembles a kind of consequentialist 'override' of a deontological duty. For example, Michael Moore offers a tripartite account of the structure of morality, in which there is a background of consequentialist reasons, a set of deontological permissions and deontological duties, and finally the possibility of a consequentialist override of those deontological duties beyond a certain threshold.[66] As with the notion of a consequentialist override, sufficiently compelling wider considerations overcome what would otherwise be a convincing proposition: that liberty of conscience, construed conformably with other basic liberties, should be respected. That cannot always be right because there will be circumstances where absurd or undesirable consequences, which themselves undermine the exercise and development of the moral powers, will ensue if wider social considerations are excluded altogether. Of course, the possibility of religious practice harming the common interest to the required degree is unlikely to be extremely frequent. Locke expresses a similar expectation as follows:

> I say, first, no opinions contrary to human society, or to those moral rules which are necessary to the preservation of civil society, are to be tolerated by the magistrate. But of these, indeed, examples in any Church are rare. For no sect can easily arrive to such a degree of madness as that it should think fit to teach, for doctrines of religion,

[64] Rawls, *A Theory of Justice* (n 11) 97; Rawls, *A Theory of Justice (Revised Edition)* (n 11) 83.
[65] ibid.
[66] MS Moore, *Placing Blame: A General Theory of the Criminal Law* (Oxford: Oxford University Press, 1997); MS Moore, 'Patrolling the Borders of Consequentialist Justifications: The Scope of Agent-Relative Restrictions' (2008) 27 *Law and Philosophy* 35. For an interpretation of this and an alternative account, see MH Kramer, 'Michael Moore on Torture, Morality, and Law' (2012) 25 *Ratio Juris* 472.

> such things as manifestly undermine the foundations of society and are, therefore, condemned by the judgement of all mankind; because their own interest, peace, reputation, everything would be thereby endangered.[67]

Nonetheless, it will sometimes be necessary to restrict practices pursuant to liberty of conscience in the common interest. The importance of taking into account such wider considerations is apparent from the hypothetical example of a religious activity, justified by a particular belief, that involves dumping oil in the river, an environmentally damaging move that nonetheless does not interfere with the basic liberties of any other human (for example, no humans live downstream of the water). Indirect harms – such as that the pollution harms the environment in which humans live more generally, or that it harms a food source – might be too remote to be captured in the compatibility analysis. This underscores the importance of the necessity stage as protecting those conditions 'the disruption of [which] is a danger for the liberty of all'.[68] But it is unlikely to be controversial that it should be possible to limit this practice pursuant to a general law that bans dumping of pollutants in rivers. Such a limitation, although impairing a basic liberty, would be necessary – not for the 'greater net sum of social and economic advantages', but rather for the concrete reason of protecting the environment, as well as animals, despite the absence of any impact on the basic liberties of other humans, which lies squarely within the common interest in a clean environment.

It may also be conceivable that such regulation may be necessary where a religious practice severely invades a right or liberty that might not be acknowledged within the framework as 'basic'. For example, consider that a certain religious belief requires its adherents to take video footage of people in their homes through windows. Assuming *arguendo* that privacy is not accepted as a basic liberty (though this may be open to question), this religious practice does not interfere with another person's basic liberty. However, it is arguably necessary in the common interest to prevent filming of people in their homes so any law that prohibited such filming would therefore prevail over the liberty of conscience claim of the adherents to this religious belief. It might be argued that such privacy is not truly in the 'common' interest because there might be some who do not need it because they are in no real danger – those who live on isolated farms, those who keep their blinds drawn at all times, or those rich enough to live behind gated mansions whose windows are out of view. But it is recalled that by 'common' we mean *generally* everyone, not every single person in a strict sense. Those who are not affected naturally fall outside the relevant category.

The issue of necessity in the common interest is ultimately one of drawing the line – to what extent should basic liberties prevail over the common interest, or to what extent should the common interest prevail over basic liberties? Viewed against the wider philosophical and theoretical landscape, the framework adopts

[67] Locke (n 22) 34.
[68] Rawls, *A Theory of Justice* (n 11) 212–13; Rawls, *A Theory of Justice (Revised Edition)* (n 11) 186–87.

a middle ground approach that is considered to be best suited to vindicate the importance of respect for moral personality. At one end of this spectrum is Adrian Vermeule's 'common good constitutionalism'.[69] Vermeule claims that constitutional rights should be 'delimited by … a conception of justice that is itself ordered to the common good'; the common good does not 'override' rights but rather 'defines their boundaries all along'.[70] However, this approach seems to leave rights up to the vicissitudes of the common good and not be reconcilable with respect for moral personality, which entails a level of protection for basic liberties that is not dictated by a potentially fluctuating common good. On my account, what animates the protection of liberty of conscience is this respect for moral personality, not the convenience of the common good.

However, the common good – or common interest, in the language of the framework, adopted from Rawls – still plays an important role, and that fact distinguishes the account from those at the opposite end of the spectrum who place rights on a kind of pedestal over the general welfare. For example, Dworkin in *Taking Rights Seriously*, which sets forth the view that rights should serve as 'trumps', states that rights may be overcome where the 'cost to society would not be simply incremental, but would be of a degree far beyond the cost paid to grant the original right, a degree great enough to justify whatever assault on dignity or equality might be involved'.[71] But this approach seems to set the bar too high. The common interest in a functioning society, a premise for the exercise and development of the moral powers, may not be adequately protected if the cost to society of an exercise of a right has to be 'of a degree *far beyond* the cost paid to grant the original right involved'.[72] Rather, the balancing assessment looks to the necessity of protecting the common interest, and is not tilted heavily in favour of the right.

B. Assessing Necessity in the Common Interest

Necessity in the common interest involves an evaluative assessment comparing the law with the end pursued, which invokes the debates over balancing, including the contentiousness about the appropriateness of structured proportionality. For example, Megan Pearson argues that an approach based on proportionality 'is the best way to resolve … conflicts between non-discrimination and freedom of religion'.[73] She lauds proportionality's 'fact-specific nature' as allowing 'subtle distinctions to be made between cases'.[74] Thus, while '[i]ssues about the appropriate balance between religious liberty and non-discrimination are not straightforward

[69] A Vermeule, *Common Good Constitutionalism* (Cambridge: Polity Press, 2022).
[70] ibid 24.
[71] Dworkin, *Taking Rights Seriously* (n 41) 241.
[72] ibid.
[73] M Pearson, *Proportionality, Equality Laws, and Religion: Conflicts in England, Canada, and the USA* (Abingdon: Routledge, 2019) 1.
[74] ibid 72.

and there is no advantage in artificially making them so', proportionality 'can recognise this and provide answers tailored to the particular facts'.[75]

Proportionality originated in Germany, before spreading around the world.[76] The approach taken to the concept of proportionality can vary to some extent between countries. In the UK the test has been set out by Lord Reed in *Bank Mellat v Her Majesty's Treasury (No 2)*:

> it is necessary to determine (1) whether the objective of the measure is sufficiently important to justify the limitation of a protected right, (2) whether the measure is rationally connected to the objective, (3) whether a less intrusive measure could have been used without unacceptably compromising the achievement of the objective, and (4) whether, balancing the severity of the measure's effects on the rights of the persons to whom it applies against the importance of the objective, to the extent that the measure will contribute to its achievement, the former outweighs the latter.[77]

Although widely used, proportionality is controversial. One problem identified with it in the scholarly literature is that it stipulates a series of overlapping questions, which makes the analysis highly repetitive.[78] Other criticisms of proportionality focus on the requirement of balancing that is at the heart of the test. Although some kind of balancing may be unavoidable in a human rights context when assessing limitations on qualified rights, there is a question as to what should be balanced and how. The final stage of the proportionality test could be viewed as a balancing of incommensurables – in the UK context, the severity of the measure's effects against the importance of the objective. An alternative approach is to compare means and ends, as at the earlier stages of the proportionality test. Intermediate scrutiny and strict scrutiny in the US constitutional law context do this by asking whether, respectively, a law is substantially related to an important government interest or a law is narrowly tailored to further a compelling government interest.[79]

While these tests do first assess a government interest to determine if it is important or compelling, the comparison that is then made is between that end and the means employed. These tests do not seek to balance the importance of the interest against the effects of the law. Prior to the introduction of the *Smith* test by the US Supreme Court in 1990[80] – a test that will be discussed further in Chapter 4 – the test of narrow tailoring to a compelling state interest (strict scrutiny) as employed in cases such as *Sherbert v Verner* and *Wisconsin v Yoder*

[75] ibid.

[76] See G Huscroft et al, 'Introduction' in G Huscroft et al (eds), *Proportionality and the Rule of Law: Rights, Justification, Reasoning* (Cambridge: Cambridge University Press, 2014).

[77] *Bank Mellat v Her Majesty's Treasury* (n 63) [74].

[78] See AL Bendor and T Sela, 'How Proportional Is Proportionality?' (2015) 13 *International Journal of Constitutional Law* 530, 538.

[79] See RW Galloway, 'Means-Ends Scrutiny in American Constitutional Law' (1988) 21 *Loyola of Los Angeles Law Review* 449.

[80] *Employment Division v Smith* (1990) 494 US 872 (Supreme Court of the United States).

seemed to work well as a test for evaluating claims to free exercise.[81] This approach focuses on the availability of possible alternatives to assess the fit between the means chosen and the end pursued. Neither approach – proportionality or means-ends scrutiny – is necessarily inconsistent with addressing the necessity question. Nor, as I noted in the previous section, does the necessity stage require judicial supremacy in the adjudication of human rights issues. However, means-end analysis represents a more appropriate method of assessing this kind of question than proportionality, given the weighing of incommensurables at the final balancing stage of proportionality that invests a very high level of discretion in a court. This final balancing stage of the test seems ill suited to be performed by the judiciary, because courts are not well placed to 'balance' the severity of the measure's effects against the importance of the objective.[82]

In response to this problem, Shipra Chordia argues that 'incommensurability may be considered inherent to judicial decision-making' because it is found in 'numerous' areas of law.[83] However, there is a difference in the nature of the task between judicial review for constitutionality and other areas of law, since not all judicial decision-making involves reviewing laws and determining their validity or compatibility with human rights. Other areas of law in which incommensurability is said to arise do not necessarily have those stakes.[84] There may also be a basis within some other tests for comparisons to take place, whereas no such basis is apparent in proportionality. Ruth Chang describes how comparability proceeds with respect to an evaluative 'covering consideration'.[85] At the balancing stage of proportionality, there is nothing in the terms of the test that relates the items being balanced; it is simply a matter of which is said to outweigh the other. Moreover, attempts by scholars to discern an unstated common criterion have failed.[86]

As a result, the likely tendency for judges at the balancing stage of proportionality is to supply their own moral or political considerations in order to make the required comparison. Stavros Tsakyrakis observes that 'there is no way to accept the notion that values [at the final balancing stage of proportionality] are commensurable without a moral argument, that is, an argument that relates them and justifies degrees of priority'.[87] Indeed, Chordia seems to accept the 'centrality of normative or moral reasoning to the final balancing stage of proportionality

[81] *Sherbert v Verner* (1963) 374 US 398 (Supreme Court of the United States); *Wisconsin v Yoder* (1972) 406 US 205 (Supreme Court of the United States). See also A Barak, *Proportionality: Constitutional Rights and Their Limitations* (Cambridge: Cambridge University Press, 2012) 344.

[82] See, eg, S Tsakyrakis, 'Proportionality: An Assault on Human Rights?' (2009) 7 *International Journal of Constitutional Law* 468, 471–75.

[83] S Chordia, *Proportionality in Australian Constitutional Law* (Alexandria, NSW: Federation Press, 2020) 58.

[84] Chordia gives the example of damages in a tort judgment, but such a judgment only affects the parties to the case: ibid.

[85] See R Chang, 'Incommensurability (and Incomparability)' in H LaFollette (ed), *The International Encyclopedia of Ethics* (Oxford: Blackwell, 2013) 5–8.

[86] See FJ Urbina, 'Incommensurability and Balancing' (2015) 35 *Oxford Journal of Legal Studies* 575, 591.

[87] Tsakyrakis (n 82) 474.

analysis'.[88] But that raises a problem of institutional competence: courts are not well placed to make highly discretionary comparisons of values that are informed by subjective, personally chosen moral or political criteria.

The incommensurability problem also undercuts the main argument advanced for proportionality: that its steps of analysis create transparency. For example, Evelyn Douek claims that '[o]ne of the key promises of structured proportionality is that it will make judicial reasoning more constrained and transparent' as '[t]he step-by-step nature of the testing' is 'methodical and not "approached as a matter of impression … pronounced as a conclusion, absent reasoning"'.[89] However, because it invests judges with such a large discretion at its final stage, the proportionality test is better understood as opaque, rather than transparent. Timothy Endicott explains that, at this final stage, '[t]he attractive structure of the judicial role crumbles at that point into an unstructured, opaque choice, when the task involves balancing the unbalanceable'.[90]

Due to this unease about proportionality's mode of balancing, it is better to approach necessity using a means-ends analysis that first assesses whether an end is in the common interest and then assesses the necessity of the means to that end. It is also important to stress the importance of the first stage of the framework, which requires evaluating the compatibility of the claim with the rights of others before turning to balancing at the second necessity stage. Compatibility analysis takes place first because it involves assessing the scope of a right to avoid a clash with another right, rather than using balancing to reconcile the clash. This reflects a 'basic distinction in modern constitutional theory between the scope of the constitutional right and the justification for its limitation'.[91]

IV. Conclusion

On the account offered in this book, liberty of conscience is not absolute. In Chapter 3, I have set out the bases for its possible limitation, consistent with the rationale for liberty of conscience established in Chapter 2. Provided that there is a non-negligible burden on liberty of conscience, the right is engaged. It can be limited in either of two ways: first, by construing it compatibly with the rights of others where they involve the exercise and development of the moral powers – in particular, consistently with the central range of application of other basic liberties; or, second, when this is necessary in the common interest, since a functioning society underpins the possibility of exercising and developing the moral powers. In short, the justification of liberty of conscience also serves as the basis for discerning its limits.

[88] Chordia, *Proportionality in Australian Constitutional Law* (n 83) 59.

[89] E Douek, 'All Out of Proportion: The Ongoing Disagreement about Structured Proportionality in Australia' (2019) 47 *Federal Law Review* 551, 552, 557.

[90] T Endicott, 'Proportionality and Incommensurability' in Huscroft et al (eds) (n 76) 311, 328.

[91] Barak (n 81) 8–9.

4

Liberty of Conscience and Neutrality

This chapter addresses the relevance of 'neutrality' to the book's analysis of liberty of conscience. One sense of neutrality has already been discussed in Chapter 2, in which I considered possible rationales for liberty of conscience, of which 'state neutrality' is one. In this chapter I discuss two other possible meanings of neutrality: neutrality as non-establishment, which is sometimes identified as an implication of liberty of conscience; and neutrality as no purpose to limit exercise, as employed by the US Supreme Court[1] (I also consider a similar purpose test adopted by the High Court of Australia,[2] though not termed 'neutrality'). In Section I, I disambiguate 'neutrality', before briefly addressing non-establishment in Section II, and then turning in Section III to a critique of the purpose test in US and Australian law to show that this form of neutrality places emphasis on less morally relevant matters and should be avoided.

I. Disambiguating Neutrality

What does a state's 'neutrality' towards religion (or other comprehensive doctrine) require? The notion seems to evoke some sense that the state keeps a hands-off approach in relation to religion (or comprehensive doctrine). Yet that sense can be interpreted in different ways. To explore this, it is helpful to have regard to the decision of the Supreme Court of Canada in *Mouvement Laïque Québécois v Saguenay*,[3] a case in which it was held that reciting prayer at municipal council meetings was not permitted under the Quebec Charter. This case has been selected to illustrate certain problems with pinning down the meaning of neutrality. It contains the following dictum by Gascon J:

> [T]he state must not interfere in religion and beliefs. The state must instead remain neutral in this regard. This neutrality requires that the state neither favour nor hinder any particular belief, and the same holds true of non-belief … It requires that the state abstain from taking any position and thus avoid adhering to a particular belief.[4]

[1] See *Employment Division v Smith* (1990) 494 US 872 (Supreme Court of the United States); *Church of the Lukumi Babalu Aye v City of Hialeah* (1993) 508 US 520 (Supreme Court of the United States).

[2] See *Kruger v Commonwealth* (1997) 190 CLR 1 (High Court of Australia).

[3] [2015] 2 SCR 3.

[4] ibid [72].

This dictum highlights the difficulty with defining neutrality, because in the span of four sentences, it appears to invoke neutrality in 10 different senses. There are several distinctions that may be drawn within the concept of neutrality set forth by Gascon J:

- The requirement not to 'favour' and the requirement not to 'hinder' may be viewed as two distinct issues. The requirement not to favour a particular belief (or non-belief) might be thought to align with notions of non-establishment. In contrast, the requirement not to hinder a belief may be seen as more traditionally the territory of liberty of conscience protections.
- There is a distinction relating to whether the favouring or hindering of a particular belief (or non-belief) relates only to the actual holding of a belief (or non-belief), or its manifestation through conduct motivated by the belief (or non-belief). As I argue in Chapters 2 and 3, I do not consider it realistic to protect liberty of conscience without extending protection to the manifestation of beliefs. However, in speaking only of not favouring or hindering a belief (or non-belief), as distinct from conduct, there is an ambiguity about this aspect of neutrality as defined by Gascon J.
- There is also a distinction between neutrality of purpose and effect. When Gascon J says that the state should not favour nor hinder any particular belief (or non-belief), does it mean that the state should not have the purpose of favouring or hindering any particular belief (or non-belief), or does this requirement extend to state laws not having the effect of favouring or hindering any particular belief (or non-belief), even if that was not the purpose? The latter idea may be significantly broader than the former, as it captures unintentional or incidental effects of laws, which may include general laws, as will be discussed further below.
- The quote goes on to say that neutrality 'requires that the state abstain from taking any position and thus avoid adhering to a particular belief'. This can be viewed as a different sense yet again of neutrality, and one that seems to mean that the state must, in its own actions, avoid acting on the basis of a belief. However, once again there is a question about whether it relates to effect or purpose. Is it enough that officials do not have in mind adherence to a particular belief or non-belief as the purpose for the action that they take, or is it also necessary that they avoid taking an action that happens to align with a particular belief or non-belief, being adherence in effect?

Despite the simple sounding words used by Gascon J in the short quotation, once all the distinctions within the concept of neutrality are taken into account, the dictum appears to raise 10 distinct possible senses of neutrality towards religion, which are as follows:

(1) The state not having the purpose of favouring the holding of religious belief or non-belief in its actions.

(2) The state not favouring the holding of religious belief or non-belief in the effect of its actions.
(3) The state not having the purpose of hindering the holding of religious belief or non-belief in its actions.
(4) The state not hindering the holding of religious belief or non-belief in the effect of its actions.
(5) The state not having the purpose of favouring the manifestation of religious belief or non-belief in its actions.
(6) The state not favouring the manifestation of religious belief or non-belief in the effect of its actions.
(7) The state not having the purpose of hindering the manifestation of religious belief or non-belief in its actions.
(8) The state not hindering the manifestation of religious belief or non-belief in the effect of its actions.
(9) The state not having the purpose of adhering to religious belief or non-belief in its actions.
(10) The state not adhering to religious belief or non-belief in the effect of its actions.

Senses (1)–(2) and (5)–(6) relate to what is usually regarded as non-establishment, which will be addressed in Section II. Senses (9)–(10) are similar to the philosophical ideas of neutrality of justification and neutrality of effect, discussed in Chapter 2, whose workability has been questioned by Kramer, Nehushtan and others. Senses (3)–(4) and (7)–(8) can be understood as forms of liberty of conscience protections. Senses (3)–(4) relate to the holding of belief, rather than its manifestation, and senses (7)–(8) relate to manifestation. Sense (8) corresponds to the analysis for the interference with liberty of conscience in Chapter 3, in which the liberty is engaged if there is a non-*de minimis* interference with manifestation of beliefs, as does sense (4).

In Section III, I will consider sense (7) – the state not having the purpose of hindering manifestation of a religious belief or non-belief (neutrality as no purpose to limit exercise). This is similar to concepts that have appeared in the case law in some jurisdictions, such as the United States and Australia (though the purpose test employed in religious freedom jurisprudence in Australia is technically not called 'neutrality'). The US Supreme Court, interpreting the Free Exercise Clause, considers whether the impugned law has the object of restricting religious exercise. However, in the US constitutional jurisprudence it is significant that much is inferred about the purpose of a law from its effect,[5] blurring some of the distinction between senses (7) and (8). Nonetheless, at least in theory, the US Supreme Court's test focuses on the purpose of the law in the specified sense.

[5] See *Lukumi* (n 1).

II. Neutrality as Non-Establishment

Religious establishment has been described by Laborde as 'usually' referring to 'an institutionalised system of state-conferred advantages onto one church or religious group'.[6] In other words, it is commonly taken to be an antonym for the 'separation' of religion and state.[7] The prohibition of establishment is closely linked to ideas of secularism, itself a contested concept without a universal definition. In France, it is tied to ideas of laïcité,[8] and in the United States, to the 'wall of separation' between church and the state advocated for by Jefferson,[9] though in India, for example, the concept of secularism has entailed a far more 'permeable' wall between religion and the state.[10] The extent of state support required to constitute 'establishment' may vary between legal systems with prohibitions of religious establishment. For example, in Australia, the High Court interpreted the prohibition of establishment under section 116 of the Constitution as only prohibiting the creation of a national religion; accordingly, funding religious schools did not constitute a violation.[11]

The concepts of non-establishment and liberty of conscience are not wholly unrelated. According to Laborde, 'symbolic' establishment in the form of ceremonial and other similar recognition of religion is unlikely to violate religious freedom in itself given the lack of practical impact on egalitarianism.[12] She writes that 'nothing in orthodox political liberalism prevents a religious majority from entrenching its symbols within the state, provided members of religious minorities are otherwise treated as free and equal citizens (according to principles of

[6] C Laborde, 'Political Liberalism and Religion: On Separation and Establishment' (2013) 21 *Journal of Political Philosophy* 67, 68.

[7] ibid.

[8] See generally E Daly, 'The Ambiguous Reach of Constitutional Secularism in Republican France: Revisiting the Idea of Laïcité and Political Liberalism as Alternatives' (2012) 32 *Oxford Journal of Legal Studies* 583; M Hunter-Henin, 'Why the French Don't Like the Burqa: Laïcité, National Identity and Religious Freedom' (2012) 61 *International and Comparative Law Quarterly* 613; M Hunter-Henin, *Why Religious Freedom Matters for Democracy: Comparative Reflections from Britain and France for a Democratic 'Vivre Ensemble'* (Oxford: Hart Publishing, 2020) Ch 2.

[9] See generally DL Dreisbach, *Thomas Jefferson and the Wall of Separation between Church and State* (New York: New York University Press, 2002); TJ Gunn, 'Religious Freedom and Laïcité: A Comparison of the United States and France' [2004] *Brigham Young University Law Review* 419. The 'wall of separation' metaphor has been employed by the US Supreme Court: see *Everson v Board of Education* (1947) 330 US 1 (Supreme Court of the United States), 16. See also generally *Lemon v Kurtzman* (1971) 403 US 602 (Supreme Court of the United States). However, the US case law has shifted towards a weaker approach in recent years: see SH Barclay, 'The Religion Clauses after *Kennedy v Bremerton School District*' (2023) 108 *Iowa Law Review* 2097, discussing *Kennedy v Bremerton School District* (2022) 142 S Ct 2407 (Supreme Court of the United States).

[10] See, eg, R Bhargava, 'What Is Indian Secularism and What Is It For?' (2002) 1 *India Review* 1, 29.

[11] *Attorney-General (Vic) ex rel Black v Commonwealth* (1981) 146 CLR 559 (High Court of Australia). For criticism of this case as 'not the High Court's finest piece of constitutional jurisprudence', see L Beck, '*Attorney-General (Victoria) Ex Rel Black v Commonwealth*: The High Court's Attempt to Make the Establishment Clause of the *Australian Constitution* Mean Very Little' in R Barker et al (eds), *Law and Religion in the Commonwealth* (Oxford: Hart Publishing, 2022) 149.

[12] Laborde (n 6) 86.

justice)'.[13] David Miller, for one, considers that a 'liberal establishment' might be possible.[14] Javier García Oliva and Helen Hall, writing in the UK context, even contend that the limited form of establishment that exists in England, Wales and Scotland has significant social and constitutional benefits.[15]

However, more substantial state support for religion could be viewed as creating inequality in a way that has an impact on liberty of conscience. Locke, in his *Letter Concerning Toleration* of 1689, points out that there may be a risk of religious persecution if there is an inadequate separation between church and state:

> This only I say, that, whencesoever their authority be sprung, since it is ecclesiastical, it ought to be confined within the bounds of the Church, nor can it in any manner be extended to civil affairs, because the Church itself is a thing absolutely separate and distinct from the commonwealth. The boundaries on both sides are fixed and immovable. He jumbles heaven and earth together, the things most remote and opposite, who mixes these two societies, which are in their original, end, business, and in everything perfectly distinct and infinitely different from each other. No man, therefore, with whatsoever ecclesiastical office he be dignified, can deprive another man that is not of his church and faith either of liberty or of any part of his worldly goods upon the account of that difference between them in religion.[16]

Locke is right to discern at least a risk that if there is not such a separation, religious leaders empowered with state authority may frustrate liberty of conscience. In addition, establishment in respect of certain beliefs might express to those who hold other beliefs that those beliefs are not equally respected.[17] The experience of State Shintō in prewar Japan illustrates the risk that religious establishment may become associated with persecution of other religions, while the postwar experience (in which a stronger separation of religion and state was adopted at the constitutional level) shows the potential social utility of non-establishment.[18] As we have seen, some courts, including the European Court of Human Rights,[19] have discerned an implication of neutrality in the sense of a form of non-establishment in respect of religion from the protection of liberty of conscience. However, despite the potential connections between non-establishment and liberty of conscience, they remain distinct concepts. States with at least symbolically established religions

[13] ibid 82. See also, defending a 'weak form' of establishment, R Ahdar and I Leigh, 'Is Establishment Consistent with Religious Freedom?' (2004) 49 *McGill Law Journal* 635.

[14] D Miller, 'What's Wrong with Religious Establishment?' (2021) 15 *Criminal Law and Philosophy* 75.

[15] J García Oliva and H Hall, *Religion, Law and the Constitution: Balancing Beliefs in Britain* (Abingdon: Routledge, 2017).

[16] J Locke, *First Letter Concerning Toleration* (William Popple tr, 1689) 15.

[17] See F Ahmed, 'What Establishment Expresses' (2022) 20 *International Journal of Constitutional Law* 818. See also N Tebbe, *Religious Freedom in an Egalitarian Age* (Cambridge, MA: Harvard University Press, 2017) Chs 6, 10.

[18] See G Baldwin and A Hatano, 'The Diffusion of Religious Freedom in Japan' (2026) 21 *Asian Journal of Comparative Law* (forthcoming).

[19] See, eg, *Lautsi v Italy* (2010) 50 EHRR 42 (European Court of Human Rights). See also *In the matter of an application by JR87* [2025] UKSC 40.

can still protect liberty of conscience, as the example of the UK, with its established Church of England,[20] demonstrates. Indeed, in a state with religious establishment, protection of liberty of conscience may be even more valuable, since it may prove important to safeguarding the rights of practitioners of other religions than that embedded in state policy. Nonetheless, although such linkages remain important, the argument for liberty of conscience developed in this book proceeds separately from the concept of non-establishment.

III. Neutrality as No Purpose to Limit Exercise

What about the sense of neutrality employed by the US Supreme Court? The starting point is the 1990 case of *Employment Division v Smith*, which concerned the claimants' religious use of peyote,[21] having resulted in their dismissal from employment. The question raised in the proceedings was whether finding this use to be 'misconduct' disqualifying them from receipt of Oregon unemployment compensation benefits violated the Free Exercise Clause of the First Amendment. The claim was dismissed on the basis that the criminal law prohibition of peyote was constitutionally valid. Scalia J, delivering the opinion of the US Supreme Court, said that the right of free exercise did not relieve an individual of the obligation to comply with a 'valid and neutral law of general applicability'.[22] Applying a balancing test was inappropriate, according to Scalia J:

> To make an individual's obligation to obey … a law contingent upon the law's coincidence with his religious beliefs, except where the State's interest is 'compelling' – permitting him, by virtue of his beliefs, 'to become a law unto himself' – contradicts both constitutional tradition and common sense.[23]

Although *Smith* changed the test for free exercise to one of neutrality and general applicability, the opinion of the Court authored by Scalia J creatively reinterpreted the relevant precedents rather than formally overruling them.[24] However, it was not altogether clear what neutrality, or indeed general applicability, meant in

[20] See generally García Oliva and Hall, *Religion, Law and the Constitution* (n 15); Hunter-Henin, *Why Religious Freedom Matters for Democracy* (n 8) Ch 3.

[21] See also the earlier decision of *Employment Division v Smith* (1988) 485 US 660 (Supreme Court of the United States). On Native American religious practices, and how the First Amendment has sometimes failed to protect them (as arguably exemplified by *Smith*), see MD McNally, *Defend the Sacred: Native American Religious Freedom beyond the First Amendment* (Princeton, NJ: Princeton University Press, 2020).

[22] *Employment Division v Smith* (n 1) 879. *cf* the different test set out in *Sherbert v Verner* (1963) 374 US 398 (Supreme Court of the United States).

[23] *Employment Division v Smith* (n 1) 885. As noted previously, Scalia J was quoting the outdated – though not formally overruled – case of *Reynolds v United States* (1879) 98 US 145 (Supreme Court of the United States).

[24] This reinterpretation has led to charges of 'dishonesty' and 'revisionism' from scholars: see, eg, MW McConnell, 'Free Exercise Revisionism and the *Smith* Decision' (1990) 57 *University of Chicago Law Review* 1109; JM Oleske Jr, 'Free Exercise (Dis)Honesty' [2019] *Wisconsin Law Review* 689.

Smith, though *Lukumi* clarified that the question of neutrality was whether the law was directed at limiting religious practice.[25] Delivering the opinion of the Court in that case, Kennedy J explained that

> if the object of a law is to infringe upon or restrict practices because of their religious motivation, the law is not neutral … There are, of course, many ways of demonstrating that the object or purpose of a law is the suppression of religion or religious conduct.[26]

In other words, the neutrality of a law is determined by its 'object'; it is not neutral if this object is the 'suppression of religion or religious conduct'. Kennedy J went on to say that '[t]o determine the object of a law, we must begin with its text, for the minimum requirement of neutrality is that a law not discriminate on its face'.[27] However, '[f]acial neutrality is not determinative. … Official action that targets religious conduct for distinctive treatment cannot be shielded by mere compliance with the requirement of facial neutrality'.[28] Although this provided some clarity around neutrality, the meaning of general applicability remains more uncertain.[29]

In *Lukumi*, the use of the words 'sacrifice' and 'ritual' in the city's prohibition on animal slaughter was not conclusive of facial discrimination, because of their possible secular meanings.[30] However, Kennedy J nonetheless found that the law was not neutral, on two bases. First, the record compelled the conclusion that 'suppression of the central element of the Santeria worship service' was the object.[31] Second, the effect of the law suggested that it was targeting religious practices, given that 'almost the only conduct subject to [the ordinances] is the religious exercise of Santeria church members'.[32] The ordinances were not generally applicable either because they were 'underinclusive' – they 'fail[ed] to prohibit nonreligious conduct that endangers these interests [of protecting the public health and preventing cruelty to animals] in a similar or greater degree than Santeria sacrifice does'.[33] Since the ordinances were neither neutral nor of general applicability, they had to survive strict scrutiny to be valid.[34] They did not, because they were 'overbroad or underinclusive', and '[t]he proffered objectives [were] not

[25] *Lukumi* (n 1) 533.
[26] ibid.
[27] ibid.
[28] ibid 534.
[29] On the ongoing confusion, see, eg, Z Rothschild, 'Free Exercise Partisanship' (2022) 107 *Cornell Law Review* 1067, 1091; SC Pill, 'The False Promise of Expanded Religious Liberty Rights after the COVID-19 Cases and *Fulton v City of Philadelphia*' (2023) 31 *William & Mary Bill of Rights Journal* 825, 839–50. General applicability is usually found to be missing when a law is 'under-inclusive' due to the existence of individualised exceptions, official discretion, or other limitations on the reach of the law: see *Employment Division v Smith* (n 1) 884; *Lukumi* (n 1) 543. In practice, this question overlaps considerably with neutrality, particularly if a lack of neutrality is discerned by a law's differential treatment of religion, relative to secular issues.
[30] *Lukumi* (n 1) 533–35.
[31] ibid 534–35.
[32] ibid 535.
[33] ibid 543.
[34] ibid 546.

pursued with respect to analogous nonreligious conduct, and those interests could be achieved by narrower ordinances that burdened religion to a far lesser degree'.[35]

A similar purpose-based approach, although not called 'neutrality', was utilised in Australia in the case of *Kruger v Commonwealth*.[36] *Kruger* related to a 1918 ordinance empowering the 'Chief Protector of Aborigines' to undertake the care, custody, or control of any Aboriginal or 'half-caste' person if 'in his opinion it is necessary or desirable in the interests of the Aboriginal or half-caste for him to do so', as well as to 'cause any Aboriginal or half-caste to be kept within the boundaries of any reserve or Aboriginal institution'.[37] The resulting abductions of large numbers of Indigenous children from their families have come to be known as the Stolen Generations.[38] The ordinance was challenged on various grounds before the High Court of Australia – almost 80 years after it was made and 40 years after it was repealed in 1957. In respect of the challenge under section 116 of the Australian Constitution, which protects (among other things) the free exercise of religion, the claim was that the removal of Indigenous children violated the free exercise clause because it interfered with their ability to practise religion. However, in the result the ordinance was found not to violate section 116 because it did not have the purpose of prohibiting the free exercise of religion.

The reasoning in *Kruger* was different from previous cases of the High Court that addressed section 116.[39] It turned on the use of the word 'for' in the phrase 'any law … for prohibiting the free exercise of any religion' in section 116 of the Australian Constitution. This word was now read to mean, as Gummow J put it, that '[t]he question becomes whether the Commonwealth has made a law in order to prohibit the free exercise of any religion, as the end to be achieved'.[40] Most members of the Court found that the ordinance did not have that purpose,[41] while Gaudron J did not consider that whether the ordinance had the proscribed purpose could 'presently be determined' and reached no decision on the issue.[42] Dawson J and McHugh J rejected the claim on the different basis that section 116 did not apply to the Northern Territory, the jurisdiction in which the ordinance was made.[43] In the result, the reading of section 116, alongside the rejection of other bases of challenge, meant that the ordinance was found to be constitutional. In this way, the US and Australian approaches to religious freedom

[35] ibid.

[36] *Kruger* (n 2).

[37] ibid 33–35. See also Aboriginals Ordinance 1918 (NT), ss 6, 16.

[38] See generally National Inquiry into the Separation of Aboriginal and Torres Strait Islander Children from Their Families, *Bringing Them Home* (Commonwealth of Australia, 1997).

[39] See *Krygger v Williams* (1912) 15 CLR 366; *Adelaide Company of Jehovah's Witnesses v Commonwealth* (1943) 67 CLR 116. For criticism of the purpose test, see L Beck, 'The Case against Improper Purpose as the Touchstone for Invalidity under Section 116 of the Australian Constitution' (2016) 44 *Federal Law Review* 505.

[40] *Kruger* (n 2) 160. See also ibid 40, 60–61, 86.

[41] ibid 40, 60–61, 86–87, 161.

[42] ibid 134.

[43] ibid 60, 141–42.

converged in the 1990s, with both focusing on the presence of a state purpose to limit religious exercise.

As in the US, the purpose test adopted in Australia was not compelled by precedent: although consonant with the approach to the establishment clause taken by several members of the Court in the *DOGS Case*,[44] it departed, without explanation, from the approach of the Court to the free exercise clause taken in *Jehovah's Witnesses*. Unlike the reasoning in *Kruger*, this was a justificatory analysis that treated the purpose of the law as merely an aspect of assessing an interference with free exercise.[45] The members of the Court in *Kruger* were seemingly aware of the discontinuity with precedent. As Gaudron J said – considering the dicta of Latham CJ in *Jehovah's Witnesses* – purpose was (now) 'the only matter to be taken into account in determining whether a law infringes s 116'.[46] However, it was not made clear for what reason the approach in *Jehovah's Witnesses* had been rejected.

Despite the similarities between the US and Australian tests, there is a potential difference in the tests relating to how searching the inquiry in relation to purpose can be. In the US, courts have in recent times increasingly managed to find proscribed purposes under the First Amendment's neutrality test due to some creative (and at times rather strained) readings of the impugned laws, as will be discussed further in the case studies in Chapters 5 and 6. Much depends on what approach a court takes to discerning the purpose of a law. This directs attention to an ambiguity under the purpose test as articulated by the High Court of Australia in *Kruger* – namely, how deep courts are willing to dig to find a proscribed purpose. Is a court just looking at the face of the legislation, or beyond it, at extrinsic materials?[47] Or does the court infer the proscribed purpose from the mere fact of differential treatment, as the US Supreme Court often does?

Notwithstanding such ambiguities, a central difficulty with this concept of neutrality – focusing on the presence of a purpose of hindering the manifestation of religious belief – is that it does not appear applicable to the moral-personality-based approach set out in Chapters 2 and 3, and indeed it seems to be less morally relevant than the considerations identified by that approach. In short, it does not seem to matter much – to either the compatibility of a claim to liberty of conscience with the rights of others or to necessity in the common interest – whether the state has the purpose of limiting exercise. As such, this is not a point that specifically arises in the framework. Certainly, if a state is maliciously targeting a religious practice, it is very likely to fail to demonstrate the necessity of its measures in the common interest. However, establishing such a failure arguably does not require recourse to this concept of purpose.

[44] See *Attorney-General (Vic) (Ex rel Black) v Commonwealth* (1981) 146 CLR 559, 579 (Barwick CJ), 598 (Gibbs J), 609 (Stephen J), 615–16 (Mason J), 653 (Wilson J).

[45] See *Jehovah's Witnesses* (n 39) 132 (Latham CJ).

[46] *Kruger* (n 2) 132 (Gaudron J).

[47] See N Van Wees, 'Judicial Review of Legislators' Motives' (2017) 45 *Federal Law Review* 681.

Focusing on purpose to limit exercise as the main criterion for assessing liberty of conscience claims is less than optimal. That is particularly apparent when one considers two possible problems: neutral laws that have a heavy, unjustified burden on freedom of religion; and practices of a particular religion that merit a specific response. As to the first, I will put forward three examples, beginning with a hypothetical. Imagine that a legislature banned the consumption of carrots out of an erroneous health concern, and a religion existed for which carrot consumption was an important practice. Despite the negligible, indeed mistaken, justification for the ban, and the burden it imposed on a religious practice, since the law's purpose was health related it would be upheld under this kind of neutrality test. This very clearly unjust hypothetical example demonstrates the problem with a test of neutrality as no purpose to limit exercise. As Thomas Nagel observes,

> there may be cases of state action not intentionally aimed against a particular community of conviction which nevertheless foreseeably damages it to such an extent and so directly that positive responsibility must be acknowledged, and the action's legitimacy rendered doubtful.[48]

In *Smith*, the impugned unemployment law had a severe impact on a religious practice – resulting in the Native American claimants who had used peyote being ineligible for compensation – with what might be viewed as a relatively negligible justification, depending on one's view of drug laws (the justification may not be quite as negligible as the carrot ban). Viewed from the perspective of the framework in this book, neither banning nor restricting unemployment insurance on the basis of the personal use of peyote seems likely to be necessary in the common interest or to interfere with the rights of others; personal peyote use, arguably at least, is a victimless crime. As Megan Pearson points out in her analysis of *Smith*,

> [i]t provides no justification to those affected by the interference with religious practices other than that the religion was not deliberately targeted, which may be of little comfort. It is indifferent to the fact that the law imposes a harsher burden on people such as Smith than on someone who uses peyote for merely recreational reasons.[49]

However, in the absence of any purpose of limiting religious practice, and given also its general applicability, the law in question was found to be necessarily constitutional under the Free Exercise Clause.

The *Kruger* case in Australia offers an additional example. This, too, is a situation where a law's lack of a proscribed purpose seems less morally relevant to the question of whether it wrongly interfered with liberty of conscience than the matters addressed by the moral framework. The seemingly drastic interferences with the liberty of conscience resulting from the abductions of Indigenous children, removing them from the communities within which their traditional

[48] T Nagel, *Equality and Partiality* (Oxford: Oxford University Press, 1991) 167.

[49] M Pearson, *Proportionality, Equality Laws, and Religion: Conflicts in England, Canada, and the USA* (Abingdon: Routledge, 2017) 39.

religious practices were presumably possible, were immune from constitutional challenge because the law was found not to have the proscribed purpose of prohibiting religious exercise. In contrast, the abductions could not be justified under the framework offered in this book, since there was no evidence supporting the view that the apparent interference with liberty of conscience was necessary in the common interest or the claim to liberty of conscience was incompatible with the rights of others. A law directed at the safety of children who actually needed protection might be a different matter; but the blanket authorisation of removals, with minimal safeguards, that applied only to Indigenous children could not have met this standard.

One issue in the *Kruger* proceedings was the lack of evidence before the Australian High Court as to the impact on the religious practice of the Indigenous children. (As Benjamin Saunders and Dan Meagher point out, the failure to determine or agree these facts before questions were reserved for the consideration of the Full Court was 'procedurally unusual'.[50]) Some members of the High Court acknowledged that there may well have been an effect on religious practice, but they did not consider it necessary to pursue the issue because they were applying a purpose test. For example, Toohey J stated that

> [i]t may well be that an effect of the Ordinance was to impair, even prohibit the spiritual beliefs and practices of the Aboriginal people in the Northern Territory, though this is something that could only be demonstrated by evidence. But I am unable to discern in the language of the Ordinance such a purpose.[51]

Gummow J (with whom Dawson J agreed on this point) wrote:

> The withdrawal of infants … from the communities in which they would otherwise have been reared, no doubt may have had the effect, as a practical matter, of denying their instruction in the religious beliefs of their community. Nonetheless, there is nothing apparent in the 1918 Ordinance which suggests that it aptly is to be characterised as a law made in order to prohibit the free exercise of any such religion, as the objective to be achieved by the implementation of the law.[52]

In other words, no matter how extreme and unmerited the interference with liberty of conscience may be, this was not relevant to the courts in either *Smith* or *Kruger* because the test applied by the courts focused on state purpose to limit exercise, and there was said to be no such purpose. However, such a criterion fails to address a situation where the law has a large impact on people's liberty of conscience with little justification. The examples of *Smith* and *Kruger* suggest that the focus should instead lie where it does in the moral framework set out in Chapters 2 and 3 – on questions of the necessity in the common interest of the state action that interferes with the claim for liberty of conscience, and the

[50] BB Saunders and D Meagher, 'Taking Seriously the Free Exercise of Religion under the Australian Constitution' (2021) 43 *Sydney Law Review* 287, 301, citing *Kruger* (n 2) 48–49 (Dawson J).

[51] *Kruger* (n 2) 86.

[52] ibid 161.

compatibility of a claim for liberty of conscience with the rights of others. Since these examples involve interference with conscience that is unlikely to be defensible on either basis, they would appear to be impermissible interferences under the moral framework.

In offering these examples, I accept that there could be other rights potentially implicated in the scenarios described. However, that does not seem to reduce or alter the liberty of conscience issue presented by the cases. The fact that several rights may be violated by, say, the abduction of Indigenous children in *Kruger* does not mean that the liberty of conscience violation is any less important or serious. Moreover, courts are limited to act on the rights that are constitutionally protected and cannot necessarily respond to infringements of general liberty unless there is a very broad liberty right in the constitution.[53] This point is particularly clear in respect of *Kruger*, where the failure to find that religious freedom was violated contributed to the consequence that the ordinance authorising the abductions of Aboriginal children was found by the majority to be constitutionally valid.

The other difficulty, which further demonstrates the lack of moral relevance of a law's purpose of restricting religious practice, is that it is entirely possible to imagine a religious practice that merits being targeted. I will again put forward three examples. As the first example, which is hypothetical, imagine a religion that requires its adherents to carry around a ceremonial metal object. This object has to be carried everywhere. However, that causes a problem, as adherents to the religion are carrying the object into rooms with magnetic resonance imaging (MRI) machines, causing potentially hazardous consequences. The legislature is aware of the problem and, deliberately targeting these religious practitioners, decides to ban bringing metal objects (including the ceremonial object) into MRI rooms. Under an approach focusing on purpose to limit exercise, such a law would be invalid despite the fact that it is (according to the moral framework) necessary in the common interest from the standpoint of safety and security concerns. If the targeting were malicious, that might seem to be morally relevant, but such a law could presumably not be justified under the common interest, so it adds little to study the legislators' motives. If the targeting is justified by necessity in the common interest, as here, it appears that we should accept the interference with liberty of conscience, despite the lack of neutrality.

My second example is more dramatic, but further illustrates the pitfalls of a focus on the purpose of a law that interferes with liberty of conscience. Consider as an example a religious group that engages in terrorism – a far from unknown possibility in the real world, which has seen religiously inspired violence in recent decades from, for example, the Islamic terror groups Al-Qaeda, Hamas,

[53] It may be acknowledged that sometimes there are such broad rights enshrined in constitutions and human rights instruments. Art 13 of the 1947 Japanese Constitution may be an example. This right provides as follows: 'All of the people shall be respected as individuals. Their right to life, liberty, and the pursuit of happiness shall, to the extent that it does not interfere with the public welfare, be the supreme consideration in legislation and in other governmental affairs.' However, there can sometimes be a tendency for such very general rights to be interpreted in a way that does not give them strong effect.

and (so-called) 'Islamic State',[54] and the Aum Shinrikyo religious group in Japan, which perpetrated a deadly sarin gas attack in 1995 in the Tokyo subway system.[55] In the hypothetical example that I put forward, there are laws against terrorism, but imagine that the laws are not working, because the practitioners of this religion are willing to incur punishment for terrorist acts (or even to die in their commission) – after all, they believe such acts to constitute an important religious ritual. Thus, to prevent the terrorist acts, laws are needed to ban the preparatory steps leading to them.

Due to a peculiarity of this religion, albeit a convenient one, exactly a month before an act of terrorism, members of the group ritualistically tie a black ribbon to a tree. Responding to this, the government passes a law banning the antecedent step of tying a black ribbon to a tree, in order to prevent the members from going through with their act (and to allow law enforcement to arrest anyone participating in this step). The result is that many lives are saved, because, according to its beliefs, the religious group is unable to follow through with its act of terrorism if the ribbon is taken down. Although there is presumably no impact on the rights of others from tying black ribbons to trees, a liberty of conscience claim against such a law would fail at the second stage of the moral framework because the limitation is 'necessary'. It is clear that the law targets a religious practice, so it is not neutral in the sense of there being no purpose to limit exercise, but it is morally justified.

Finally, in *Lukumi* the animal sacrifice in that case may well have been precisely the kind of religious practice that merited targeting by a non-neutral law, given the moral value, increasingly recognised, of protecting the lives of animals.[56] Although the issue may be viewed as complex and more contestable than the hypothetical examples, it is at least possible that under the moral framework the interference with liberty of conscience in *Lukumi* would have been supported either by compatibility (on the basis of animal basic liberties, if these were accepted) or the necessity in the common interest of protecting sentient life. In the examples given, the fact that a law has the object of restricting a religious practice does not much seem to matter as much as the considerations identified by the moral framework: the necessity of a limitation of liberty of conscience in the common interest, and whether the claim to liberty of conscience interferes with another basic liberty.

[54] See, eg, D Snow and S Byrd, 'Ideology, Framing Processes, and Islamic Terrorist Movements' (2007) 12 *Mobilization: An International Quarterly Review* 119; G Baldwin, 'Support for Terrorism and Freedom of Association' [2024] 4 *European Human Rights Law Review* 342; G Baldwin, 'The Lawfulness of Citizenship Deprivation: Comparing Australia and the UK' (2025) 14 *Laws* 12.

[55] See, eg, T Okumura et al, 'Report on 640 Victims of the Tokyo Subway Sarin Attack' (1996) 28 *Annals of Emergency Medicine* 129; A Sugiyama et al, 'The Tokyo Subway Sarin Attack Has Long-Term Effects on Survivors: A 10-Year Study Started 5 Years after the Terrorist Incident' (2020) 15 PLoS ONE e0234967; E Baffelli, 'Did Aum Shinrikyō Really End?' in M Stausberg et al (eds), *The Demise of Religion: How Religions End, Die, or Dissipate* (London: Bloomsbury, 2020).

[56] See, eg, MC Nussbaum, *Justice for Animals: Our Collective Responsibility* (New York: Simon & Schuster, 2023); RN Fasel, *More Equal Than Others: Humans and the Rights of Other Animals* (Oxford: Oxford University Press, 2024); JO Adenitire and R Fasel, *Animals and the Constitution: Towards Sentience-Based Constitutionalism* (Oxford: Oxford University Press, 2025).

Admittedly, under the US Supreme Court's own approach, neutrality and general applicability are only the first step of the legal inquiry and, in theory, at least, the subsequent strict scrutiny stage should catch many of these kinds of cases. However, the US Supreme Court's strict scrutiny analysis has often been very cursory, and in *Masterpiece Cakeshop* this step was skipped altogether in the opinion of the Court[57] (with a *post facto* attempt at explaining this odd omission being offered in *Kennedy v Bremerton School District*[58]). In *Lukumi* the absence of neutrality and general applicability of the impugned law was taken to largely explain the failure at the strict scrutiny stage,[59] so there is a risk that placing emphasis on these matters will lead to the strict scrutiny assessment being an afterthought. In the Australian case law, as shown in *Kruger*, there is apparently no second stage of the test, indicating all the more the pitfalls of judicial reliance on a test of no purpose to limit exercise.

In the US, the neutrality test has become robust, and some commentary suggests that the US Supreme Court has transformed the Free Exercise Clause into a broad 'equality right' rather than the 'liberty right' it had been under earlier precedents, as expansive understandings of differential treatment towards religion are taken to demonstrate non-neutral purposes.[60] Critics argue that religion has acquired a status akin to 'most favoured nation' in international trade law, such that 'if a statute provides any exemptions to the regulation at issue for secular reasons, then religious activity must be accorded an exemption as well'.[61] The US Supreme Court case of *Carson v Makin* serves as a significant example of the potential breadth of neutrality as a test.[62] In that case, it was held that a system of school vouchers offered by the state of Maine, which were not available for religious private schools, violated the Free Exercise Clause. As the dissenting opinions noted, that seemed to mean that the state was required to fund religious institutions, in potential

[57] *Masterpiece Cakeshop v Colorado Civil Rights Commission* (2018) 138 S Ct 1719 (Supreme Court of the United States).

[58] In *Kennedy*, Gorsuch J, delivering the opinion of the Court, wrote as follows in a footnote: 'A plaintiff may also prove a free exercise violation by showing that "official expressions of hostility" to religion accompany laws or policies burdening religious exercise; in cases like that we have "set aside" such policies without further inquiry': *Kennedy v Bremerton School District* (2022) 142 S Ct 2407 (Supreme Court of the United States) 2422 fn 1. However, this is clearly an explanation after the fact, since in *Masterpiece Cakeshop*, Gorsuch J did believe strict scrutiny was required, as he applied strict scrutiny in his concurring opinion: *Masterpiece Cakeshop v Colorado Civil Rights Commission* (n 57) 1734, 1737.

[59] *Lukumi* (n 1) 546.

[60] Rothschild, 'Free Exercise Partisanship' (n 29) 1099–1104. See also Z Rothschild, 'Free Exercise's Lingering Ambiguity' (2020) 11 *California Law Review Online* 282. This development was advocated for by some in the legal academy, such as Douglas Laycock, when *Smith* was originally decided: D Laycock, 'The Remnants of Free Exercise' [1990] *Supreme Court Review* 1, 49–50.

[61] M Strasser, 'COVID-19, Free Exercise, and Most Favored Nation Status' (2023) 27 *Lewis & Clark Law Review* 1, 1. See also Z Rothschild, 'Individualized Exemptions, Vaccine Mandates, and the New Free Exercise Clause' (2022) 131 *Yale Law Journal Forum* 1106; A Koppelman, 'The Increasingly Dangerous Variants of the "Most-Favored-Nation" Theory of Religious Liberty' (2023) 108 *Iowa Law Review* 2237; NS Chapman, 'The Case for the Current Free Exercise Regime' (2023) 108 *Iowa Law Review* 2115.

[62] *Carson v Makin* (2022) 142 S Ct 1987 (Supreme Court of the United States).

contravention of the Establishment Clause. However, the status of *Smith* is nonetheless shaky, in the wake of criticism in *Fulton v City of Philadelphia*,[63] which is discussed in Chapter 6. In *Mahmoud v Taylor*,[64] the Court weakened *Smith*, applying strict scrutiny for a substantial burden on religious practice in the context of education, irrespective of whether the burden was imposed by a law that was neutral and of general applicability. I return to the issue of the status of *Smith* in Chapter 7.

IV. Conclusion

This chapter has disambiguated the concept of 'neutrality' and addressed the significance of two of its possible meanings. Although neutrality as non-establishment has some linkages with liberty of conscience, neutrality as no purpose to limit exercise seems less attractive than the moral framework set out in Chapter 3. It seems to overlook that neutral laws of general applicability could heavily burden liberty of conscience in unjustified ways, or, conversely, that it might be necessary to respond non-neutrally to a problematic religious practice. The key cases from the US, a pioneer of this kind of test, also raise doubts on their facts: as a consequence of applying the test of neutrality and general applicability in the circumstances, *Lukumi* found what was arguably animal cruelty to be constitutionally protected while *Smith* found what was arguably victimless drug use not to be constitutionally protected, counterintuitive results. Meanwhile, in Australia, the *Kruger* case applied a purpose test to give constitutional imprimatur to removals of Indigenous children from their families. *Smith* and *Lukumi* have significant detractors among the current members of the US Supreme Court, but remain the law at least for now. Even if it is possible to apply a neutrality test broadly with enough judicial creativity – as the US Supreme Court has sometimes demonstrated – that does not alter the fact that the test focuses on morally less relevant questions. Indeed, it may merely exacerbate the problem.

[63] (2021) 141 S Ct 1868 (Supreme Court of the United States).

[64] (2025) 145 S Ct 2332 (Supreme Court of the United States), applying *Wisconsin v Yoder* (1972) 406 US 205 (Supreme Court of the United States).

5

Coronavirus Pandemic

From early 2020, the novel coronavirus SARS-CoV-2 swept across the world, causing millions of deaths and inflicting serious health problems on many others. Rather than seeking to eradicate the virus, most states adopted an objective of merely 'flattening the curve' of infection numbers – an objective which, despite its relative lack of ambition, was nonetheless often pursued through strong, population-wide restrictions.[1] These restrictions have presented a human rights challenge. The difficulty of balancing public health against human rights has been particularly acute in relation to liberty of conscience, as measures limiting attendance at places of worship or requiring their temporary closure have been challenged in the courts.[2] Although the legal approaches to assessing violations of religious freedom in the US and UK are different, both approaches have led to the similar result of courts taking issue with the imposition of certain public health restrictions on places of worship.

In Chapters 2, 3 and 4 of this book, I developed a theoretical framework intended to assist in ascertaining the limits of claims to liberty of conscience. In this chapter, I turn to the first case study addressing these limits, which concerns the clash between liberty of conscience and integrity of the person, as well as the common interest in public health, that is presented by the circumstances of the pandemic.

[1] See C Kenyon, 'Flattening-the-Curve Associated with Reduced COVID-19 Case Fatality Rates – An Ecological Analysis of 65 Countries' (2020) 81 *Journal of Infection* E89. For a comparison of laws addressing the coronavirus pandemic, see generally J King and OLM Ferraz (eds), *Comparing Covid Laws: A Critical Global Survey* (Oxford: Oxford University Press, 2026).

[2] In the US and UK, see generally *Dolan v Secretary of State for Health and Social Care* [2020] EWHC 1786 (Admin) (Administrative Court) (*Dolan*); *Dolan v Secretary of State for Health and Social Care* [2021] 1 WLR 2326 (Court of Appeal Civil Division) (*Dolan appeal*); *Philip v Scottish Ministers* 2021 SLT 559 (Outer House of the Court of Session); *South Bay United Pentecostal Church v Newsom (No 1)* (2020) 140 S Ct 1613 (Supreme Court of the United States); *Roman Catholic Diocese v Cuomo* (2020) 141 S Ct 63 (Supreme Court of the United States). For analysis from the author, see G Baldwin, 'The Coronavirus Pandemic and Religious Freedom: Judicial Decisions in the United States and United Kingdom' (2021) 26 *Judicial Review* 297; G Baldwin, 'Positive Obligations to Protect the Public under Human Rights Law' (2025) 30 *Judicial Review* 232. For detailed discussion of the US cases, including at lower court level, see J Blackman, 'The "Essential" Free Exercise Clause' (2021) 44 *Harvard Journal of Law & Public Policy* 637. In this chapter, I address only the US Supreme Court decisions on the issue. These decisions came through what is called the 'shadow docket', involving requests for emergency relief, rather than the 'merits docket'. For an explanation on the distinction between the shadow docket and merits docket, see SC Pill, 'The False Promise of Expanded Religious Liberty Rights after the COVID-19 Cases and *Fulton v City of Philadelphia*' (2023) 31 *William & Mary Bill of Rights Journal* 825, 863–65. In the UK, because the UK Supreme Court (as distinct from the Judicial Committee of the Privy Council) has not considered the issue, I refer to lower court decisions in England and Scotland.

Applying the framework to the reasoning of courts in the US and UK,[3] it will be shown that the conclusion of some courts – that closures of, or attendance limits upon, places of worship intended to protect lives are in violation of protections for liberty of conscience – is not the morally preferable position according to both the compatibility and necessity stages of the framework developed in this book.

This chapter has five sections. In Section I, I address the significance of the integrity of the person within the framework, arguing that it should be considered a basic liberty. In Section II, I outline the judicial decisions considering coronavirus restrictions on attendance at places of worship in the US and UK. In both countries, courts initially declined relief against the restrictions, but the judicial approach later shifted, and some challenges to restrictions were upheld on religious freedom grounds. In Section III, I consider the cases through the lens of compatibility, which will highlight the flaws in the reasoning of these later cases, because compatibility analysis permits limitation of liberty of conscience on the basis of the protection of integrity of the person. Specifically, it is doubtful that the interference with liberty of conscience presented by requiring worship to go online temporarily went to the central range of application of liberty of conscience, while the spread of the virus that was potentially exacerbated by in-person religious gatherings went to the central range of application of integrity of the person. In Section IV, I evaluate these decisions by reference to necessity in the common interest, which will demonstrate further pitfalls because of the clear common interest in public health that justifies the limitation of liberty of conscience in the circumstances, particularly when the interference does not go to the central range of application of that basic liberty.

[3] Although I focus on the US and UK, the clash between liberty of conscience and coronavirus restrictions was a major legal issue in many jurisdictions throughout the world: see, eg, NT Phuong, 'Religion, Law, State, and Covid-19 in Vietnam' (2020) 8 *Journal of Law, Religion and State* 284; M Gur-Arye and S Shakargy, 'Solidarity, Religious Freedom and COVID-19: The Case of the Ultra-Orthodox Sects in Israel' (2021) 50 *Netherlands Journal of Legal Philosophy* 203; AM Piwko, 'Islam and the COVID-19 Pandemic: Between Religious Practice and Health Protection' (2021) 60 *Journal of Religion and Health* 3291; OT Shemudara and VO Ayeni, 'Law and Religion: The Challenges of Citizens as a Result of Covid-19 Pandemic in Nigeria' (2021) 3 *International Review of Law and Jurisprudence* 166; A Fornerod, 'Freedom of Worship during a Public Health State of Emergency in France' (2021) 10 *Laws* 15; J Tengatenga et al, '*Zimitsani Moto*: Understanding the Malawi COVID-19 Response' (2021) 10 *Laws* 20; G Androutsopoulos, 'The Right of Religious Freedom in Light of the Coronavirus Pandemic: The Greek Case' (2021) 10 *Laws* 14; B Bird, 'COVID-19 and Religious Freedom in Canada' (2022) 64 *Journal of Church and State* 621; GA du Plessis and A Portaru, 'Restrictions to Religious Worship during COVID-19: A Bird's-Eye View of Court Decisions from Selected European Countries and the European Court of Human Rights' (2022) 64 *Journal of Church and State* 641; BR Lara, 'Two Years Later: A Critical Analysis of the Impact of Spanish Law about COVID-19 on Religious Freedom' (2022) 64 *Journal of Church and State* 683; CS Pratiwi, 'Indonesia's Legal Policies amid Covid-19' (2022) 6 *Journal of Southeast Asian Human Rights* 182; Ł Skoczylas et al, 'Restrictions on Religious Practices in Selected European Countries during the COVID-19 Pandemic: A Legal-Sociological Study from Poland's Experiences' (2023) 7 *Society Register* 35; C Burke, 'COVID-19 and Korea: Viral Xenophobia through a Legal Lens' (2023) 16 *International Journal for Religious Freedom* 91; DP Petri and T Flores, 'The Impact of COVID-19 on Religious Regulation in Colombia, Cuba, Mexico, and Nicaragua' (2023) 16 *International Journal for Religious Freedom* 31; C Mikoski, 'Churches and COVID-19: Key Trends in Congregational Life since the Pandemic' (2025) 16 *Religions* 759. But, for a different dimension of the issue, see RF Baggaley et al, 'Impact of the COVID-19 Pandemic on Communal Religious Worshippers' Mental Health and the Benefits of Positive Religious Coping' (2024) 10 *Heliyon* e39093.

In Section V, I conclude that the restrictions on places of worship prior to widespread vaccination – despite interfering with liberty of conscience – were justifiable during the coronavirus pandemic on an emergency basis under both compatibility and necessity analysis. The case law from the US and UK that is opposed to this conclusion fails to reflect the moral position established by the framework.

I. A Basic Liberty of Integrity of the Person

Before turning to analyse this case study, it is necessary to consider the significance of integrity of the person. The idea that the state should seek to protect its citizens from physical harm is a fundamental one. In common law systems, this idea is reflected in the law of battery and assault, both in tort (trespass to the person) and the criminal law. It is also an aspect of constitutional or human rights law in many systems, such as through the right to life under Article 2 of the European Convention on Human Rights,[4] the right to private life under Article 8,[5] and the prohibition on torture and inhuman or degrading treatment or punishment in Article 3.[6] Philosophers have long understood the importance of physical safety. For example, for Thomas Hobbes in *Leviathan*, the significance of a sovereign was precisely that the sovereign could ensure the safety of the public; this was worth trading for the liberty entailed in living in the state of nature.[7] In the state of nature, life was solitary, poor, nasty, brutish and short; the very point of the state was to alleviate these features.[8]

However, there are differing possible accounts of why integrity of the person ought to be protected (and, as will be seen, it may be that several of these accounts express valid reasons for that position). In the present account, I put forward the view that integrity of the person is a condition of moral personality, because it is often not possible to exercise and develop the moral powers in circumstances of physical insecurity. Rawls specifies that the 'rights and liberties specified by the liberty and integrity (physical and psychological) of the person' are basic liberties within the first principle of justice.[9] That is because these liberties are, according to Rawls, 'necessary if the other basic liberties are to be properly guaranteed'.[10]

[4] See, eg, *McCann v United Kingdom* (1996) 21 EHRR 97 (European Court of Human Rights).

[5] Art 8 has been interpreted as protecting the 'physical and psychological integrity of a person': see *Pretty v United Kingdom* (2002) 35 EHRR 1, [61]. On the breadth of Art 8, as interpreted by the European Court of Human Rights, in protecting health and well-being, see, eg, *Verein KlimaSeniorinnen Schweiz v Switzerland* (2024) 79 EHRR 1 (European Court of Human Rights) [519]. However, on the reducibility of bodily integrity to notions of autonomy, see J Herring and J Wall, 'The Nature and Significance of the Right to Bodily Integrity' (2017) 76 *Cambridge Law Journal* 566.

[6] See, eg, *Gäfgen v Germany* (2011) 52 EHRR 1 (European Court of Human Rights).

[7] T Hobbes, *Leviathan or The Matter, Forme and Power of a Commonwealth Ecclesiasticall and Civil* (1651).

[8] ibid Ch XIII.

[9] J Rawls, *Justice as Fairness: A Restatement* (E Kelly ed, Cambridge, MA: Harvard University Press, 2001) 44.

[10] ibid 113.

Thus, Rawls endorses the position that, as a necessary underpinning of the other basic liberties, integrity of the person must itself be protected as a basic liberty. Of course, this is open to possible objection on the basis that it may well be that there are other such conditions, including those not acknowledged by Rawls, such as food, shelter and health care. However, for present purposes such matters are set aside as I focus on confirming Rawls's inclusion of integrity of the person as a basic liberty, since other possible conditions do not arise in the case studies. Rawls explains that integrity of the person 'includes freedom from psychological oppression and physical assault and dismemberment'.[11] Although it is not necessary to consider in detail the nature of integrity of the person, the account that I offer shares the view of Rawls that it extends to psychological integrity.

The argument advanced here is that a basic liberty of integrity of the person is necessary for recognition respect for moral personality because of a sufficient tendency for interference with integrity of the person to impair the development and exercise of the moral powers. Rawls's argument that integrity of the person needs to be protected in order to guarantee the other basic liberties is sound insofar as there is a clear relationship between integrity of the person and the other basic liberties. For the same reason, integrity of the person is essential to the development and exercise of the moral powers. A person cannot, say, exercise political liberties nor effectively develop and exercise the moral power of the capacity for a sense of right and justice if, in, say, seeking to vote, she faces a campaign of psychological terror by people determined to disenfranchise her. Nor can a person exercise liberty of conscience nor develop and exercise the moral power of the capacity for a conception of the good if he faces violence for holding particular religious views. It is plain, then, that integrity of the person is required to enable persons 'adequately to develop and fully exercise' the moral powers.[12]

Although these examples of threatened violence in order to deter the exercise of other basic liberties are particularly illustrative of the significance of integrity of the person to the other basic liberties, it is not necessary that the impairment of integrity of the person take place with the *intention* of adversely affecting the exercise of another basic liberty. Consider the example of a person who is stabbed by a mugger and hospitalised, and as a result is unable to attend a place of worship for several weeks. The violation of integrity of the person, although not intended to prevent the person from attending a place of worship, nonetheless has that consequence, impairing him from developing and exercising the moral power of the capacity for a conception of the good. The same would be true if the mugger's action instead had the effect of preventing someone from voting.

As was also discussed in relation to liberty of conscience in Chapter 2, a question arises about the nature of the required relationship between integrity of the person and the development and exercise of the moral powers. When Rawls writes that integrity of the person is 'necessary if the other basic liberties are to

[11] Rawls, *A Theory of Justice (Revised Edition)* (Cambridge, MA: Harvard University Press, 1999) 53.
[12] Rawls, *Justice as Fairness: A Restatement* (n 9) 88.

be properly guaranteed', he does not elaborate on the *extent* of the relationship between interference with integrity of the person and the failure to guarantee other basic liberties. It may be accepted that interference with integrity of the person may not *always* have the effect of interfering with the exercise of other basic liberties. If a person is stabbed by a mugger and ends up in hospital, but manages to vote by mail with the assistance of others, the exercise of the right to vote has not been prevented (even though it has been made more difficult). Equally, it may be that the stabbing does not take place near an election day, so there is no interference with that particular basic liberty at all. But the fact that it may sometimes be possible to mitigate the consequences of interferences with integrity of the person does not eliminate the potential relationship that would exist between interference with integrity of the person and exercise of other basic liberties. It is this potential relationship, a *sufficient tendency* to impair the exercise and development of the moral powers, that justifies inclusion of integrity of the person as a basic liberty necessary to moral personality.

This account of why integrity of the person should be protected focuses on the importance of that integrity not intrinsically but instrumentally to moral personality. That is not to say that there cannot be compelling reasons why the integrity of the person should be protected inherently. The harmfulness of interference with integrity of the person may appear obvious when it inflicts reduced capacities on a person, whether temporarily or permanently, or results in death, or inflicts pain, though a sense of violation may result even in the absence of these features. Thus, one possible challenge to this account of integrity of the person as a basic liberty as necessary for the development and exercise of the moral powers is that it is altogether too elaborate. For example, as previously noted in Chapter 1, Tasioulas contends that it makes more sense for the right not to be tortured to be based not on the idea that torture impairs the pursuit of a conception of the good but rather on the idea that torture involves suffering.[13] What Alasdair Cochrane calls 'welfarist' accounts of human rights that explain rights by reference to interests necessary to lead a decent life offer an arguably more direct route towards explicating certain rights, including rights to bodily integrity.[14]

However, the potential existence of multiple pathways to establishing rights does not detract from the reasoning advanced above. It is clear that interference with integrity of the person can and does undermine the exercise and development of the moral powers and, for that reason, there is good reason to think that on that basis, integrity of the person is a basic liberty. In this regard, the present account has

[13] J Tasioulas, 'Human Rights, Universality and the Values of Personhood: Retracting Griffin's Steps' (2002) 10 *European Journal of Philosophy* 79, 93.

[14] A Cochrane, 'From Human Rights to Sentient Rights' (2013) 16 *Critical Review of International Social and Political Philosophy* 655, 661–62, citing MC Nussbaum, 'Capabilities and Human Rights' (1998) 66 *Fordham Law Review* 273; A Buchanan, *Justice, Legitimacy, and International Relations: Moral Foundations for International Law* (Oxford: Oxford University Press, 2004); S Caney, 'Global Poverty and Human Rights: The Case for Positive Duties' in T Pogge (ed), *Freedom from Poverty as a Human Right: Who Owes What to the Very Poor?* (Oxford: Oxford University Press, 2007).

affinities with aspects of the work of other theorists, such as Drucilla Cornell, who considers bodily integrity as a condition necessary for a minimum degree of individuation,[15] and Henry Shue, in explaining basic rights as rights that are essential to the enjoyment of other rights.[16] Shue identifies three basic rights, being physical security, subsistence, and liberty, as underpinning all other rights.[17] The reasoning in this account, although drawing on moral personality, resembles Shue's approach in noting the importance of physical security to the realisation of all other rights.

Rawls's terse justification of integrity of the person does not address some of the other complexities involved in the protection of that integrity. For example, whether 'bodily integrity' can be separated from the mind, such that it refers only to 'physical inviolability', is contested.[18] Rawls sidesteps this issue of dualism, and thus whether the mind can be considered as part of 'bodily integrity', by specifying that he is referring to the integrity of the person both physical and psychological. Rawls also does not broach the issue of the integrity of the person of a pregnant woman who has, on one view, another person in her womb (or, at least, a future person), while retaining her own right to integrity of the person.[19] Nussbaum, in contrast, specifically defines 'choice in matters of reproduction' as an aspect of bodily integrity.[20] For present purposes, it is not necessary to resolve the significance of reproductive rights to bodily integrity. Nor is it necessary to address whether a right to integrity of the person might extend to some provision of health care.

A further complexity is consent. When an interference with integrity of the person occurs with freely given consent, one might think that there is no real impairment to the development and exercise of the moral powers. A consensual hug between friends is of a different character from an unwanted hug by a stranger. What might be alarming and violative becomes harmless, or even beneficial, due to the presence of consent. Equally, being pierced with a knife during a medical procedure undertaken with informed consent is of a different character from being stabbed by the mugger. Sometimes, it should be noted, consent might be provided by another, such as a parent of a young child. For example, in the case of *Gillick v West Norfolk and Wisbech Area Health Authority*, Lord Scarman in the UK House of Lords explained the limits of such a proposition as that

> [a]s a matter of law the parental right to determine whether or not their minor child below the age of sixteen will have medical treatment terminates if and when the child achieves a sufficient understanding and intelligence to understand fully what is proposed.[21]

[15] D Cornell, *The Imaginary Domain: Abortion, Pornography and Sexual Harassment* (Abingdon: Routledge, 1995) 4, 51.

[16] H Shue, *Basic Rights: Subsistence, Affluence, and US Foreign Policy: 40th Anniversary Edition* (Princeton, NJ: Princeton University Press, 2020).

[17] ibid 1, 3.

[18] See M Patosalmi, 'Bodily Integrity and Conceptions of Subjectivity' (2009) 24 *Hypatia* 125, 133.

[19] ibid 134–35.

[20] See MC Nussbaum, *Women and Human Development: The Capabilities Approach* (Cambridge: Cambridge University Press, 2000) 78–80.

[21] *Gillick v West Norfolk and Wisbech Area Health Authority* [1986] AC 112 (United Kingdom House of Lords) 188–89.

There are also limits to the legitimacy of consent. One is capacity. A person who is intoxicated, mentally ill or otherwise incapacitated generally cannot consent.[22] Other factors may vitiate consent, such as lack of information, duress or a power imbalance. Moreover, other limits may apply even with seemingly valid consent. If a person agreed to be stabbed by the mugger for some irrational reason, it seems doubtful that the mugger's action would cease to be wrongful. The quality of consent, viewed against the nature of what is being consented to, is therefore relevant. Some of these matters were elaborated upon in the UK Supreme Court case of *Montgomery v Lanarkshire Health Board*, where informed consent in a medical context was said to require consideration of risks, benefits and alternatives to the medical treatment.[23] The issue of consent offers a complicating factor in any account of integrity of the person; the presence of consent, or even perhaps merely its reasonable anticipation, affects the question of whether there has been interference with that basic liberty.

Moreover, accepting integrity of the person as a basic liberty is not to conceive of it as absolute, but rather to accept it as subject to the same potential limitations for compatibility and necessity as liberty of conscience itself, particularly outside the central range of application of the basic liberty, as discussed in Chapter 3. The state may, for example, engage in invasive searches of the person if justified pursuant to the reasonable suspicions of the police, since such searches may be necessary for the common interest in law enforcement.[24] Another example of where we do not consider an interference with integrity of the person as wrongful, even though such an interference has technically occurred, is normal jostling in a public transport setting. Sometimes it has been suggested that there is implied consent to this by boarding public transport, but even if the person involved has, say, never ridden a bus before and was not aware of the possibility of jostling, we would likely still not entertain the claim that the state should intervene to prevent such jostling.

It might be that the absence of intention by others in a public transport setting to interfere with integrity of another person (unlike, say, a mugger who is intending to harm the integrity of another or is reckless as to it) is relevant. However, some forms of intentional interference done with the pretext of the public transport setting that would not be permissible, such as needless shoving, but passing closely by others to exit a train might well be intentional and yet not viewed as wrongful. In the UK case of *Collins v Wilcock*, Lord Goff expressed the view that there was a general exception covering such circumstances because it was 'physical conduct which is generally acceptable in the ordinary conduct of daily life'.[25] It is

[22] See, eg, A Clough, 'Finding the Balance: Intoxication and Consent' (2019) 40 *Liverpool Law Review* 49.

[23] *Montgomery v Lanarkshire Health Board* [2015] AC 1430 (Supreme Court of the United Kingdom) [89].

[24] See, eg, *Gillan v United Kingdom* (2010) 50 EHRR 45 (European Court of Human Rights). In the US context, the Fourth Amendment to the US Constitution prohibits 'unreasonable searches and seizures': see, eg, *Katz v United States* (1967) 389 US 347 (Supreme Court of the United States).

[25] [1984] 1 WLR 1172 (Divisional Court of the Queen's Bench Division) 1177.

likely that such interference would, in any case, fall well outside the central range of application of the basic liberty of integrity of the person.

II. Key Case Law

Having established bodily integrity as a basic liberty, I now turn to set out the details of the US and UK cases that concerned liberty of conscience and coronavirus restrictions. In the US Supreme Court, applications for injunctive relief against restrictions on places of worship on the basis of the Free Exercise Clause of the First Amendment were rejected in the early months of the pandemic, but then later generally granted on the basis that the restrictions imposed were not 'neutral' pursuant to the *Smith-Lukumi* test discussed in Chapter 4 of this book. In the UK courts, the question was the proportionality of the restrictions on manifestation of religion under Article 9(2) of the European Convention on Human Rights, as referred to in Chapter 3 above. Similarly to the US, initially courts rejected the claim that the restrictions were not proportionate to their legitimate end of protecting public health. However, in *Philip* the Outer House of the Court of Session found that there was a violation of Article 9 of the Convention.

A. US Case Law

As noted, the US Supreme Court initially opted to refuse the requested injunctions against the enforcement of attendance limits at places of worship. In *South Bay United Pentecostal Church v Newsom*,[26] decided on 29 May 2020, the applicants sought an injunction to enjoin enforcement of an executive order limiting attendance at places of worship in California to 25 per cent of building capacity or a maximum of 100 attendees. Roberts CJ, in his concurring opinion, reasoned that:

> Similar or more severe restrictions apply to comparable secular gatherings, including lectures, concerts, movie showings, spectator sports, and theatrical performances, where large groups of people gather in close proximity for extended periods of time. And the Order exempts or treats more leniently only dissimilar activities, such as operating grocery stores, banks, and laundromats, in which people neither congregate in large groups nor remain in close proximity for extended periods.[27]

Thomas J, Alito J, Gorsuch J and Kavanaugh J dissented. Kavanaugh J, with whom Thomas J and Gorsuch J joined, said that '[t]he basic constitutional problem is that comparable secular businesses are not subject to a 25% occupancy cap, including

[26] *South Bay (No 1)* (n 2).
[27] ibid 1613.

factories, offices, supermarkets, restaurants, retail stores, pharmacies, shopping malls, pet grooming shops, bookstores, florists, hair salons, and cannabis dispensaries'.[28] Given this, strict scrutiny was said to apply. California 'undoubtedly has a compelling interest in combating the spread of COVID-19 and protecting the health of its citizens', but it was necessary that there be 'a compelling justification for distinguishing between (i) religious worship services and (ii) the litany of other secular businesses that are not subject to an occupancy cap'.[29] According to Kavanaugh J, California had not shown such a justification: 'Assuming all of the same precautions are taken, why can someone safely walk down a grocery store aisle but not a pew? And why can someone safely interact with a brave deliverywoman but not with a stoic minister?'[30]

In *Calvary Chapel Dayton Valley v Sisolak*,[31] decided on 24 July 2020, the Court again split 5-4, with the majority dismissing an application for an injunction against Nevada's 50-person limit on religious attendance. Alito J, with whom Thomas J and Kavanaugh J joined, considered that the Governor's directive was not neutral because it 'specifically treats worship services differently from other activities that involve extended, indoor gatherings of large groups of people' – places of worship were limited to 50 persons, while other facilities hosting indoor activities like bowling alleys, breweries, fitness facilities and casinos could operate at 50 per cent capacity.[32] Alito J distinguished *South Bay* on the basis that in these facilities, 'people congregate in large groups and remain in close proximity for extended periods'.[33] The discriminatory treatment could not withstand strict scrutiny, since '[h]aving allowed thousands to gather in casinos, the State cannot claim to have a compelling interest in limiting religious gatherings to 50 people'.[34] Gorsuch J and Kavanaugh J each wrote similar dissents.

However, after those decisions, the US Supreme Court's composition changed, with Ginsburg J passing away on 18 September 2020 and Barrett J being confirmed to join the Court by the US Senate on 26 October 2020. All of a sudden, the Court began granting injunctions, beginning with the *Roman Catholic Diocese v Cuomo* decision on 25 November 2020.[35] The shift in approach as a result of a new appointment to the Court underscores concerns about the politicisation of the US judiciary. For example, Zalman Rothschild documents in an empirical study that

[28] ibid 1614.
[29] ibid 1614–15.
[30] ibid 1615.
[31] (2020) 140 S Ct 2603.
[32] ibid 2605.
[33] ibid 2609.
[34] ibid 2608.
[35] *Roman Catholic Diocese* (n 2). For discussion, see G Baldwin, 'The Pandemic and the First Amendment' (*UK Constitutional Law Association Blog*, 8 December 2020) http://ukconstitutionallaw.org/2020/12/08/guy-baldwin-the-pandemic-and-the-first-amendment.

> in deciding free exercise challenges by religious plaintiffs to COVID-19 lockdown orders, 0% of Democratic-appointed judges sided with religious plaintiffs, 66% of Republican-appointed judges sided with religious plaintiffs, and 82% of Trump-appointed judges sided with religious plaintiffs.[36]

The *Roman Catholic Diocese* case concerned 10- and 25-person occupancy limits on attendance at religious services in New York. The *per curiam* of Thomas, Alito, Gorsuch, Kavanaugh and Barrett JJ said that 'the regulations cannot be viewed as neutral because they single out houses of worship for especially harsh treatment' relative to businesses.[37] Further, the measures failed strict scrutiny because of their restrictiveness.[38] Gorsuch J and Kavanaugh J each wrote separate concurrences. Roberts CJ and Breyer J each dissented on the basis that the designations had changed and the places of worship were no longer subject to the challenged restrictions. Sotomayor J, with whom Kagan J joined, dissented on the basis that the prior cases provided a 'clear and workable rule' to state officials – '[t]hey may restrict attendance at houses of worship so long as comparable secular institutions face restrictions that are at least equally as strict' – and New York's restrictions satisfied this rule.[39]

In the second *South Bay United Pentecostal Church v Newsom* case,[40] decided on 5 February 2021, the Court granted an injunction against a prohibition on indoor worship services, but refused the application with respect to percentage capacity limitations and a prohibition on singing and chanting during indoor services. Roberts CJ and Barrett J, with whom Kavanaugh J joined, concurred in the partial grant of the application for injunctive relief. Gorsuch J, with whom Thomas J and Alito J joined, would have granted the injunction in full. Kagan J, with whom Breyer J and Sotomayor J joined, dissented, stating that 'the State's policies treat worship just as favorably as secular activities (including political assemblies) that, according to medical evidence, pose the same risk of COVID transmission'.[41] She said that the Court required the State to 'treat worship services like secular activities that pose a much lesser danger'.[42]

The last of this series of applications for injunctive relief relating to state coronavirus restrictions was *Tandon v Newsom*,[43] decided on 9 April 2021. The Court granted an injunction against limits on religious gatherings in homes to three households because

> California treats some comparable secular activities more favorably than at-home religious exercise, permitting hair salons, retail stores, personal care services, movie

[36] Z Rothschild, 'Free Exercise Partisanship' (2022) 107 *Cornell Law Review* 1067, 1068.
[37] *Roman Catholic Diocese* (n 2) 66.
[38] ibid 67.
[39] ibid 79.
[40] *South Bay United Pentecostal Church v Newsom (No 2)* (2021) 141 S Ct 716.
[41] ibid 720.
[42] *Roman Catholic Diocese* (n 2) 720.
[43] *Tandon v Newsom* (2021) 141 S Ct 1294 (Supreme Court of the United States).

> theaters, private suites at sporting events and concerts, and indoor restaurants to bring together more than three households at a time.[44]

Kagan J, with whom Breyer J and Sotomayor J joined, dissented, noting that the State 'has adopted a blanket restriction on at-home gatherings of all kinds, religious and secular alike'.[45] Roberts CJ also would have denied the application (but did not write a dissent on this occasion).

B. UK Case Law

The UK cases showed a similar pattern of rejecting human rights challenges to coronavirus restrictions in the first few months of the pandemic. These initial challenges were brought in respect of the original lockdown regulations in England: the Health Protection (Coronavirus, Restrictions) (England) Regulations 2020, made by the Secretary of State for Health on 26 March 2020,[46] required that any person responsible for a place of worship ensure that the place of worship was closed, with the exception of certain permitted uses listed at regulation 5(6), such as funerals, broadcast of acts of worship and the provision of support services or urgent public support services. Regulation 7 prohibited gatherings of more than two people in any public place, with the exception of certain specified purposes, which did not include attendance at an act of worship.

In *R (Hussain) v Secretary of State for Health & Social Care*,[47] an application for interim relief was heard and decided on 21 May 2020, challenging the Health Protection (Coronavirus, Restrictions) (England) Regulations 2020. The claimant complained that the restrictions prevented collective prayer at the Barkerend Road Mosque, and in particular the Jumu'ah or Friday afternoon prayer, and further this was the case during Ramadan (which had commenced on 23 April 2020).[48] He sought interim relief in the form of an order prohibiting enforcement of regulations 5, 6 and 7 so far as they prohibited attendance at Friday prayers at Barkerend Road Mosque, on the basis of Article 9 of the European Convention on Human Rights.[49] Swift J accepted that 'the cumulative effect of the restrictions contained in the 2020 Regulations is an infringement of the Claimant's right to manifest his religious belief by worship, practice or observance' given the religious obligation to attend Friday prayers.[50]

[44] ibid 1297.
[45] ibid 1298.
[46] SI 2020/250. See generally J Brown and E Kirk-Wade, *Coronavirus: A History of 'Lockdown Laws' in England* (House of Commons Library, 2021).
[47] [2020] EWHC 1392 (Admin).
[48] ibid 6–7. For analysis of the closure of mosques during the pandemic in the UK, see A Al-Astewani, 'To Open or Close? COVID-19, Mosques and the Role of Religious Authority within the British Muslim Community: A Socio-Legal Analysis' (2021) 12 *Religions* 11.
[49] *Hussain* (n 47) [8]–[9].
[50] ibid [11].

However, significantly, Swift J observed that the interference concerned 'only one aspect of religious observance', and did not render the claimant's Article 9 rights 'illusory', though the interference that did exist was 'an important matter'.[51] Further, 'the duration of the interference will be finite'.[52] Swift J also cited a document published by the British Board of Scholars and Imams stating that 'government directives would take priority' in the context of the pandemic and lifting the obligation of Jumu'ah from UK Muslims.[53] He concluded that if the matter went to trial, it was 'very likely' that the Secretary of State would succeed on the submission that 'interference with the Claimant's Article 9 rights as a result of the 2020 Regulations is justified', and therefore the strong prima facie case required for interim relief was not established.[54] That was because '[t]he Covid-19 pandemic presents truly exceptional circumstances, the like of which has not been experienced in the United Kingdom for more than half a century', and the regulations rested on scientific advice about the contagiousness of the virus at gatherings indoors.[55]

Dolan v Secretary of State for Health and Social Care,[56] decided on 6 July 2020, was a judicial review challenge in the High Court against the same regulations. Lewis J refused permission to apply for judicial review on all grounds.[57] Following the hearing on 2 July 2020, regulations were made at 10am on 3 July 2020 that permitted places of worship to hold acts of communal worship for up to 30 people with effect from 4 July 2020.[58] Thus, the judge adjourned consideration of the Article 9 issue to determine whether the claim had become academic.[59] He then refused permission to advance this ground in an order sealed on 22 July 2020.[60] An application for permission to appeal the order refusing permission to apply for judicial review was made to the Court of Appeal and heard on 29 and 30 October 2020, before Lord Burnett of Maldon, King LJ and Singh LJ, who delivered a joint judgment on 1 December 2020. Because of the repeal of the regulations, the challenge had become academic, and the Court of Appeal did not consider it appropriate to consider the merits of the argument under Article 9 given the possible continuation of the claim in *Hussain*.[61]

After these initial human rights challenges brought in the English courts, activity shifted north to Scotland. The Health Protection (Coronavirus) (Restrictions and Requirements) (Local Levels) (Scotland) Amendment (No 11) Regulations

[51] ibid [12].
[52] ibid [13].
[53] ibid [14]–[16].
[54] ibid [18].
[55] ibid [19].
[56] *Dolan* (n 2).
[57] ibid [114]–[118].
[58] ibid [87].
[59] ibid.
[60] *Dolan appeal* (n 2) [25].
[61] ibid [39]–[42], [98]–[100].

2021[62] entered into force on 8 January 2021. These regulations required places of worship to close in 'level 4' areas in Scotland, except for certain permitted uses such as funerals or broadcasting acts of worship. The challenge in *Philip*, decided on 24 March 2021 by Lord Braid in the Outer House of the Court of Session, was brought by Reverend Dr William Philip and 26 other ministers and church leaders of Christian churches of various protestant denominations.[63] A Roman Catholic priest, Canon Thomas White, also joined the proceedings in support of the petitioners.[64] There were two issues in the case: first, a 'constitutional' issue relating to the division in Scotland between the spiritual authority of the church and the civil authority of the state, as 'the church has exclusive jurisdiction in matters spiritual, and the state has exclusive jurisdiction in matters civil'; and second, a human rights issue under the European Convention on Human Rights (principally Article 9).[65] This chapter focuses on the latter (human rights) issue, as the former issue is particular to the law of Scotland.

It was common ground that there had been an interference with the right to manifest religion.[66] Lord Braid found that the regulations interfering with the right to manifest religion were prescribed by law, and had a legitimate aim '[i]nsofar as they pursue the protection of public health and preservation of life'.[67] Turning to justification, the regulations were prescribed by law.[68] They were accepted to have a legitimate aim '[i]nsofar as they pursue the protection of public health and preservation of life'.[69] Since 'the closure of places of worship combined with the stay at home requirement will inevitably reduce human interaction', there was a rational connection between the regulations and the aim.[70] However, there were less intrusive means of 'reducing risk to a significant extent' given the possibility of 'effective mitigation measures', 'good ventilation' and 'admit[ting] a limited number of people for communal worship'.[71] In case he was wrong about less intrusive means, Lord Braid found that the regulations failed the balancing stage because 'mitigating factors are known to reduce the risk of transmission,

[62] SSI 2021/3.
[63] *Philip* (n 2) [1].
[64] ibid [4].
[65] ibid [1], [73]. Lord Braid concluded that proportionality should be used as the test for deciding the separation of spiritual and civil authority issue, such that 'any interference in worship by the state will be lawful if (and only if) it is a proportionate and necessary response to a civil matter in which the state is entitled to legislate': [79]. As a result, the issue was said to follow the outcome of the proportionality analysis under Art 9 of the European Convention on Human Rights. For background on this issue, see *Percy v Board of National Mission of the Church of Scotland* [2006] 2 AC 28 (United Kingdom House of Lords). For analysis of its treatment in *Philip*, see J McGowan, 'Public Health, Proportionality, and the "Freedom of Halie Kirk": On *Philip v Scottish Ministers*' [2022] *Public Law* 545; G Baldwin, 'Banning Public Worship during the Pandemic?' (*UK Constitutional Law Association Blog*, 12 April 2021) https://ukconstitutionallaw.org/2021/04/12/guy-baldwin-banning-public-worship-during-the-pandemic/.
[66] *Philip* (n 2) [96].
[67] ibid [99].
[68] ibid [98].
[69] ibid [99].
[70] ibid [103].
[71] ibid [115].

even indoors' and the right to manifest one's religion was 'an important right to which much weight must be attached'.[72]

III. Compatibility Analysis

The compatibility stage of the framework raises the question of how the rights of others – those who are sought to be protected by restrictions designed to inhibit the spread of the coronavirus – enter into consideration in adjudicating a claim to liberty of conscience. We have seen that integrity of the person is a basic liberty on equal footing with liberty of conscience within the moral framework. The first question posed by the framework therefore concerns the interaction between liberty of conscience in respect of the closure of places of worship or the reduction of attendance levels at those places of worship, and the rights of others to integrity of the person, which may be affected, as a result of the increased propagation of the virus, through the religious exercise of others in choosing to gather for worship.[73] Largely, this issue was overlooked in the cases, and the absence of reasoning on this point is effectively highlighted by this aspect of the framework.

In the US case law, it does not seem possible to consider the rights of others affected by religious practice – at least in the first stage of the *Smith-Lukumi* test – because of the focus on whether the law limiting religious freedom is neutral and of general applicability. In focusing on the nature of the law, especially the law's object, this test does not offer much basis to consider the rights of those that the law may be protecting against religious practice. Questions of justification do arise in the strict scrutiny analysis, but this strict scrutiny analysis, at least in some recent cases, has been either skipped altogether,[74] or treated briefly and almost as an afterthought in which possible justifications are summarily dismissed. (Richard Fallon describes the US Supreme Court's current understanding of strict scrutiny as a 'nearly categorical prohibition', rather than the more even balancing approach it previously has been.[75]) Thus, in the coronavirus restrictions cases before the US Supreme Court, the rights of others – their lives and integrity of the person as safeguarded by reducing virus transmission – did not expressly factor in the analysis.

That is so despite some recognition in US Supreme Court case law of the importance of bodily integrity. In *Union Pacific Railway Co v Botsford*, the Court, in an opinion delivered by Gray J, stated: 'No right is held more sacred, or is more carefully guarded by the common law than the right of every individual to

[72] ibid [119]–[120].

[73] On the constitutional significance of how the coronavirus SARS-CoV-2 spreads through gatherings, see CM Corbin, 'Religious Liberty in a Pandemic' (2020) 70 *Duke Law Journal Online* 1.

[74] See, eg, *Masterpiece Cakeshop v Colorado Civil Rights Commission* (2018) 138 S Ct 1719 (Supreme Court of the United States).

[75] RH Fallon, Jr, 'Strict Judicial Scrutiny' (2007) 54 *UCLA Law Review* 1267, 1302–1303.

the possession and control of his own person'.[76] In *Cruzan v Director, Missouri Department of Health*, the Court, in an opinion delivered by Rehnquist CJ, stated that '[e]very human being of adult years and sound mind has a right to determine what shall be done with his body'.[77] The dissenting opinion of Breyer, Sotomayor and Kagan JJ in the abortion rights case of *Dobbs v Jackson Women's Health Organization* cited these and other precedents, and observed that 'the Court has restricted the power of government to interfere with a person's medical decisions or compel her to undergo medical procedures or treatments'.[78] However, the uncontrolled spread of a deadly virus also represents a potentially significant interference with integrity of the person, albeit in a more indirect way. Accordingly, this issue does seem as though it could have been relevant to the analysis at the strict scrutiny stage, should the Court have been minded to consider it.

In the UK, the rights of others are more relevant to the inquiry. That is because Article 9(2) of the European Convention on Human Rights permits limiting religious manifestation 'for the protection of the rights and freedoms of others' (as well as for the 'protection of … health'). But, apart from when quoting Article 9,[79] the 'rights and freedoms of others' were never mentioned by Lord Braid in *Philip*. This is a strange omission as the 'rights and freedoms of others', including their right to life, would seem to be important to assessing the permissibility of restrictions designed to protect people's lives from the coronavirus. The failure to consider the rights and freedoms of others is striking as they have been taken into account many times by the European Court of Human Rights and UK domestic courts when considering limitations under Article 9(2).[80] The respondents also cited Article 2, though it is not entirely clear from Lord Braid's summary what argument was being made about it.[81] In his comment on *Philip*, Alan Greene correctly observes that '[i]n a pandemic, the state has a positive obligation to protect people's right to life under Article 2 ECHR'.[82]

[76] (1891) 141 US 250 (Supreme Court of the United States) 251.

[77] (1990) 497 US 261 (Supreme Court of the United States) 269, quoting Cardozo J, at the time on the Court of Appeals of New York, in *Schloendorff v Society of New York Hospital* (1914) 211 NY 125, 129-30, 105 NE 92 (Court of Appeals of New York).

[78] (2022) 142 S Ct 2228 (Supreme Court of the United States) 2328. See also *Rochin v California* (1952) 342 US 165 (Supreme Court of the United States); *Winston v Lee* (1985) 470 US 753 (Supreme Court of the United States); *Washington v Harper* (1990) 494 US 210 (Supreme Court of the United States).

[79] *Philip* (n 2) [90].

[80] See, eg, *Kosteski v Former Yugoslav Republic of Macedonia* (2007) 45 EHRR 31 (European Court of Human Rights); *Leela Förderkreis EV v Germany* (2009) 49 EHRR 5 (European Court of Human Rights); *Schilder v The Netherlands* App no 2158/12 (ECtHR, 16 October 2012). See also the discussion in Chapter 7 below of *R (Williamson) v Secretary of State for Education and Employment* [2005] 2 AC 246 (United Kingdom House of Lords).

[81] *Philip* (n 2) [94].

[82] A Greene, 'Closing Places of Worship and COVID-19: Towards a Culture of Justification?' (2021) 25 *Edinburgh Law Review* 393, 395. See also A Greene, *Emergency Powers in a Time of Pandemic* (Bristol: Bristol University Press, 2020).

That is because the state has a positive obligation under Article 2 to respond to threats to the right to life, and a pandemic is undoubtedly such a threat. To quote the European Court of Human Rights in the case of *Öneryildiz v Turkey*: the 'positive obligation to take all appropriate steps to safeguard life for the purposes of Art 2 entails above all a primary duty on the state to put in place a legislative and administrative framework designed to provide effective deterrence against threats to the right to life'.[83] In that case there was a 'real and immediate risk to a number of persons living near' a particular rubbish tip and consequently the Turkish authorities 'had a positive obligation under Art 2 of the Convention to take such preventive operational measures as were necessary and sufficient to protect' them.[84] Since infection with a virus is a threat to life,[85] in the circumstances of a pandemic the Article 2 positive obligation would seem to be relevant. That much has been repeatedly acknowledged by the European Court of Human Rights, for example in *Le Mailloux v France*,[86] *Terheş v Romania*,[87] *Fenech v Malta*,[88] *Communauté Genevoise D'Action Syndicale (CGAS) v Switzerland*[89] and *Pasquinelli v San Marino*.[90] Similarly, Resolution 2338 (2020) of the Parliamentary Assembly of the Council of Europe on 'The impact of the Covid-19 pandemic on human rights and the rule of law', adopted on 13 October 2020, states as follows:

> Although primarily a public health crisis, the Covid-19 pandemic is also an unprecedented challenge for human rights and the rule of law – both of which remain applicable even in times of national emergency. *The positive obligations under the European Convention on Human Rights (ETS No. 5, the Convention) require States to take measures to protect the life and health of their populations.* This imperative does not, however, give States a free hand to trample on rights, suppress freedoms, dismantle democracy or violate the rule of law. Even during a state of emergency, the Convention continues to set limits, thereby ensuring respect for common European fundamental standards. (emphasis added)

Thus, an apparent deficiency of the *Philip* judgment is that the argument was not even considered that the rights of others – in particular, their right to

[83] *Öneryildiz v Turkey* (2005) 41 EHRR 20 (European Court of Human Rights) [89].

[84] ibid [101].

[85] *GN v Italy* App no 43134/05 (ECtHR, 1 December 2009); *Oyal v Turkey* (2010) 51 EHRR 30 (European Court of Human Rights).

[86] App no 18108/20 (ECtHR, 3 December 2020) [9].

[87] App no 49933/20 (ECtHR, 20 May 2021) [40].

[88] App no 19090/20 (ECtHR, 1 March 2022) [104].

[89] (2024) 78 EHRR 22 (European Court of Human Rights) [84]. The Court in *CGAS* (at Chamber level) went on – in a 4–3 vote – to find that the lockdown measures in Switzerland violated Art 11 of the Convention. However, the Grand Chamber subsequently, in 2023, found that the application by CGAS was inadmissible due to failures to comply with the six-month time limit for applications and to exhaust domestic remedies: *Communauté Genevoise D'Action Syndicale (CGAS) v Switzerland* App no 21881/20 (ECtHR, 27 November 2023).

[90] (2025) 80 EHRR 8 (European Court of Human Rights) [104]. See also P Järvinen and V Vikman, '*Pasquinelli and Others v San Marino* – The Momentous Competing Interests of the Community as a Whole against Healthcare Workers Refusing the Covid-19 Vaccine' (*Strasbourg Observers*, 4 October 2024) https://strasbourgobservers.com/2024/10/04/pasquinelli-and-others-v-san-marino-the-momentous-competing-interests-of-the-community-as-a-whole-against-healthcare-workers-refusing-the-covid-19-vaccine/.

life – may justify the limitation on manifestation of religious beliefs imposed by the coronavirus restrictions. It might be argued that Lord Braid implicitly took into account the rights of others by addressing the legitimate aim said to be served by the coronavirus restrictions in Scotland, which was accepted by the respondent as involving the 'protection of public health and preservation of life'.[91] But it seems to alter the analysis to consider that there was only one right under threat in the circumstances. Failing to identify the protection of the rights of others as a legitimate aim may weaken the connection between means and ends at the necessity stage of the proportionality test, and reduce the weight assigned to the objective pursued in the final balancing stage. Instead of recognising that the state was in an invidious position in needing to address rights under both Articles 2 and 9, the analysis proceeded from an incorrect premise and failed to take account of the importance of life as a right under the European Convention on Human Rights.

Interestingly, though, the existence of positive obligations owed to the population as a whole, or to 'broad and undefined… sector[s]' thereof, was disputed by the Administrative Court in the case of *R (Gardner) v Secretary of State for Health and Social Care*, decided on 27 April 2022.[92] Does this decision rescue the analysis in *Philip*? The *Gardner* case concerned certain government policy documents in early 2020 during the coronavirus pandemic relating to care homes, especially those directing the discharge of hospital patients into care homes without testing, isolation or other appropriate measures.[93] The Administrative Court, in a judgment of the Court to which both Bean LJ and Garnham J contributed, found that two documents issued by the Secretary of State for Health and Social Care and Public Health England were irrational in the administrative law sense 'in failing to advise that where an asymptomatic patient (other than one who had tested negative) was admitted to a care home, he or she should, so far as practicable, be kept apart from other residents for 14 days'.[94]

Although finding for the claimants overall, the Court rejected a human rights challenge relating to Article 2 positive obligations. Central to the Court's reasoning was a narrow understanding of the operational obligation under Article 2 derived from the facts of existing cases that had considered it. After reviewing various cases of UK courts and the European Court of Human Rights, the Court opined that 'a real and immediate risk to life is a necessary but not sufficient factor for the existence of an Article 2 operational duty'.[95] The Court stated that 'generally', it was necessary for there to be an 'assumption by the State of responsibility for the welfare and safety of particular individuals, of whom prisoners, detainees under mental health legislation, immigration detainees and conscripts are paradigm

[91] *Philip* (n 2) [99].

[92] [2022] PTSR 1338 (England and Wales High Court). For critical commentary, see VL Moore and LD Graham, '*R (Gardner and Harris) v Secretary of State for Health and Social Care and Others* [2022] EWHC 967: Scant Regard for Covid-19 Risk to Care Homes' (2022) 30 *Medical Law Review* 734.

[93] *Gardner* (n 92) [6]–[7], [10], [18]–[19].

[94] ibid [298].

[95] ibid [250(i)].

examples since they are under State control'.[96] However, it then acknowledged that there were cases where that factor was not present and an operational obligation was still found. The Court thus stated that:

> the duty may exist even in the absence of an assumption by the State of responsibility, where State or municipal authorities have become aware of dangerous situations involving a specific threat to life which arise exceptionally from risks posed by the violent and unlawful acts of others (*Osman*) or man-made hazards (*Oneryildiz, Kolyadenko*) or natural hazards (*Budayeva*), or from appalling conditions in residential care facilities of which the authorities had become aware (*Nencheva, Campeanu*).[97]

It also accepted that the operational obligation may arise 'where State or municipal authorities engage in activities which they know or should know pose a real and immediate risk'.[98] The Court's framing of these cases seems to seek to confine the test for the Article 2 operational obligation by reference to various categories of existing cases, rather than treating these cases as what they are: examples of the application of the test that do not necessarily limit its potential application to future cases. The gloss placed upon the test by the Administrative Court stands in contrast with the approach of the European Court, which said, for example, in *Cannavacciuolo v Italy* that Article 2 positive obligations arise 'in the context of any activity, whether public or not, in which the right to life may be at stake'.[99]

The Court in *Gardner* concluded its analysis with a suggested limitation of the Article 2 operational obligation test by reference to the concept of a 'broad and undefined' sector of the population, stating as follows:

> There is no authority of the Strasbourg court which has gone as far as holding that a State is under an operational duty to take all reasonable steps to avoid the real and immediate risk to life posed by an epidemic or pandemic to as broad and undefined a sector of the population as residents of care homes for the elderly. There is no clear and consistent line of Strasbourg authority which indicates that such a duty exists and we cannot be at all confident – indeed we gravely doubt – that the ECtHR would be willing to declare that it does. We should keep pace with the Strasbourg jurisprudence, but not run past it and disappear into the distance. The Defendants did not, in our view, owe the Article 2 operational duty for which the Claimants contend.[100]

The Court's reference to a clear and consistent line of Strasbourg authority seems somewhat out of place, as although 'clear and constant jurisprudence' from Strasbourg is often said to require UK courts to follow that jurisprudence,[101] the absence of such jurisprudence does not mean that a UK court cannot act. The principles governing when UK courts can go beyond Strasbourg were discussed by the Administrative Court in *Gardner*, quoting *R (AB) v Secretary of State for*

[96] ibid [250(ii)].
[97] ibid [250(iii)].
[98] ibid [250(iv)].
[99] (2025) 81 EHRR 15 (European Court of Human Rights) [376].
[100] *Gardner* (n 92) [252].
[101] *R (Ullah) v Special Adjudicator* [2004] 2 AC 32 (United Kingdom House of Lords) [20].

Justice.[102] In that case, Lord Reed, with whom the other Justices agreed, stated that '[i]n situations which have not yet come before the European court', courts are expected to 'aim to anticipate, where possible, how the European court might be expected to decide the case, on the basis of the principles established in its case law'.[103] The Court added that '[t]he application of the Convention by our domestic courts, in such circumstances, will be based on the principles established by the European court, even if some incremental development may be involved'.[104]

As to what the European Court would have been willing to find on the basis of established principles, it is significant that the Administrative Court did not cite any of the relevant cases of the European Court, mentioned above, that acknowledged Article 2 positive obligations in the context of the coronavirus pandemic, many of which had been handed down by the time of the decision. Further, in a meaningful sense, the Administrative Court's decision departs from the established principles of the operational obligation by finding an implied limitation of it. Nothing in the language of Article 2 restricts the right to 'defined sectors' of the population, and to do so seems to be contrary to Article 1 of the Convention, which states the obligation of the contracting parties to 'secure to *everyone* within their jurisdiction the rights and freedoms defined in Section I of this Convention' (emphasis added).

Although not strictly speaking a UK case, the analysis of the Judicial Committee of the Privy Council in *Suraj v Attorney General of Trinidad and Tobago*[105] – handed down in June 2022 – offers some support for the position that the right to life should be considered when assessing lockdown restrictions, contrary to the reasoning in *Philip*, and that positive obligations may be owed to the population, contrary to the reasoning in *Gardner*. This case involved a challenge to coronavirus restrictions on religious gatherings under section 4 of the Trinidad and Tobago Constitution, which protects various rights including 'freedom of conscience and religious belief and observance'. Lord Sales and Lord Hamblen, with whom Lord Reed, Lord Hodge and Lady Rose agreed, found that these restrictions were proportionate, and expressly noted the right to life of the population as a whole in its reasoning, stating as follows:

> [T]he Board is satisfied that the interference with the appellants' rights was proportionate and hence consistent with those rights and involved no violation of them. The Rules were promulgated on the basis of expert scientific advice against a background of considerable uncertainty about how the disease was transmitted and how best to counter its spread. The public interest in issue, *the protection of the right to life and the health of the whole population*, was an especially important one. In the Board's view, the Rules struck a fair balance between the rights of the appellants and the general interest of the

[102] [2022] AC 487. See also *R (Elan-Cane) v Secretary of State for the Home Department* [2023] AC 559 (Supreme Court of the United Kingdom) [101].
[103] *AB* (n 102) [59].
[104] ibid.
[105] [2023] AC 337.

> community and were plainly a proportionate means of protecting the public interest in the circumstances. The Board takes the same view of this as the Court of Appeal of England and Wales in *R (Dolan) v Secretary of State for Health and Social Care* in relation to similar restrictions on gatherings.[106] (emphasis added and citation omitted)

Gardner is also difficult to square with a growing body of environmental case law, which not infrequently addresses threats to sectors of the population or indeed the whole population. In *Verein KlimaSeniorinnen Schweiz v Switzerland*,[107] the European Court found that states have positive obligations under Article 8 of the European Convention on Human Rights (relevantly, protecting private and family life and the home) to respond to climate change (an Article 2 issue was not decided). The Court was concerned to limit possible proceedings in relation to climate change with a tightened test of standing, but nonetheless it is apparent that the Court was prepared to acknowledge positive obligations in respect of an issue that affected the population as a whole. In *Cannavacciuolo*, a pollution issue potentially affecting millions of people gave rise to positive obligations under Article 2.[108] The viewpoint that positive obligations do not extend to 'broad and undefined … sector[s]' of the population is therefore unsound, and does not overcome the critique of *Philip* for ignoring Article 2 positive obligations.

As we have seen, the framework calls for attention to compatibility with the rights of others as the first question to be addressed, before turning to a balancing analysis under necessity. Viewed from the standpoint of compatibility, there was a clash between the right to integrity of the person of those in the community who may have been affected by the increased transmission of the coronavirus resulting from the exercise of religion in this case, and the right to liberty of conscience of those who sought to gather to practise their religion. Did the interference go to the central range of liberty of conscience? On the one hand, it concerned worship, which is undoubtedly an important matter. John Inazu writes that '[t]he shutdown and social distancing orders … not only restricted free exercise but also curtailed what many people consider to be the core of that exercise: religious worship'.[109]

However, there may be some reason to doubt this analysis, since worship was not wholly prohibited, but merely transferred online, and even this only on a temporary basis. In other words, in assessing whether to uphold a limitation on the manifestation of religious belief in order to protect life, it would be important to consider how much the right to manifest religious belief was actually limited. The UK cases demonstrated markedly different approaches to that issue. Swift J downplayed the extent of the burden in *Hussain*:

[106] ibid [100]. For a decision of the European Court rejecting a religious freedom claim relating to pandemic restrictions, see also *Spînu v Romania* App no 29443/20 (ECtHR, 11 October 2022) (European Court of Human Rights).

[107] (2024) 79 EHRR 1.

[108] For further discussion of these cases, see G Baldwin, 'Positive Obligations to Protect the Population under Human Rights Law' (2025) 30 *Judicial Review* 232.

[109] J Inazu, 'COVID-19, Churches, and Culture Wars' (2022) 18 *University of St Thomas Law Journal* 307, 307.

> [T]he interference relied on in these proceedings concerns only one aspect of religious observance – attendance at communal Friday prayers. This is not to diminish the significance of that requirement, yet it is relevant to the scope of the interference that is to be justified. In submissions it was suggested that the inability to attend Friday prayers in a mosque rendered the Claimant's Article 9 rights to manifest his religious belief illusory. The Claimant's evidence does not make that case good, albeit it is clear that the Claimant considers, and I accept, that the interference that does exist is an important matter.[110]

Lord Braid took the opposite tack:

> I accept the evidence of the petitioners and of the additional party that worship in their faiths cannot properly take place on-line, by means of internet platforms. The respondents have produced various Decrees and other documents issued to Bishops … giving advice as to alternative means of celebration of the liturgy, but these can best be described as 'work-arounds' during the pandemic (and are time-limited). The same can be said of other on-line broadcasts and services. These are best viewed as an alternative to worship, rather than worship itself. While certain church practices – the reading of prayer, preaching and teaching – may be observed, or even, in the case of live streaming, participated in to a certain extent, on a computer screen or a television whilst alone, in the solitude of one's own home, that does not amount to collective worship. The essential features of worship identified above – including communion and baptism – cannot take place by those means.[111]

The logic of this passage seems to be that unless online worship has all the features of worship in person, it is not even worship at all, but merely an alternative to it.[112] But this seems like an overstatement. Those who worked from home during the pandemic were still working – not engaged in an 'alternative' to work – even though they might not be able to engage in every aspect of what they would usually do in the office. In the same way, when much of what happens during religious services did indeed move online during the lockdowns, it seems more apposite to acknowledge that, although there are limitations, what takes place online is still 'worship'. The odd language here obscured a point that should have been relevant to assessing the proportionality of Scotland's restrictions: that the temporary burden of coronavirus restrictions, although significant, was not completely inhibiting religious manifestation, but instead putting religious practice on similar footing to a wide range of other activities that were taken online during the coronavirus lockdowns.

[110] *Hussain* (n 47) [12].
[111] *Philip* (n 2) [61].
[112] The *per curiam* in *Roman Catholic Diocese* made a similar point, stating that the challenged restrictions, if enforced, would cause 'irreparable harm' since many would be unable to attend in person, and although watching services on television would be possible, 'remote viewing' was not the same as personal attendance as 'Catholics who watch a Mass at home cannot receive communion, and there are important religious traditions in the Orthodox Jewish faith that require personal attendance': *Roman Catholic Diocese* (n 2) 67–68.

This temporariness forms another important part of the compatibility stage of analysis within the framework, because it, too, suggests that the interference with liberty of conscience here did not go to the central range of application of that basic liberty. Legal responses to public health crises vary depending on the circumstances. In the pandemic, there was little reason to doubt that restrictions would be lifted as soon as the circumstances allowed. However, the cases exhibited differing approaches to the significance of this temporariness.[113] In most of the US decisions, the temporary character of the restrictions was not even mentioned. In his concurring opinion in the second *South Bay* case, Gorsuch J addressed the argument that the temporariness of the restrictions was relevant to their constitutionality. Considering the point briefly, he doubted that this temporariness offered any kind of justification:

> No doubt, California will argue on remand, as it has before, that its prohibitions are merely temporary because vaccinations are underway. But the State's 'temporary' ban on indoor worship has been in place since August 2020, and applied routinely since March. California no longer asks its movie studios, malls, and manicurists to wait. And one could be forgiven for doubting its asserted timeline. Government actors have been moving the goalposts on pandemic-related sacrifices for months, adopting new benchmarks that always seem to put restoration of liberty just around the corner. As this crisis enters its second year – and hovers over a second Lent, a second Passover, and a second Ramadan – it is too late for the State to defend extreme measures with claims of temporary exigency, if it ever could.[114]

The rhetorical emphasis on the crisis entering its second year – as though that demonstrates how unacceptable any invocation of temporariness is – may seem surprising, because serious crises often last much longer than a year; sometimes they go on for several years. The coronavirus pandemic has been perhaps the worst public health crisis in 100 years, if not longer, so the notion that it needed to be over in less than a year seems to evince a lack of perspective. The pandemic has in fact eased relatively quickly due to the unprecedented speed at which vaccines were developed. The position that governments are only given a narrow window of time in which to respond to a crisis of this kind before their response ceases to be temporary is odd, and Gorsuch J does not offer any explanation for why that should be so.

In the two cases in the UK, the courts addressed the issue of temporariness in different ways. In *Hussain*, Swift J emphasised that 'the duration of the interference will be finite' since the regulations were due to expire in September 2020 and also had to be reviewed every three weeks.[115] There was also a government 'route map' that envisaged lifting restrictions on attendance at public places, including places

[113] On the normative relevance of temporariness, see, eg, B Ackerman, 'The Emergency Constitution' (2004) 113 *Yale Law Journal* 1029; J Ferejohn and P Pasquino, 'The Law of the Exception: A Typology of Emergency Powers' (2004) 2 *International Journal of Constitutional Law* 210.

[114] *South Bay (No 2)* (n 40) 720.

[115] *Hussain* (n 47) [13].

of worship, in early July.[116] This contrasts with the approach in *Philip*. In assessing proportionality, Lord Braid took into account the temporary character of the restrictions, but went on to say as follows:

> As for severity of effect, it is all too easy to argue, as the respondents in effect do, that 'it doesn't really matter' that places of worship are closed because it's only for a short period, and those who wish to do so can go on-line. The first of those points is valid to an extent, although it should be pointed out that 3 weeks became 6 became 9, and that by the time the Regulations (we are told) will be revoked or amended with effect from 26 March 2021 they will have been in force for 11 weeks.[117]

Again, 11 weeks is not a particularly long period of time in the span of a global pandemic. Linked to this question of the temporariness of the restrictions was also a difference of approach about whether to address restrictions that were about to be lifted or had even already been lifted. In *Philip*, Lord Braid found the restrictions invalid on 24 March 2021 even though public worship was due to be permitted from 26 March 2021 anyway.[118] However, in the *Dolan* appeal, the academic nature of the challenge against the repealed restrictions meant that permission to bring a claim for judicial review was granted only in respect of the vires ground, since it would serve the public interest to consider it given that new regulations continued to be made under the same enabling power.[119] In *Roman Catholic Diocese*, the Court issued an injunction even though the restrictions had been lifted in the relevant areas, because of the 'constant threat' that they would be reimposed.[120]

In these circumstances, it seems doubtful that the interference with liberty of conscience constituted by the restrictions on in-person worship went to its central range of application, since it was still possible to undertake many of the activities associated with worship online, and the interference was on a temporary basis. At the same time, the risk to the right to integrity of the person of others would go to its central range, as it was a risk of death as a result of transmission of the coronavirus due to the exercise of religion. In a clash between liberty of conscience outside its central range and the right to bodily integrity within it, the latter would necessarily prevail, offering a compelling reason to consider that the restrictions should have prevailed over liberty of conscience. However, even if the clash is viewed as being between the two rights in their central range, avoiding a risk of death would be more closely connected with the exercise and development of the moral powers than attending worship in person. Rutledge J, delivering the opinion of the US Supreme Court in *Prince v Massachusetts*, a 1944 case relating to a free exercise challenge to a child welfare law, wrote that '[t]he right to practice religion freely does not include liberty to expose the community or the child to communicable

[116] ibid.
[117] *Philip* (n 2) [3], [58], [121], [133]–[134].
[118] ibid [3].
[119] *Dolan appeal* (n 2) [41]–[42].
[120] *Roman Catholic Diocese* (n 2) 68.

disease or the latter to ill health or death'.[121] That observation remains correct: liberty of conscience cannot be a licence to put others in danger.

In summary, then, the framework directs attention in its compatibility stage to the rights of others affected by religious practice. That is an important issue here, where the lives of others were potentially put at risk through spread of the coronavirus. Yet in the cases, there was a lack of consideration of the rights of others. That omission in the context of the Free Exercise Clause is not surprising, because the focus of the *Smith-Lukumi* test is elsewhere, illustrating the problems with that test, though it was still theoretically possible for this point to be taken up at the strict scrutiny stage. In the UK, it is more surprising, because the 'rights and freedoms of others' constitute an express basis for limiting the right to manifest religious belief under Article 9(2). Positive obligations under Article 2 may also be relevant in this context, notwithstanding the view of the Administrative Court in *Gardner*. Of course, positive obligations under Article 2 cannot serve as a blank cheque. States cannot automatically justify any action designed to increase public safety by reference to the right to life, as is plain from European Court of Human Rights case law in the terrorism context.[122] But when considering the validity of restrictions designed to protect life, Article 2 would seem to merit mention. In this sense, the coronavirus restriction cases represent a situation in which religious practices harmed, or at least put at risk, the bodily integrity of others, albeit indirectly.

Also relevant to the compatibility analysis was the temporary nature of the restrictions. Most of the US decisions overlooked the temporary nature of the restrictions completely, while Gorsuch J in the second *South Bay* decision was dismissive of it.[123] In the UK, temporariness was emphasised by Swift J in *Hussain*,[124] but Lord Braid in *Philip* said it was 'all too easy' to cite the temporariness of the restrictions.[125] Yet it seems apparent that the longer restrictions run, the heavier the burden on religious freedom may be, which makes temporariness an important consideration in the proportionality analysis. That much was clear at the time, but after widespread vaccination and a lifting of lockdown restrictions – which have not returned in the years since – the impatience of courts, in being unable to abide a brief period of restrictions during a genuine crisis, is all the more striking. Taking these matters into account, there was reason to doubt whether the interference with liberty of conscience went to the central range of application. Since a threat to life undoubtedly does go to the central range of application of integrity of the person, that offered good reason to consider that the claims to liberty of conscience should have failed.

[121] *Prince v Massachusetts* (1944) 321 US 158 (Supreme Court of the United States) 166–67.

[122] See, eg, *A v United Kingdom* (2009) 49 EHRR 29 (European Court of Human Rights).

[123] *South Bay (No 2)* (n 40) 720.

[124] *Hussain* (n 47) [13].

[125] *Philip* (n 2) [121].

IV. Necessity Analysis

Although it has been concluded that compatibility with the rights of others is a sufficient basis on which to resolve the issue of coronavirus lockdown restrictions, if that were not the case the next step would be to consider whether the restrictions were necessary in the common interest. For completeness, it is desirable to do so anyway. Rawls expressly acknowledged public health as a matter in the common interest – and it undoubtedly is so since it affects the population generally – so the question is whether the restrictions were necessary for that matter.[126]

However, one significant point of difference between the analysis called for by necessity and that undertaken by the courts in the UK and US, which it is helpful to flag at the outset, is that the use of comparisons between the regulation of secular and religious activities, a feature of the case law of both jurisdictions, is of limited relevance. Instead, the question is fundamentally one of closeness of connection between the measures adopted – ranging between closure of places of worship and restrictions on numbers in attendance – and the end identified as being in the common interest, which is public health. It seems plain that there was a sufficiently close connection given the considerable risk of transmission of the virus from the restricted gatherings, at least at a time prior to effective treatments or vaccines for the coronavirus. It was in the common interest to seek to prevent transmission, and the interference with liberty of conscience, which did not go to the central range of application for the reasons given above, was necessary in that common interest.

There was, in any case, a difference between the US and UK cases in how much emphasis was placed on comparisons. These comparisons were particularly important in the US because they are relevant to neutrality – that is, whether the object of a law is the 'suppression of religion or religious conduct' – whereas in the UK they form only part of a wider proportionality analysis. In both jurisdictions, different approaches emerged about how to compare like with like, and the comparisons have seemed malleable and uncertain. This, in turn, 'can lead to unpredictable and inconsistent results'.[127] In the US, the position as it is apparently supposed to be was spelled out in *Tandon*. The *per curiam* said that 'government regulations are not neutral and generally applicable, and therefore trigger strict scrutiny under the Free Exercise Clause, whenever they treat any comparable secular activity more favorably than religious exercise', where '[c]omparability is concerned with the risks various activities pose'.[128]

In this regard, the legal issue under the neutrality and general applicability test is not whether religious exercise is 'essential' or not. For example, Thomas Berg writes that '[s]tates cannot place worship in a more restricted category on the basis

[126] Rawls, *A Theory of Justice (Revised Edition)* (n 11) 83.

[127] 'Constitutional Constraints on Free Exercise Analogies' (2021) 134 *Harvard Law Review* 1782, 1783.

[128] *Tandon v Newsom* (n 43) 1296.

that it is nonessential',[129] but this seems to miss the point – rather, the issue is the risk level posed by different activities. However, despite this professed focus in *Tandon* on activities that were comparable in the sense of risk level, that approach was not applied by the majority in the prior decision of *Roman Catholic Diocese*. The *per curiam* in that case said:

> In a red zone, while a synagogue or church may not admit more than 10 persons, businesses categorized as 'essential' may admit as many people as they wish. And the list of 'essential' businesses includes things such as acupuncture facilities, camp grounds, garages, as well as many whose services are not limited to those that can be regarded as essential, such as all plants manufacturing chemicals and microelectronics and all transportation facilities. … The disparate treatment is even more striking in an orange zone. While attendance at houses of worship is limited to 25 persons, even non-essential businesses may decide for themselves how many persons to admit.[130]

No analysis was included that explained why, for example, meeting one-on-one with an acupuncturist carried a comparable risk profile to gathering indoors in a group. The concurrences showed the same flaw, with those in the majority in these cases invoking secular examples that were less restricted than the religious activities. For example, Gorsuch J, pointing out that essential businesses had no capacity restrictions, said that according to the Governor of New York, 'it may be unsafe to go to church, but it is always fine to pick up another bottle of wine, shop for a new bike, or spend the afternoon exploring your distal points and meridians'.[131] He added sarcastically: 'Who knew public health would so perfectly align with secular convenience?'[132] But walking into a shop to buy a bottle of wine and then walking out again does not have the same risk profile as gathering indoors with other people for an extended period. As Caroline Corbin notes, 'the science … suggests worship services and activities like shopping are not comparable'.[133] Kavanaugh J, concurring in the grant of injunctive relief in *Roman Catholic Diocese*, similarly complained that '[i]n a red zone, for example, a church or synagogue must adhere to a 10-person attendance cap, while a grocery store, pet store, or big-box store down the street does not face the same restriction'.[134] Again, this reasoning is not permissible according to the test as later stated in *Tandon* because the comparison is not differentiated according to risk.

Hence, Sotomayor J argued in her dissent in *Roman Catholic Diocese* that New York applied similar or more severe restrictions to comparable secular gatherings like lectures, concerts, movie showings, spectator sports, and theatrical performances, 'where large groups of people gather in close proximity for extended

[129] TC Berg, 'Religious Freedom amid the Tumult' (2022) 17 *University of St Thomas Law Journal* 735, 740.
[130] *Roman Catholic Diocese* (n 2) 66.
[131] ibid 69.
[132] ibid.
[133] Corbin (n 73) 19.
[134] *Roman Catholic Diocese* (n 2) 73.

periods of time', and treated more leniently only dissimilar activities such as operating grocery stores, banks and laundromats, 'in which people neither congregate in large groups nor remain in close proximity for extended periods'.[135] She added that Gorsuch J did not 'even try to square his examples with the conditions medical experts tell us facilitate the spread of COVID-19: large groups of people gathering, speaking, and singing in close proximity indoors for extended periods of time'.[136]

But questionable applications of the *Smith-Lukumi* test might not be confined to these later cases. In *Calvary Chapel*, which Berg describes as a 'far more troubling' case than *South Bay*,[137] the Court prior to its change of composition declined to enjoin enforcement of Nevada's 50-person limit on religious attendance even though casinos (as well as restaurants, bars and gyms) were allowed up to 50 per cent of their capacity, including for shows. No one in the majority wrote to explain the Court's order, so it is not apparent what their reasoning was. In dissent, Alito J objected that

> [a] church, synagogue, or mosque, regardless of its size, may not admit more than 50 persons, but casinos and certain other favored facilities may admit 50% of their maximum occupancy – and in the case of gigantic Las Vegas casinos, this means that thousands of patrons are allowed.[138]

Kavanaugh J claimed that the 'risk of COVID-19 transmission is at least as high' in venues like casinos as in religious services because 'people congregating … often linger at least as long as they do at religious services'.[139] On this occasion, the concerns seem valid and it is at best doubtful that neutrality was shown.

Because the test in the UK is proportionality, these comparisons between the regulation of secular activities and religious activities are less important, but they may still be relevant. In the early decision of *Hussain* the claimant pointed to other activities permitted by the regulations, such as 'taking exercise, including with one member of another household; visiting parks and open spaces for recreation; visiting houses in connection with the purchase, sale, rental of a residential property; going to local tips and recycling centres', but Swift J said that there was a

> qualitative difference in terms of the risk of transmission of the virus between a situation such as a religious service where a number of people meet in an enclosed space for a period of an hour or more, and the transitory briefer contact likely in a setting such as that of shopping in a garden centre.[140]

However, in *Philip* Lord Braid drew a quite strained comparison when finding that the regulations were not proportionate. He accepted that 'it is difficult to draw a meaningful comparison between places of worship and some premises

[135] ibid 79. See also *South Bay (No 1)* (n 2) 1613.
[136] *Roman Catholic Diocese* (n 2) 79.
[137] Berg (n 129) 741.
[138] *Calvary Chapel* (n 31) 2604.
[139] ibid 2610.
[140] *Hussain* (n 47) [20], [23].

which are exempt from the requirement to close, such as bicycle shops' but said that 'a more meaningful comparison can perhaps be drawn with the continued use of cinemas as jury centres' because '[l]ike places of worship, they involve people from different households coming together repeatedly to congregate indoors in a confined area'.[141] But there was little explanation of this comparison, and it raises questions: a jury comprises only a few people, so why did these jury centres have a similar risk profile to gathering in a place of worship? Further, to focus only on juries – one example – in circumstances where more obvious activities that are similar in risk level to gathering in places of worship, such as watching a movie at the cinema, attending a sports stadium and gathering in a conference centre, were all prohibited, seems like cherry-picking.

The analysis of whether regulation is discriminatory towards religion can potentially capture something important, in that negative discriminatory treatment of religion may be problematic when it lacks justification. But comparisons drawn between secular and religious activities prove malleable, with judges in both the US and the UK fastening upon implausible comparators to reach the seeming desired outcome. That is perhaps inevitable in the US, where the *Smith-Lukumi* test implies that even harsh restrictions on religious exercise should be upheld, provided that they are neutral and of general applicability, as discussed in Chapter 4. Perhaps the majority of the US Supreme Court shied away from that implication, applying strained comparisons with dissimilar secular activities in order to injunct severe restrictions on religious exercise. Nonetheless, the strained reasoning evident in many of the US and the UK cases illustrates the limitations of such comparisons. That makes it unfortunate that in the US they are a central feature of the *Smith-Lukumi* test. In contrast, the use of comparisons between the regulation of secular and religious activities in the UK cases of *Hussain* and *Philip* was far briefer and less significant to the analysis.

At times, it seemed that members of the US Supreme Court were particularly concerned about the severity of the restrictions that were being imposed on religious practice. For example, in the second *South Bay* decision, Roberts CJ said nothing about neutrality and general applicability, only expressing the view that the state's determination that 'the maximum number of adherents who can safely worship in the most cavernous cathedral is zero … appears to reflect not expertise or discretion, but instead insufficient appreciation or consideration of the interests at stake'.[142] Similarly, Roberts CJ in *Roman Catholic Diocese* stated that '[n]umerical capacity limits of 10 and 25 people … do seem unduly restrictive',[143] while Kavanaugh J observed that 'New York's 10-person and 25-person caps on attendance at religious services in red and orange zones (which are areas where COVID-19 is more prevalent) are much more severe than most other States'

[141] *Philip* (n 2) [114].
[142] *South Bay (No 2)* (n 40) 717.
[143] *Roman Catholic Diocese* (n 2) 75.

restrictions'.[144] These observations do not seem consistent with the first stage of the *Smith-Lukumi* test, in which the issue is not the severity of restrictions, but their neutrality and general applicability.

Nonetheless, the severity of the restrictions does matter very much in relation to the second stage of the test (strict scrutiny), which applies if a law is not neutral and of general applicability. It is also relevant to the necessity in the common interest inquiry within the framework, which aligns significantly with this kind of test, because it requires assessing the means against the end. That may make it surprising that in *Roman Catholic Diocese*, the *per curiam*'s strict scrutiny analysis was very brief: two paragraphs. The *per curiam* first of all accepted that '[s]temming the spread of COVID-19 is unquestionably a compelling interest'.[145] However, it went on to say that it was 'hard to see how the challenged regulations can be regarded as "narrowly tailored"' because

> [t]hey are far more restrictive than any COVID-related regulations that have previously come before the Court, much tighter than those adopted by many other jurisdictions hard-hit by the pandemic, and far more severe than has been shown to be required to prevent the spread of the virus at the applicants' services.[146]

But the fact that some other states have looser restrictions does not demonstrate that the measures were not narrowly tailored, since those states may have underreacted. Noting the size of the churches and synagogues in question, the *per curiam* said that 'there are many other less restrictive rules that could be adopted to minimize the risk to those attending religious services'[147] – that is, the Court considered that the state could do less to 'minimise' the risk, though it seems to be implicit that such measures would not necessarily be as effective as the caps that the state imposed. The point appeared to be that lesser measures would minimise the risk *enough*, though it was not clear how the Court drew this line. The crux of the proportionality analysis in *Philip* was, similarly, a conclusion that the state could do less. After considering a number of factors, the judge concluded that there were less intrusive means available:

> [T]he respondents have failed to show that no less intrusive means than the Regulations were available to address their aim of reducing risk to a significant extent. Standing [*sic*] the advice they had at the time, they have not demonstrated why there was an unacceptable degree of risk by continuing to allow places of worship which employed effective mitigation measures and had good ventilation to admit a limited number of people for communal worship. They have not demonstrated why they could not proceed on the basis that those responsible for places of worship would continue to act responsibly in the manner in which services were conducted, and not open if it was not safe to do so; in other words, why the opening of churches could not have been left to guidance. Even if I am wrong in reaching that conclusion, the respondents have in any event

[144] ibid 72–73.
[145] ibid 67.
[146] ibid.
[147] ibid.

> not demonstrated why it was necessary to ban private prayer, the reasons which were given for that recommendation being insufficient to withstand even the lowest degree of scrutiny.[148]

This is peculiar reasoning because the test under *Bank Mellat* is supposed to be whether a less intrusive measure could have been used 'without unacceptably compromising the achievement of the objective'.[149] Yet it seems obvious that the less intrusive measure that Lord Braid is suggesting – opening places of worship with mitigation measures – would be less effective at preventing transmission than a closure of places of worship, so clearly it compromises the objective. Perhaps the question is whether it compromises the objective 'unacceptably'. This seems, again, to boil down to a value judgement about whether it would be acceptable for the state to take less effective measures that are less intrusive. As Mark Movsesian observes, the decision in *Philip*, like those of the US Supreme Court, involved 'intuitive judgments' on '[w]hether a public-health measure goes too far', and 'a judge with contrary views could just as plausibly have drawn the lines differently'.[150]

Given the resemblance in these cases between the less intrusive means stage of proportionality and the strict scrutiny stage of the *Smith-Lukumi* test, it seems correct to say that there are 'affinities' between the tests in the US and UK.[151] However, the affinities have limitations, as the approach did differ in certain respects. First, the role of comparisons was much larger in the US cases because of the first stage of the *Smith-Lukumi* test. If a law is neutral and of general applicability then, unlike in the UK, the court does not reach tailoring. Second, the tailoring analysis (when reached) tended to be cursory in the US cases, whereas in *Philip* balancing – employed in some form in the third and fourth stages of the *Bank Mellat* test – was the focus of the exercise. Third, the final stage of proportionality in the UK was different from tailoring in the US. This balancing exercise weighs not merely ends and means as in the case of strict scrutiny, but the effect on rights against the importance of the objective. In *Philip*, this final stage offered another reason for Lord Braid to conclude that the law was invalid – one even more in the nature of a value judgement, since this stage of proportionality is often criticised as a weighing of incommensurables, as discussed in Chapter 3.

The courts also differed on how much leeway or deference to grant the executive in the circumstances. Swift J in *Hussain* allowed the Secretary of State 'a suitable margin of appreciation to decide the order in which steps are to be taken to reduce the reach and impact of the restrictions',[152] but Lord Braid in *Philip* considered that the margin of appreciation, while 'still a relevant factor at several of the stages',

[148] *Philip* (n 2) [115].
[149] *Bank Mellat v Her Majesty's Treasury (No 2)* [2014] AC 700 (Supreme Court of the United Kingdom) [74].
[150] ML Movsesian, 'Law, Religion, and the COVID-19 Crisis' (2022) 37 *Journal of Law and Religion* 9, 15.
[151] ibid 11, 21, 24.
[152] *Hussain* (n 47) para 21.

was 'not the complete answer to a challenge that a decision or legislation is not proportionate'.[153] He also did not consider that the court should defer to the expertise of the executive:

> As regards whether the decision involved a scientific judgment best left to an executive armed with expertise and experience not available to the court, I do not consider that the decision can be categorised in that way. As the petitioners point out, the science is not in dispute. It is accepted that Covid-19 is an extremely serious and highly transmissible disease which can result in serious illness and death. The scientific material on which the respondents based their decision is either available to the court or ought to have been made available. It should also be pointed out that also not in dispute is that mitigating measures such as social distancing, face masks, hand washing and good ventilation are known to reduce the risk of transmission.[154]

The *per curiam* in *Roman Catholic Diocese* struck a similar note. It accepted that '[m]embers of this Court are not public health experts, and we should respect the judgment of those with special expertise and responsibility in this area', but said that, 'even in a pandemic, the Constitution cannot be put away and forgotten'.[155] As Shlomo Pill puts it, the Court 'declined to defer to health officials' judgments about the comparability of burdened religious and exempted secular activities in terms of viral spread risks'.[156] Cass Sunstein describes this non-deferential approach favourably as an 'anti-*Korematsu*',[157] referring to a case during World War II addressing the internment of Japanese-Americans in which the US Supreme Court failed to invalidate the practice.[158] However, the analogy Sunstein draws between coronavirus restrictions and ethnically-targeted wartime detention seems wildly inapposite.

In dissent, Sotomayor J highlighted the severity of the situation in the US at that time, saying that the 'Justices of this Court play a deadly game in second guessing the expert judgment of health officials about the environments in which a contagious virus, now infecting a million Americans each week, spreads most easily'.[159] Sotomayor J's criticisms have salience. Although it is true that courts cannot abdicate their role in adjudicating rights violations, even in exceptional circumstances, because of the risk of abuse and overreach, courts' oversight role should

[153] *Philip* (n 2) [100].
[154] ibid [111].
[155] *Roman Catholic Diocese* (n 2) 68.
[156] SC Pill, 'The False Promise of Expanded Religious Liberty Rights after the COVID-19 Cases and *Fulton v City of Philadelphia*' (2023) 31 *William & Mary Bill of Rights Journal* 825, 862.
[157] CR Sunstein, 'Our Anti-*Korematsu*' (2021) 1 *American Journal of Law and Equality* 221.
[158] *Korematsu v United States* (1944) 323 US 214 (Supreme Court of the United States).
[159] *Roman Catholic Diocese* (n 2) 79. Roberts CJ had a similar approach in the first *South Bay* decision, stating that '[w]here … broad limits are not exceeded, [politically accountable officials] should not be subject to second-guessing by an "unelected federal judiciary," which lacks the background, competence, and expertise to assess public health and is not accountable to the people': *South Bay (No 1)* (n 2) 1613–14. In the second *South Bay* decision, he again emphasised that 'federal courts owe significant deference to politically accountable officials with the "background, competence, and expertise to assess public health"', but said that '[d]eference, though broad, has its limits': *South Bay (No 2)* (n 40) 716–17.

be conducted carefully. In particular, they should at least factor in as a significant consideration when restrictions are made on a temporary basis to address an emergency.[160] Properly analysed within the necessity stage of the framework, such emergency restrictions would have been justified by the common interest in mitigating a public health crisis. In addition to compatibility, necessity offers another basis for defeat of the claims.

The theoretical analysis in Chapter 3 establishes that liberty of conscience should not be regarded an absolute right. It is necessarily subject to certain limitations for compatibility with the basic liberties of others or necessity in the common interest. Nor is it thought to be an absolute right in US or UK law. However, the non-absolute nature of liberty of conscience seemed at times to be forgotten in the US coronavirus cases. In *Roman Catholic Diocese*, Gorsuch J wrote that 'we may not shelter in place when the Constitution is under attack'.[161] As above, the *per curiam* said that 'even in a pandemic, the Constitution cannot be put away and forgotten'.[162] That is one characterisation of what is at stake. But the opposing view is that the US Constitution would only be under attack or forgotten if it were accepted that there was an absolute right to religious exercise irrespective of the circumstances, and the right has never been construed in that way in US constitutional law. That view says that given the circumstances of a pandemic, it is legitimate to accept temporary restrictions on an emergency basis to protect people's lives. As Goldberg J, delivering the US Supreme Court's opinion in *Kennedy v Mendoza-Martinez* in 1963, famously said: 'while the Constitution protects against invasions of individual rights, it is not a suicide pact'.[163]

The UK cases tended to avoid the kind of language used by Gorsuch J, and it was clearer that what the courts were undertaking was a balancing exercise involving a qualified right that could legitimately be restricted. Lord Braid in *Philip* did not suggest that the European Convention on Human Rights was 'under attack' due to the fact that the Scottish government had struck the balance differently from the way that he would have preferred. Rather, he accepted that the matter was 'finely balanced'.[164] That acceptance was surely correct in circumstances where he was making a value judgement on which reasonable minds could differ. Viewed against the UK cases, the bombast of Gorsuch J seems even more jarring and inapposite. Of course, it is true that the courts do play a supervisory role and, even in an emergency, there have to be limits. But the issue in these cases was how to

[160] See generally RA Posner, *Not a Suicide Pact: The Constitution in a Time of National Emergency* (Oxford: Oxford University Press, 2006); O Gross and FN Aoláin, *Law in Times of Crisis: Emergency Powers in Theory and Practice* (Cambridge: Cambridge University Press, 2006); M Tushnet, 'The Political Constitutional of Emergency Powers: Parliamentary and Separation-of-Powers Regulation' (2007) 3 *International Journal of Law in Context* 275.

[161] *Roman Catholic Diocese* (n 2) 71.

[162] ibid 68.

[163] *Kennedy v Mendoza-Martinez* (1963) 372 US 144 (Supreme Court of the United States) 160.

[164] *Philip* (n 2) [126].

assess restrictions on liberty of conscience bearing in mind the possibility of valid limitations on that right.

In summary, on the issue of necessity, the comparisons employed between the regulation of secular and religious activities, which proved malleable, did little to advance the analysis. In the US cases, comparisons were often not differentiated according to risk as was later said to be required in *Tandon*.[165] However, members of the US Supreme Court pointed to less restrictive regulation of lower-risk secular activities as reason to strike down more restrictive regulation of higher-risk religious activities. The role of comparisons was at the fore in the US case law because of the *Smith-Lukumi* test, and the difficulties experienced by the Court raise further questions about this controversial test. In the UK context, where the test is proportionality, comparisons between regulation of secular and religious activities were less important. Nonetheless, to the extent that a comparison was employed in *Philip*, it too raised unanswered questions. These comparisons are only of peripheral relevance, if any relevance at all, to the necessity in the common interest analysis prescribed by the framework.

What is of significantly greater importance to necessity in the common interest is an assessment of means against ends. On this point, the tailoring analysis in the US cases tended to be very brief, whereas in *Philip* the consideration of less intrusive means was more substantial. In both jurisdictions, the courts made what was essentially a value judgement that coronavirus restrictions could be less strict and that would still be acceptable. It is difficult to discern on what basis this value judgement was made, particularly as the measures preferred by the courts were evidently going to be less effective than the measures that they had found invalid. That much was plain in *Philip*, where it was unclear how a less intrusive measure was available without 'unacceptably compromising the achievement of the objective'. From a practical standpoint, these cases suggest the critical importance of the tailoring or less intrusive means stage of the analysis – being decisive in both jurisdictions – as well as the apparent risk that that kind of analysis will lead to a court telling the government to accept less *effective* means.

V. Conclusion

Applying the framework developed in Chapters 2, 3 and 4 to responses to the coronavirus pandemic highlights the complex issues that arise at the moral level. In respect of compatibility analysis, the right to integrity of the person of others is threatened in its central range of application by the exercise of liberty of conscience in the form of religious gatherings, since this may increase the spread of SARS-CoV-2. In contrast, the lockdown restrictions did not go to the central range of

[165] On the relevance of risk, see, eg, DR Reiss and M Thomas, 'More Than a Mask: Stay-at-Home Orders and Religious Freedom' (2020) 57 *San Diego Law Review* 947, 965.

application of liberty of conscience because of the possibility of online worship and the temporary nature of the restrictions. Accordingly, the claim to liberty of conscience fails at the compatibility stage. Further, it fails at the necessity stage, as the challenged measures could be said to be necessary in the common interest in public health.

The framework therefore suggests that claims upheld by some courts should have been defeated. The US jurisprudence is particularly troubling on this front. As Mark Strasser says in his comment on the coronavirus cases, 'the [US Supreme] Court has more than fulfilled the pessimistic expectations of some who fear that free exercise jurisprudence has been torn from its moorings'.[166] In respect of the European Convention, although some states chose to derogate under Article 15 on the basis of the pandemic,[167] it arguably should not be necessary to do so at least in relation to Article 9, because a qualified right of that nature – one that refers expressly to limitations for the protection of 'health' and the 'rights and freedoms of others' – can already accommodate restrictions required to address a pandemic. That, at least, is the morally preferable position as indicated by the framework. Under the US Constitution, there is no possibility of derogating, making it all the more necessary to construe the First Amendment in a practically workable way.

[166] M Strasser, 'Covid-19, Free Exercise, and Most Favored Nation Status' (2023) 27 *Lewis & Clark Law Review* 1, 3.

[167] See Council of Europe, 'Derogations Covid-19' https://www.coe.int/en/web/conventions/derogations-covid-19.

6

Discrimination towards Same-Sex Couples

Gay people have faced a long history of terrible discrimination in many parts of the world.[1] Only recently has legal recognition of same-sex relationships become a major topic of consideration, and the spread of same-sex marriage to many countries across the world, including the United States and United Kingdom, is often viewed as a triumph of civil rights.[2] In practice, the enactment of non-discrimination obligations in respect of sexual orientation could be equally important.[3] However, such developments may be opposed by some religious believers as in tension with their convictions that homosexuality is morally wrong. As I sought to show in Chapter 2, liberty of conscience is an important right too. How do we reconcile the rights of same-sex couples with the rights of religious believers, as protected by liberty of conscience?

This chapter therefore addresses the interaction between laws prohibiting discrimination towards same-sex couples and liberty of conscience. As Kathleen Brady puts it, some of the 'bitterest battles over religious accommodation have

[1] For an overview of the persecution of gay people through history, see B Fone, *Homophobia: A History* (New York: Henry Holt, 2000). This experience of persecution has not necessarily been universal, as in some cultures homosexuality was permitted or even valued in certain contexts: see, eg, GP Leupp, *Male Colors: The Construction of Homosexuality in Tokugawa Japan* (Berkeley, CA: University of California Press, 1997).

[2] See, in the US, *Obergefell v Hodges* (2015) 576 US 644 (Supreme Court of the United States); in the UK, the Marriage (Same Sex Couples) Act 2013, which made provision for same-sex marriage in England and Wales. On religious freedom issues with the introduction of same-sex marriage, see, eg, J García Oliva and H Hall, 'Same-Sex Marriage: An Inevitable Challenge to Religious Liberty and Establishment?' (2014) 3 *Oxford Journal of Law and Religion* 25.

[3] In the UK, see the Equality Act 2010. In the US, at the federal level, non-discrimination protections in employment under Title VII of the Civil Rights Act of 1964 were extended to gay and transgender persons by the US Supreme Court in *Bostock v Clayton County* (2020) 140 S Ct 1731 (Supreme Court of the United States). The reasoning of this decision is somewhat novel, as it interpreted the protection against discrimination on the ground of 'sex' as extending to 'sexual orientation' and 'gender identity'. Gorsuch J, delivering the opinion of the Court, explained this as follows: 'An employer who fires an individual for being homosexual or transgender fires that person for traits or actions it would not have questioned in members of a different sex. Sex plays a necessary and undisguisable role in the decision, exactly what Title VII forbids. … Those who adopted the Civil Rights Act might not have anticipated their work would lead to this particular result. … But the limits of the drafters' imagination supply no reason to ignore the law's demands. When the express terms of a statute give us one answer and extra-textual considerations suggest another, it's no contest. Only the written word is the law, and all persons are entitled to its benefit': at 1737.

been in the context of same-sex marriage'.[4] Although this topic has been extensively addressed in the literature,[5] the contribution of this chapter is to employ the framework developed in Chapters 2, 3 and 4 of this book to analyse the issue. As with Chapter 5, which addressed the interaction of coronavirus restrictions and liberty of conscience, this chapter focuses on the law of the US and UK. Broadly, the view is advanced that non-discrimination should receive preference over liberty of conscience in compatibility analysis where the clash takes place outside the central range of application of liberty of conscience, but within the central range of application of non-discrimination. Further, the limitation on liberty of conscience in these circumstances is also supported by necessity in the common interest.

The chapter proceeds in four sections. In Section I, I consider the status of non-discrimination within the framework, namely whether we should accept it as a basic liberty. In Section II, I set out the cases: two cases of the US Supreme Court[6] and two cases of the UK Supreme Court[7] that consider the clash between rights to non-discrimination of same-sex couples and liberty of conscience. In Section III, I analyse these cases by reference to compatibility, concluding that all the cases except *Lee* should ideally have been resolved in favour of the same-sex couples in question on the basis of the rights of others. That is because the claims to liberty of conscience were not in the central range of application of that basic liberty, as they occurred in the commercial sphere, but the effect of the subject of the claim of liberty of conscience on a basic liberty of non-discrimination did go to its central range of application. In Section IV, I consider that the same result would be achieved through the concept of necessity in the common interest. It is in the common interest in social harmony to prohibit discrimination on the basis of sexual orientation in public contexts, and appropriately tailored restrictions on liberty of conscience to achieve this (such as non-discrimination laws) are necessary in the common interest when the interferences with liberty of conscience do not go to the central range of application of that basic liberty. In Section V, I conclude that the analysis favours the reasoning of the UK courts over that of the US courts. Whereas the UK Supreme Court reached the morally correct outcome in both cases under consideration, the US Supreme Court's approach in its two cases proves to be inconsistent with the framework advanced in this book – both because of the *Smith-Lukumi* test itself and how it is applied.

[4] KA Brady, 'The Disappearance of Religion from Debates about Religious Accommodation' (2017) 20 *Lewis & Clark Law Review* 1093, 1097.

[5] See, eg, T Shah, T Farr and J Friedman (eds), *Religious Freedom and Gay Rights: Emerging Conflicts in the United States and Europe* (New York: Oxford University Press, 2016); A Koppelman, *Gay Rights vs Religious Liberty? The Unnecessary Conflict* (New York: Oxford University Press, 2020).

[6] *Masterpiece Cakeshop v Colorado Civil Rights Commission* (2018) 138 S Ct 1719 (Supreme Court of the United States); *Fulton v City of Philadelphia* (2021) 141 S Ct 1868 (Supreme Court of the United States). See also *303 Creative LLC v Elenis* (2023) 143 S Ct 2298 (Supreme Court of the United States) (addressed below, though only briefly, as it was not decided on free exercise of religion grounds).

[7] *Bull v Hall* [2013] 1 WLR 3741 (Supreme Court of the United Kingdom); *Lee v Ashers Baking Co Ltd* [2020] AC 413 (Supreme Court of the United Kingdom).

I. A Basic Liberty of Non-Discrimination

The relevant potential basic liberty to be considered in this chapter is non-discrimination. This basic liberty is important because the case study involves clashes between liberty of conscience and non-discrimination. Although Rawls does not consider non-discrimination to be a basic liberty within the first principle of justice (the liberty principle), he acknowledges non-discrimination as an aspect of fair equality of opportunity within the second principle of justice, which also includes Rawls's famous 'difference principle'. Rawls's idea of fair equality of opportunity is nonetheless fairly robust. In *Political Liberalism*, Rawls says that 'announcements of jobs and positions can be forbidden to contain statements which exclude applicants of certain designated ethnic and racial groups, or of either sex, when these limitations are contrary to fair equality of opportunity'.[8] In *Justice as Fairness*, Rawls suggests that discrimination in university admissions would also violate this principle.[9]

However, the classification of this notion of non-discrimination under the second principle of justice is significant because the first principle has lexical priority over the second.[10] It may seem surprising that Rawls classifies non-discrimination in this subordinated way when he acknowledges its key social importance. Rawls writes in *A Theory of Justice* that '[t]here are questions which we feel sure must be answered in a certain way. For example, we are confident that religious intolerance and racial discrimination are unjust'.[11] He describes how embedding inequalities based on race and sex within the basic structure would be irrational, because in the original position, due to the veil of ignorance, '[n]o one can tell whether such principles would be to his advantage'.[12] However, for inequalities based on race and sex not to be embedded in the basic structure may seem insufficient, if discrimination on those grounds (or others) is not prevented in society at large, as Seana Shiffrin persuasively argues.[13] It seems unfortunate for Rawls to accept the unjustness of discrimination, and yet fail to include non-discrimination as a basic liberty within the first principle.

One possible explanation for Rawls's account is that discrimination is not the focus of his theory. For example, Rawls says that lack of consideration of race and gender in *A Theory of Justice* is an 'omission … but an omission is not as such a

[8] J Rawls, *Political Liberalism* (New York: Columbia University Press, 2005) 363. For debate over the merits of Rawls's concept of fair equality of opportunity, see RJ Arneson, 'Against Rawlsian Equality of Opportunity' (1999) 93 *Philosophical Studies* 77; L Lindblom, 'In Defense of Rawlsian Fair Equality of Opportunity' (2018) 47 *Philosophical Papers* 235.

[9] J Rawls, *Justice as Fairness: A Restatement* (E Kelly ed, Cambridge, MA: Harvard University Press, 2001) 11.

[10] Rawls, *Political Liberalism* (n 8) 309–10, 363–64.

[11] J Rawls, *A Theory of Justice* (Cambridge, MA: Harvard University Press, 1971) 19; J Rawls, *A Theory of Justice (Revised Edition)* (Cambridge, MA: Harvard University Press, 1999) 17.

[12] Rawls, *A Theory of Justice* (n 11) 99, 149–50; Rawls, *A Theory of Justice (Revised Edition)* (n 11) 85, 129–30.

[13] SV Shiffrin, 'Race and Ethnicity, Race, Labor, and the Fair Equality of Opportunity Principle' (2004) 72 *Fordham Law Review* 1643.

fault', because he is focused on ideal theory, and only considered limited questions in non-ideal theory.[14] However, the inclusion of a notion of non-discrimination as part of fair equality of opportunity complicates that, since there is not a total omission of such consideration. Perhaps Rawls thought it was not suited to be resolved in the original position, where the representatives are behind the veil of ignorance; it could instead be addressed by constitutional drafters or legislators once the veil is partially lifted, as Tommie Shelby suggests.[15] But that might be strange when questions of distributive justice are taken up in the original position, resulting in the adoption of the second principle of justice. The notion that the representatives in the original position are alert to economic unfairness but naïve about the possibility of discrimination is hard to accept.

Because Rawls acknowledges non-discrimination as a norm, but not one at the same level as the basic liberties, some work is required here to elucidate the issue and consider the proper status of non-discrimination. In the moral framework in this book, I recognise a right not to be discriminated against in public contexts on the basis of protected characteristics as a basic liberty, because discrimination interferes with moral personality. Non-discrimination is necessary for the development and exercise of the moral powers because discrimination has a sufficient tendency to inhibit a person's development and exercise of the moral powers by failing to treat that person as an individual. As with other basic liberties within the framework, including liberty of conscience, compatibility and necessity may operate to justify compromise of this basic liberty.

My analysis of why non-discrimination should be accepted as a basic liberty proceeds in three sections. In Section A, I analyse the nature and unfairness of discrimination, drawing particularly on the account offered by Eidelson.[16] In Section B, I assess the relationship between discrimination and respect for moral personality, contending that this respect does require a norm of non-discrimination in public contexts on the basis of protected characteristics. In Section C, I respond briefly to some other possible accounts to explain why the understanding of non-discrimination offered here should be preferred. In particular, I argue that an account of non-discrimination as a basic liberty of universal application is superior both normatively and descriptively to an account that treats it as a socially or historically contingent norm.

A. Nature and Unfairness of Discrimination

Although working out a detailed definition of discrimination is not the purpose of this book, it is necessary, as a preliminary step, to formulate a rough one to

[14] Rawls, *Justice as Fairness: A Restatement* (n 9) 66.

[15] T Shelby, 'Race and Ethnicity, Race and Social Justice: Rawlsian Considerations' (2004) 72 *Fordham Law Review* 1697, 1706–1709.

[16] See B Eidelson, *Discrimination and Disrespect* (Oxford: Oxford University Press, 2015).

guide the foregoing discussion. The definition can be stated as follows: discrimination is taken to mean treating a person *disadvantageously* because of *protected characteristics*. Non-discrimination is the right not to suffer such discrimination. These ideas require some explanation. First, there is a requirement of 'disadvantageous' treatment in this definition because positive treatment is not discrimination 'against' someone, though positive treatment of one person on a particular basis may be discriminatory against another. As Eidelson explains, 'to discriminate against someone, one must treat him differently in some dimension than others, and this differential treatment must be comparatively disadvantageous to him in some respect'.[17]

The disadvantageous treatment must take place because of protected characteristics. Roughly, these are certain personal attributes internal to the individual, as opposed to an individual's external actions, for example a person's employment record or achievements or performance in school or an exam – or, less positively, criminal record. I say 'certain' personal attributes because drawing the line as to what is protected may be difficult, and some possible protected characteristics have been the subject of significant academic debate, such as disability and philosophical beliefs.[18] In some systems, such as under the European Convention on Human Rights, very broad approaches to what might be protected are taken due to the presence of the words 'other status' in Article 14 of the Convention, though only certain 'suspect grounds' require 'very weighty reasons' for discrimination to be justified.[19]

This chapter does not seek to draw the line exactly as to what characteristics are protected, though as noted, the personal attributes that we consider should be protected usually relate to personal attributes that are internal to the individual, even if they may manifest in external action. Below, I make an argument for including natural attributes – traits where it is accurate to say people are 'born that way' – such as skin colour, sex and sexual orientation within the scope of protected characteristics, since this is relevant to the case study considered below. Sometimes, these attributes are referred to as 'immutable' attributes. In truth, mutability may coincide with the naturalness of these attributes, but it is not the whole issue (discrimination is still wrong even if these natural attributes can be altered), and some other attributes that are often protected, such as religious belief, are mutable, but we still usually consider that they merit protection because they are important to identity.[20]

[17] ibid 15.

[18] See, eg, L Vickers, *Religious Freedom, Religious Discrimination and the Workplace*, 2nd edn (Oxford: Hart Publishing, 2016) Ch 5.

[19] See generally *R (SC) v Secretary of State for Work and Pensions* [2022] AC 223 (Supreme Court of the United Kingdom) [100]–[110]. See originally *Abdulaziz v United Kingdom* (1985) 7 EHRR 471 (European Court of Human Rights).

[20] See generally C McCrudden, *Litigating Religions: An Essay on Human Rights, Courts, and Beliefs* (Oxford: Oxford University Press, 2018) 78–79.

My analysis of discrimination is focused on 'direct' discrimination,[21] including 'proxy' discrimination, in which the differential treatment is on the basis of another trait that is a proxy for the protected characteristic. As Eidelson puts it,

> the differential treatment simply has to be due, in part, to the fact that the agent regards the discriminatees differently in respect of that trait – whether or not she intends to be sensitive to this apparent difference, and whether or not she is sensitive to it only as a proxy for some other trait with which she is concerned.[22]

This concept of proxy discrimination, as a form of direct discrimination, is related to what is described in UK law as discrimination on a criterion 'indissociable' from a protected characteristic.[23] However, I do not use the concept of a proxy too restrictively. In the framework, proxy discrimination occurs when another trait serves as an *effective* proxy for a protected characteristic, for example because everyone who possesses the protected characteristic would be caught by the proxy.

I do not focus on what is called in European law 'indirect' discrimination,[24] or in American law 'disparate impact' discrimination,[25] which relates to circumstances in which a seemingly neutral policy has uneven effects on those with protected characteristics. Waldron describes how indirect discrimination may pose more complex questions philosophically than direct discrimination.[26] The case study considered in this chapter can be addressed satisfactorily on the basis of an account of direct discrimination. Consequently, although the account I offer may cover instances of indirect discrimination – to the extent that such discrimination has a sufficient tendency to impair the development and exercise of the moral powers, it might be explainable on the same normative basis – it is a more challenging question, and it proves unnecessary to consider the point for the purposes of this book.

The most important feature of discrimination is the basis on which acts of discrimination take place (as distinct from the intention or purpose underlying them). Discrimination consists in acts that are otherwise permissible – such as denying service in a commercial context, denying someone a job, denying someone a position at an educational institution – that become wrongful because they

[21] See, in the UK context, Equality Act 2010, s 13.

[22] Eidelson (n 16) 38.

[23] See, eg, *Bull v Hall* (n 7) [19]–[20].

[24] See Equality Act 2010, s 19.

[25] For the judicial origins of this doctrine in US law, see *Griggs v Duke Power Co* (1971) 401 US 424 (Supreme Court of the United States). The US Congress later codified the 'disparate impact' concept, which had originated with the US Supreme Court, in an amendment to the Civil Rights Act of 1964: see Civil Rights Act of 1991. However, disparate impact discrimination does not apply to the constitutional equal protection requirement under the Fifth and Fourteenth Amendments: *Washington v Davis* (1976) 426 US 229 (Supreme Court of the United States). Given the inconsistency, an issue later arose as to whether the disparate impact doctrine might itself be unconstitutional: see *Ricci v DeStefano* (2009) 557 US 557 (Supreme Court of the United States).

[26] J Waldron, 'Indirect Discrimination' in S Guest and A Milne (eds), *Equality and Discrimination: Essays in Freedom and Justice* (Stuttgart: F Steiner, 1985). See also Eidelson (n 16) Ch 2.

are taken on the basis of protected characteristics.[27] A key point that we might consider distinguishes discrimination from other forms of denial of opportunities or services (that is, those not taken on the basis of protected characteristics) is the unfairness of discrimination – denying service, a job, or a position at an educational position on this particular basis is unfair. However, despite the intuitiveness of the position that discrimination is unfair, where this unfairness arises from may not be immediately clear. For example, Deborah Hellman seems to be correct to say that people are often not entitled to particular opportunities, such as job opportunities (short of legal rights or other bases for forming expectations of them), so it is perhaps not useful to speak of being denied of opportunities to which one is entitled.[28]

Rather, the unfairness of discrimination, properly understood, stems from the failure of discriminatory decisions to acknowledge the potential of the individual, by instead treating the individual merely as an avatar of a group or a holder of a personal attribute on which basis the individual is disfavoured (irrespective of whether the disfavouring results from any stereotype about the group or attribute that is accurate or not). Discrimination is unfair because it treats a person as a statistic – an amalgam of attributes shared with others – rather than as a person with all the possibilities entailed in being a person, including the exercise and development of the moral powers. As will be shown, the consequence of that kind of failure is, not surprisingly, to impair the exercise and development of the moral powers of that person, and to fail to accord her recognition respect as a moral person. This point is indebted to Eidelson's insightful analysis of the philosophical foundations of wrongful discrimination. Eidelson explains the importance of treating someone as an individual as follows:

> According to this account … treating someone as an individual demands two things. First, it means paying reasonable attention to relevant ways in which a person has exercised her autonomy, insofar as these are discernible from the outside, in making herself the person she is. Second, it means recognizing that, because she is an autonomous agent, she is capable of deciding how to act for herself. When we act in accordance with these requirements, we deal with people in a way that respects the role they can play and have played in shaping themselves, rather than treating them as determined by demographic categories or other matters of statistical fate.[29]

In other words, discrimination overlooks an individual's past choices and future possibilities by treating the individual as a mere avatar of her personal attributes – it subsumes the individual within her group identity. As Dworkin writes in the context of the criminal law, 'it is unjust to put someone in jail on the basis of a judgment about a class, however accurate, because that denies his claim to equal respect as an

[27] Equality Act 2010, Pt 2, ch 1.

[28] D Hellman, *When Is Discrimination Wrong?* (Cambridge, MA: Harvard University Press, 2008) 103.

[29] Eidelson (n 16) 145.

individual'.[30] It is this dimension that supplies the unfairness of discrimination that corresponds with our moral intuitions. But to justify state intervention to address discrimination, it might well be insufficient that discrimination is unfair. It might evince what Kramer calls a 'quidnunc' mentality for the state to seek to intervene in private relations in order to ensure that everyone is treated fairly.[31] For this reason, I seek to take a further step and explain how failure to treat a person as an individual interferes with development and exercise of the moral powers, because it is in this circumstance that the state must protect non-discrimination as a basic liberty.

B. Non-Discrimination as Required by Recognition Respect for Moral Personality

The criterion for inclusion of non-discrimination as a basic liberty is more than that it is unfair, but rather that there is a sufficient tendency for such discrimination to interfere with development and exercise of the moral powers when it occurs in what I term public contexts. As outlined in Chapter 2, I advance the argument that recognition respect of persons as bearing moral personality implies respect for their development and exercise of the moral powers, which in turn necessitates the protection of liberty of conscience. Does recognition respect for moral personality also imply a right not to be discriminated against in the sense outlined above? It does, because discrimination, at least in a public context, interferes with the development and exercise of the moral powers. This development and exercise do not exist in a social vacuum, and can be affected by the treatment sustained at the hands of others.

The issue of a public context is not dealt with in detail in Eidelson's account, on which I otherwise rely rather heavily.[32] I seek to limit my argument to public contexts because although differential treatment of a person on the basis of protected characteristics in purely private relations might well be unfair, in the manner outlined above, it may not necessarily be harmful to the exercise and development of the moral powers in the particular way considered in this chapter. As an example of how this distinction operates, a preference for a particular age range in online dating would not take place in a relevantly public context; this is properly understood to be a private matter. Although a detailed account of what kind of context is 'public' will not be provided and lies beyond the scope of the book, archetypal public contexts would be education, employment and 'public accommodations', as they are termed in US law (meaning the provision of services to the public), which are the kind of places in which legal requirements of non-discrimination commonly apply.

[30] R Dworkin, *Taking Rights Seriously* (London: Bloomsbury, 2013) 27.
[31] MH Kramer, *Liberalism with Excellence* (Oxford: Oxford University Press, 2017) Ch 6.
[32] See Eidelson (n 16) 122–25.

Although this argument is harm based, that does not mean that it is a contingent one that only works in certain circumstances where harm actually eventuates from the discrimination.[33] What this objection overlooks is that the law often prohibits an activity that is dangerous regardless of whether harm eventuates, such as discharge of a firearm in public place. It is because of the risk of harm – or, expressed differently, the tendency to harm – that we regard that act as wrongful even if the harm does not transpire. As with the integrity of the person, for something to be a basic liberty there needs to be a sufficient tendency for restriction of it to impair the exercise and development of the moral powers. The requirement is not that the connection is absolute or completely uniform. As a result, discrimination is wrongful even when harm does not eventuate in a given example, because it bears a sufficient tendency to cause such harm.

There are two distinct types of harm that can stem from the failure to treat someone as an individual in a public context, which serve as the basis for finding non-discrimination to be a basic liberty: material harm and psychological harm.[34] Turning first to material harm, unfair disadvantageous treatment on the basis of protected characteristics results in material harm in the form of denial of opportunities that would be otherwise received. This form of harm entails a counterfactual analysis, focused on the denial of an opportunity in circumstances where it results from a failure to acknowledge a person as an individual, with all the potential of an individual. One possible form of the harm is a total bar to an opportunity, such that, for example, a person of a disfavoured skin colour is turned away entirely from certain opportunities. But even if the odds of succeeding at attaining that opportunity are simply reduced, missing out on something that a person would otherwise have received but for skin colour still constitutes harm even if it was only a partial factor.

This harm impairs the development and exercise of the moral powers. For example, in respect of judging right and justice, a gay person blocked from political organising by the prejudice of others would be prevented from exercising his political judgements. The same is true if that scenario applied to a member of a minority religion. In respect of pursuing a conception of the good, a Black person who is barred from attending an educational institution would be impaired in developing and pursuing his conception of the good. The same is true of a woman denied entry on the basis of being a woman. These material harms can be of such an extreme nature that the European Court of Human Rights has even recognised them as constituting degrading treatment towards the disfavoured group, as in

[33] See, eg, the possible objection identified in K Lippert-Rasmussen, *Born Free and Equal? A Philosophical Inquiry into the Nature of Discrimination* (Oxford: Oxford University Press, 2014) 165. (Ultimately, Lippert-Rasmussen himself offers a harm-based account of the wrongness of discrimination.)

[34] See similarly the analysis in D NeJaime and R Siegel, 'Conscience Wars in Transnational Perspective: Religious Liberty, Third-Party Harm, and Pluralism' in S Mancini and M Rosenfeld (eds), *The Conscience Wars: Rethinking the Balance between Religion, Identity, and Equality* (Cambridge: Cambridge University Press, 2018).

Cyprus v Turkey in relation to discriminatory treatment of Greek Cypriots. In that case, the Court found a violation of Article 3, reasoning as follows:

> For the Court it is an inescapable conclusion that the interferences at issue were directed at the Karpas Greek-Cypriot community for the very reason that they belonged to this class of persons. The treatment to which they were subjected during the period under consideration can only be explained in terms of the features which distinguish them from the Turkish-Cypriot population, namely their ethnic origin, race and religion. … In the Court's opinion, and with reference to the period under consideration, the discriminatory treatment attained a level of severity which amounted to degrading treatment.[35]

As noted above, the kind of material harm under consideration, interfering with the development and exercise of the moral powers, occurs in a public context. Missing out on being invited to dinner because the host disapproves of your religion may well be highly unfair, and could even be disappointing or upsetting. But it is not quite the same as being denied an educational or professional opportunity, which has a sufficient tendency to interfere with the exercise and development of the moral powers by removing a person from circumstances that would contribute to that exercise and development. Although I do not rely specifically on the concept of autonomy, this account somewhat resembles John Gardner's view that 'duties of non-discrimination, whether on ground of immutable status or on ground of fundamental choice, are alike in being autonomy-based duties' in its emphasis on how discrimination can affect our choices.[36] He explains this idea as follows:

> [T]he familiar liberal idea of an autonomous life … is the ideal of a life substantially lived through the successive valuable choices of the person who lives it, where valuable choices are choices from among an adequate range of valuable options. Discrimination on the basis of our immutable status tends to deny us this life. Its result is that our further choices are constrained not mainly by our own choices, but by the choices of others. Because these choices of others are based on our immutable status, our own choices can make no difference to them.[37]

Although the sufficient tendency of such discrimination to harm the exercise and development of the moral powers through material disadvantage offers a justification for the inclusion of non-discrimination as a basic liberty in itself, it supplements the argument to observe that discrimination may also cause psychological impacts that further impair the exercise and development of the moral powers. Thus, even when the practical impact of discrimination on the basis of protected characteristics may not be as extreme, the sense of worthlessness, exclusion and stigmatisation imparted by discrimination in the public sphere is likely to have psychological effects that impair the development and exercise of the moral powers – consistent with the recognition, arrived at in Chapter 5, of

[35] *Cyprus v Turkey* (2002) 35 EHRR 30 (European Court of Human Rights) [309]–[310].
[36] J Gardner, 'On the Ground of Her Sex(uality)' (1998) 18 *Oxford Journal of Legal Studies* 167, 171.
[37] ibid 170–71.

psychological integrity of the person as an aspect of integrity of the person as a basic liberty. Arguably, this is so even when the issue is the provision of services by a private business.

That is because discrimination implies that someone is less worthy on the basis of their protected characteristics. The psychological harm results from the denial of, for example, an opportunity due to discrimination on the basis of protected characteristics, not having been acknowledged as an individual with the potential of an individual, which inherently designates the disfavoured group as inferior, less worthy, and less deserving. As Paul Brest recognises, discrimination may – setting aside its practical effects – 'inflict psychological injury by stigmatizing [its] victims as inferior … Recognition of the stigmatic injury inflicted by discrimination explains applications of the antidiscrimination principle where the material harm seems slight or problematic'.[38] Or as the US Supreme Court said in *Brown v Board of Education*, segregation of schools entailed 'a feeling of inferiority as to [Black children's] status in the community that may affect their hearts and minds in a way unlikely ever to be undone'.[39]

Discrimination may not necessarily affect everyone psychologically in the same way, as some may not be affected, for example due to their unusual fortitude. However, this does not matter to the analysis because all that is required to establish non-discrimination as a basic liberty is a sufficient tendency to impair the exercise and development of the moral powers. That sufficient tendency exists because it stigmatises people as not meeting the basic standards of humanity to deny them opportunities in a public context on the basis of protected characteristics – it implies, in essence, that they are not even participants in society, or, as Adenitire describes it, merely 'second-class citizens'.[40] Discriminating in a public context has this impact because the statement made by discrimination in that context is that the disfavoured have less worth and matter less, as individuals.

Discrimination, as an interference with a basic liberty, can still potentially be justified by necessity in the common interest or compatibility with other basic liberties, as discussed in Chapter 3. It is convenient at this point to consider the significance of the rationality of a discriminatory measure, and conversely, the significance of error.[41] Presumably the rationality of any discriminatory measure would be necessary in order to establish necessity, as an irrational measure is unlikely to satisfy that standard, but it may not be sufficient. After all, even an accurate generalisation about a group may be unfair if it fails to respect the potential of the individual. For example, consider an employer who declines to hire a

[38] P Brest, 'Foreword: In Defense of the Antidiscrimination Principle' (1976) 90 *Harvard Law Review* 1, 8–9.

[39] *Brown v Board of Education of Topeka* (1954) 347 US 483 (Supreme Court of the United States) 494.

[40] J Adenitire, *A General Right to Conscientious Exemption: Beyond Religious Privilege* (Cambridge: Cambridge University Press, 2020) 280.

[41] See, eg, L Alexander, 'What Makes Wrongful Discrimination Wrongful? Biases, Preferences, Stereotypes, and Proxies' (1992) 141 *University of Pennsylvania Law Review* 149.

woman because of the possibility that she will take time off work to have children. Even though this generalisation may be accurate, it is not an acceptable one that overcomes the basic liberty of non-discrimination. Although many generalisations that underlie discriminatory policies may be in error, or irrational, that is not always so; error and rationality cannot explain the problem of when discrimination should be permitted. As Miller says:

> A particular woman is not made less deserving because she happens to fall into a category of which it is true, *ex hypothesi*, that members have such-and-such probability of reduced performance in the future. ... [W]e cannot say of any particular woman we are considering for a position that she is liable to perform at a lower level because of a decision to have children. To make that decision is to fail to treat her respectfully as an individual, and potentially to commit an injustice.[42]

However, it is possible to think of examples in which discrimination would be permissible due to necessity in the common interest. An obvious one is a women's shelter that chooses only to employ women. The necessity in the common interest of establishing a truly safe refuge for women who have suffered domestic violence at the hands of men – one in which they can both be safe and feel safe – justifies discriminating against men in hiring for the staffing of the shelter. Further, although the issue of affirmative action is beyond the scope of this chapter, it may be possible that a justification for it could exist in certain circumstances on the basis of necessity.[43] Another basis on which non-discrimination as a right may potentially be overcome is its interaction with the rights of others (compatibility). This issue will be the focus of an extended analysis later in this chapter.[44]

C. Other Approaches to Non-Discrimination

It is helpful to consider briefly two issues that are relevant to other theoretical approaches to non-discrimination but do not matter on the approach to non-discrimination described in this chapter. The first is the mental state or 'animus'

[42] D Miller, *Principles of Social Justice* (Cambridge, MA: Harvard University Press, 2001) 168–69.

[43] For the debate, see, eg, K Lippert-Rasmussen, *Making Sense of Affirmative Action* (Oxford: Oxford University Press, 2020).

[44] It is not difficult to imagine some circumstances in which it is at least arguable that liberty of conscience should prevail over non-discrimination in the circumstances of a clash between them. For example, choices about the staffing of a church would be core to religious practice, and hence to the exercise and development of the moral powers, and within the central range of application of the basic liberty of liberty of conscience. There is therefore a potentially strong argument that discrimination against gay people in that context, if connected with religious belief, may be permissible on the basis of liberty of conscience as a basic liberty prevailing over the basic liberty of non-discrimination. However, where the circumstances are further removed from core circumstances of religious practice, such as in the commercial sphere, the situation becomes more complex, as discussed below.

of the perpetrator of the discrimination.[45] Mental state is not relevant as this is a harm-based account that focuses on the injury to the moral personality of those discriminated against (where such injury may result from both material and psychological harm). Moreover, an account that focused on mental state might have some unattractive features as it could fail to identify the wrongs of those who believe that they are acting beneficially, rather than out of animus. Consider a society, Discriminatia, in which leaders belonging to ethnic group A pass laws allowing shops to deny service to members of ethnic group B out of concern that they are wasting too much of their money. This 'benign', albeit paternalistic, motivation does not avoid the breach of the basic liberty on the account offered above, in a way that aligns with our intuitions about the wrongfulness of discrimination.

The second issue that is not relevant within this account is the role of social conditions as informing what is wrongful discrimination. Treating non-discrimination as a basic liberty means that it is a general norm within a society, and not contingent on social conditions. This places the proposed norm in tension with the approach of those who might argue that the history and current social status of groups inform when discrimination is wrongful. For example, Hellman contends that 'a history of mistreatment and the current social status of people with a particular characteristic are relevant to whether instances of differentiation are wrong'.[46] Her account is that discrimination is wrong when it 'demeans'.[47] According to Hellman,

> differentiating on the basis of features that define a historically mistreated group or a group that currently occupies a low social position is more likely to demean than doing so on the basis of other features. This is because the history and current status of the group concerned affects the meaning of the distinction drawing.[48]

However, these claims raise doubts for several reasons. First, it seems unclear whether discrimination truly becomes any less wrong in the absence of historical mistreatment or low current social status. I give a hypothetical example to illustrate this. Imagine that in country Pluralia there is an ethnic group C that has never been discriminated against before and occupies high social status. They have been tolerated or even venerated by the majority group D, because the religion practised by group D regards group C extremely favourably. But the new president of Pluralia, a member of group D who does not subscribe to this religion, has long hated group C, and as soon as he takes office he immediately enacts discriminatory legislation against them, banning members of group C from working or attending educational institutions. Is this not wrongful discrimination because group C has not faced historical injustice and occupies a high social status? Clearly, this is wrongful discrimination.

[45] For mental-state-based accounts, see generally Alexander (n 41); RJ Arneson, 'What Is Wrongful Discrimination?' (2006) 43 *San Diego Law Review* 775. For critical discussion of such accounts, see, eg, Lippert-Rasmussen (n 33) Ch 4; Hellman (n 28) Ch 6.

[46] Hellman (n 28) 14.

[47] ibid 33.

[48] ibid 57.

It seems apparent that discrimination can be wrongful even without issues of history or social status. An approach that fixates on historical discrimination and social status therefore risks giving a free pass to enacting discrimination in the present. Indeed, as Hellman concedes, discrimination may be wrong even the first time – thus, she claims that her reliance on history constitutes a 'rule of thumb', not an 'absolute requirement'.[49] She gives an example that highlights the limitations of her approach:

> Suppose the government were to decide to deny freckled people the right to vote. Treating people with freckles differently than those without freckles does not carry any baggage, if you will, so that this distinction – though arbitrary and stupid – would likely not demean, except that something vital is at stake. If justice requires that all adults have the right to vote, then restricting the franchise to those without freckles is unjust – and derivatively may also be demeaning. This instance of treating freckled people differently, as it violates justice, may express contempt for the equal humanity of the freckled. As this is an action of government, a good case can be made that this differentiation demeans freckled people.[50]

This acknowledgement of the limitations of Hellman's approach is welcome, as it seems clear that her focus on history and social status cannot adequately explain the wrongfulness of this discrimination against freckled people. It leads to the surprising conclusion that denying people with freckles the right to vote would 'likely not demean' except because of the application of an undefined notion of justice. What if the discrimination against freckled people had been less significant than a denial of their voting rights? Would this change the analysis? Hellman does not say. But, even as a 'rule of thumb', it is apparent that an emphasis on history or current social status lacks explanatory power for when discrimination is unjust in the case of even obvious examples.[51]

As a second objection, there are obvious practical issues with Hellman's reliance on history and social status. Courts cannot be expected to inquire into which social groups have suffered historical mistreatment or have a particular current social status to determine when discrimination is wrongful. Hellman accepts, rightly, that laws need to be general.[52] But this point diminishes the explanatory usefulness of her conception of when discrimination is wrongful, as it cannot explain – indeed, does not try to explain – legal approaches that establish general norms of non-discrimination that apply to all groups with protected

[49] ibid 57.

[50] ibid 53.

[51] A further difficulty with Hellman's account is that it seemingly cannot explain why past discrimination against particular groups – on which the wrongfulness of present discrimination is said to rest – was wrongful at the time that it first occurred, because at that time there was no history of discrimination. A possible corollary is that Hellman's account may be unable to explain why past discrimination was ever wrongful.

[52] Hellman (n 28) 37.

characteristics.[53] Moreover, the issue is no less problematic if we take Hellman to be providing a purely moral account that does not explain the law, if there is any suggestion for moral duties to guide behaviour. Individuals cannot be expected to structure their relations by reference to something that may be highly subjective or debatable, namely the relative social status or historical treatment of particular groups. In short, this approach provides a vague and unworkable standard.

As a third objection, Hellman does not grapple with the fact that her approach risks creating double standards in which discrimination becomes permissible against some groups but not others, based on their historical treatment or social status. Those double standards might be justified on some basis, but such justification is needed: the apparently unfair nature of double standards cannot simply be ignored. Yet this point is not taken at all in Hellman's analysis. Adopting an egalitarian Rawlsian perspective, a relevant guiding principle seems to be that no one should be treated as a second-class citizen – that is, equality is the moral entitlement of everyone. An approach to non-discrimination that reflects these ideas is to be preferred to one that treats non-discrimination as a contingent norm. Our intuition is that it is inherently unfair to judge people on the basis of protected characteristics. That intuition is not a contingent one.

II. Key Case Law

In two key US cases, *Masterpiece Cakeshop* (concerning a refusal to provide a wedding cake for a same-sex couple) and *Fulton* (concerning a refusal to certify same-sex couples to be foster parents), free exercise of religion has been given a robust scope of operation in interactions with the right to non-discrimination of same-sex couples despite the apparently narrow test adopted by the US Supreme Court in *Smith*. In each case, the free exercise claim under the First Amendment, challenging laws under which it was alleged that the conduct in question constituted discrimination, succeeded, though with sometimes elusive and complicated reasoning. In the UK, a different approach to the clash between conscience and non-discrimination has been adopted. In *Bull*, the UK Supreme Court resolved this clash in favour of a same-sex couple being denied service at a hotel, ruling with a decisiveness that has eluded the US Supreme Court. Nonetheless, the UK Supreme Court has been careful not to overreach and, in *Lee*, it sided with the

[53] See, eg, *R (Steinfeld) v Secretary of State for International Development* [2020] AC 1 (Supreme Court of the United Kingdom). This case concerned a law pursuant to which civil partnerships were only available to same-sex couples, and not to opposite-sex couples. The UK Supreme Court issued a declaration of incompatibility under the Human Rights Act 1998, s 4, applying Art 14 taken with Art 8 of the European Convention, in respect of this law. The equal application of non-discrimination principles to opposite-sex couples and same-sex couples is a feature of the law that Hellman's theory cannot adequately explain.

proprietor in relation to the refusal to make a cake supporting same-sex marriage, because the issue was the message on the cake, not the attributes of the customer.

A. US Case Law

Masterpiece Cakeshop concerned a bakery in Lakewood, Colorado.[54] Jack Phillips (the baker), who owned and operated the shop, was a devout Christian.[55] One of his religious beliefs was that 'God's intention for marriage from the beginning of history is that it is and should be the union of one man and one woman'.[56] Charlie Craig and Dave Mullins (the same-sex couple) entered his shop in 2012 and told the baker that they were interested in ordering a cake for 'our wedding'.[57] The baker responded that he did not 'create' wedding cakes for same-sex weddings.[58] He later explained to the mother of one member of the couple that this was due to his religious convictions.[59]

The Colorado Anti-Discrimination Act prohibited discrimination on the basis of sexual orientation as well as other protected characteristics. The Act relevantly provided as follows:

> It is a discriminatory practice and unlawful for a person, directly or indirectly, to refuse, withhold from, or deny to an individual or a group, because of disability, race, creed, color, sex, sexual orientation, marital status, national origin, or ancestry, the full and equal enjoyment of the goods, services, facilities, privileges, advantages, or accommodations of a place of public accommodation.[60]

The Act defined 'public accommodation' broadly to include any 'place of business engaged in any sales to the public and any place offering services … to the public', but excluded 'a church, synagogue, mosque, or other place that is principally used for religious purposes'.[61]

The same-sex couple filed a discrimination complaint against Masterpiece Cakeshop and the baker, stating that they had been denied 'full and equal service' at the bakery due to their sexual orientation.[62] The Civil Rights Division found probable cause that the baker had violated non-discrimination law and referred the case to the Civil Rights Commission.[63] The Commission sent the case to an Administrative Law Judge, who ruled against the baker and Masterpiece

[54] *Masterpiece Cakeshop* (n 6) 1724.
[55] ibid.
[56] ibid.
[57] ibid.
[58] ibid.
[59] ibid.
[60] ibid 1725.
[61] ibid.
[62] ibid.
[63] ibid 1726.

Cakeshop.[64] The Commission then heard an appeal, affirming the decision in full.[65] An appeal to the Colorado Court of Appeals was dismissed, and the Colorado Supreme Court declined to hear the case.[66] The baker sought review before the US Supreme Court, which granted certiorari.[67]

The US Supreme Court, by majority, overturned the Commission's decision. Kennedy J delivered the opinion of the Court, which Roberts CJ and Breyer, Alito, Kagan and Gorsuch JJ joined. He resolved the case on the basis that the 'Commission's treatment of [the baker's] case has some elements of a clear and impermissible hostility toward the sincere religious beliefs that motivated [the baker's] objection', according to the record of the Commission's formal, public hearings; there had also been requests for cakes with anti-gay marriage symbolism in which refusals of service had not been considered discriminatory.[68] Kennedy J noted that one of the seven members of the Commission said the following:

> Freedom of religion and religion has been used to justify all kinds of discrimination throughout history, whether it be slavery, whether it be the holocaust, whether it be – I mean, we – we can list hundreds of situations where freedom of religion has been used to justify discrimination. And to me it is one of the most despicable pieces of rhetoric that people can use to – to use their religion to hurt others.[69]

These statements were found to have 'cast doubt on the fairness and impartiality of the Commission's adjudication of [the baker's] case'.[70] Kennedy J noted that the Court had previously held in *Lukumi* that, under the Free Exercise Clause, the government cannot impose regulations that are 'hostile to the religious beliefs of affected citizens and cannot act in a manner that passes judgment upon or presupposes the illegitimacy of religious beliefs and practices'.[71] He held that 'the Commission's consideration of [the] case was neither tolerant nor respectful of [the baker's] religious beliefs', and therefore the Court was required to 'draw the inference that [the baker's] religious objection was not considered with the neutrality that the Free Exercise Clause requires'.[72]

The US Supreme Court's decision in *Fulton* concerned Catholic Social Services (CSS), a foster care agency in Philadelphia. The City of Philadelphia stopped referring children to CSS after a newspaper story reported that the agency would not certify same-sex couples to be foster parents on the basis of its religious beliefs.[73] The City claimed that the refusal of CSS to certify same-sex couples violated a non-discrimination provision in its contract with the City and the

[64] ibid.
[65] ibid.
[66] ibid 1726–27.
[67] ibid 1727.
[68] ibid 1729–30.
[69] ibid 1729.
[70] ibid 1730.
[71] ibid 1731.
[72] ibid.
[73] *Fulton* (n 6) 1875.

non-discrimination requirements of Philadelphia's Fair Practices Ordinance.[74] The City informed CSS that it would renew its foster care contract with the agency only if it agreed to certify same-sex couples.[75]

The City's actions were challenged under the Free Exercise Clause and Free Speech Clause of the First Amendment.[76] In respect of the Free Exercise Clause, the District Court denied preliminary relief on the basis that the contractual non-discrimination requirement and the Fair Practices Ordinance were neutral and generally applicable.[77] The Court of Appeals for the Third Circuit affirmed this decision.[78] It reasoned that although the contract between the parties had expired, the City could require the inclusion of language prohibiting discrimination on the basis of sexual orientation as a condition of contract renewal as this language was neutral and generally applicable.[79] In respect of the Free Speech Clause, both courts considered that the claims to free speech were unlikely to succeed because CSS performed certifications under a government program.[80]

The US Supreme Court reversed this decision. The opinion of the Court, written by Roberts CJ and joined by Breyer, Sotomayor, Kagan, Kavanaugh and Barrett JJ, said that it was 'plain that the City's actions have burdened CSS's religious exercise by putting it to the choice of curtailing its mission or approving relationships inconsistent with its beliefs'.[81] *Smith* did not apply because the non-discrimination rules in question were not 'generally applicable'.[82] Citing *Smith*, the opinion stated that a 'law is not generally applicable if it "invite[s]" the government to consider the particular reasons for a person's conduct by providing "a mechanism for individualized exemptions"'.[83] Moreover, citing *Lukumi*, the opinion stated that a law 'also lacks general applicability if it prohibits religious conduct while permitting secular conduct that undermines the government's asserted interests in a similar way', by being underinclusive.[84] Section 3.21 of the standard foster care contract on which the City relied relevantly provided as follows:

> **Rejection of Referral.** Provider shall not reject a child or family including, but not limited to, ... prospective foster or adoptive parents, for Services based upon ... their ... sexual orientation ... unless an exception is granted by the Commissioner or the Commissioner's designee, in his/her sole discretion.

Thus, the opinion concluded that section 3.21 incorporates 'a system of individual exemptions, made available in this case at the "sole discretion" of the

[74] ibid.
[75] ibid 1875–76.
[76] ibid 1876.
[77] ibid.
[78] ibid.
[79] ibid.
[80] ibid.
[81] ibid.
[82] ibid 1877.
[83] ibid.
[84] ibid.

Commissioner'.[85] The City also relied on the Fair Practices Ordinance, which prohibited 'deny[ing] or interfer[ing] with the public accommodations opportunities of an individual or otherwise discriminat[ing] based on his or her race, ethnicity, color, sex, sexual orientation, ... disability, marital status, familial status', or several other protected categories.[86] However, the opinion found that 'foster care agencies do not act as public accommodations in performing certifications'.[87]

Turning to strict scrutiny, the City relied on three government interests: maximising the number of foster parents; protecting the City from liability; and ensuring equal treatment of prospective foster parents and foster children.[88] Roberts CJ stated that the City failed to show that granting CSS an exception would put the goals of maximising foster families and minimising liability at risk, since '[i]f anything, including CSS in the program seems likely to increase, not reduce, the number of available foster parents', and it was 'only speculation that it might be sued over CSS's certification practices'.[89] In relation to the equal treatment of prospective foster parents and foster children, Roberts CJ merely noted that '[t] he creation of a system of exceptions under the contract undermines the City's contention that its non-discrimination policies can brook no departures'.[90]

B. UK Case Law

Steven Preddy and Martyn Hall were a same-sex couple in a civil partnership who made plans to visit Cornwall. Preddy made a telephone booking at the Chymorvah Private Hotel in Marazion, of a double bedroom for two nights.[91] The hotel was owned by Peter and Hazelmary Bull (the hotel owners), devout Christians who believed 'that the only divinely ordained sexual relationship is that between a man and a woman within the bonds of matrimony'.[92] At the relevant time, the online booking form stated as follows: 'Here at Chymorvah we have few rules, but please note, that out of a deep regard for marriage we prefer to let double accommodation to heterosexual married couples only – thank you'.[93] Preddy did not see this clause because he booked by telephone and Hazelmary Bull did not inform him of it.[94]

When the same-sex couple arrived at the hotel, a person who helped run the hotel informed them that the double-bedded rooms were for married couples only.[95] Even though the couple were in a civil partnership, he said 'that [they] were

[85] ibid 1878.
[86] ibid 1880.
[87] ibid.
[88] ibid 1881.
[89] ibid 1882.
[90] ibid.
[91] *Bull v Hall* (n 7) [9].
[92] ibid.
[93] ibid.
[94] ibid [10].
[95] ibid.

Christians and did not believe in civil partnerships and that marriage is between a man and a woman and therefore we could not honour their booking'.[96] The denial of service was said to be 'very hurtful' to the couple, who then found another hotel.[97] Their deposit was returned.[98] The lower courts found that the actions of the hotel constituted direct discrimination under regulation 3(1) of the Equality Act (Sexual Orientation) Regulations 2007.[99] Although there was interference with the right to manifest religion under Article 9 of the European Convention on Human Rights, this interference was considered to be justified.[100]

The UK Supreme Court unanimously dismissed the appeal, but split 3-2 on whether the discrimination was direct (under regulation 3(1)) or indirect (under regulation 3(3)). As Lady Hale put it, '[the hotel owners] state that they did not discriminate against [the same-sex couple] on the ground of their sexual orientation but on the ground that they were not married to one another. They have applied exactly the same policy to unmarried opposite sex couples'.[101] Lady Hale placed emphasis on the fact that the couple were in a civil partnership in finding that there was direct discrimination.[102] Lords Toulson and Kerr agreed that it was direct discrimination, though their reasoning differed partially from that of Lady Hale, which will be addressed further below. The distinction between direct discrimination and indirect discrimination is relevant because direct discrimination cannot be justified, whereas indirect discrimination can be justified.[103]

However, if the hotel's actions were not direct discrimination, it was not in dispute that they amounted to indirect discrimination, since, as Lady Hale said, '[t]he policy of letting double-bedded rooms only to married couples, while applied to heterosexual and homosexual people alike, undoubtedly puts homosexual people as a group at a serious disadvantage when compared with heterosexuals, as they cannot enter into a status which [the hotel owners] would regard as marriage'.[104] This indirect discrimination could not be justified: because 'same sex couples can enter into a mutual commitment which is the equivalent of marriage, the suppliers of goods, facilities and services should treat them in the same way'.[105] In relation to Article 9, the interference was justified to protect the rights of others, namely those of the same-sex couple not to be discriminated against.[106] As the Court was unanimous on indirect discrimination, in the result the appeal was unanimously dismissed.

[96] ibid.
[97] ibid.
[98] ibid.
[99] SI 2007/1263; ibid [12]–[13].
[100] ibid.
[101] ibid [17].
[102] ibid [29].
[103] For the current law (not in force at the time of the circumstances in *Bull*), see Equality Act 2010, ss 13, 19. On the potential inflexibility of UK law on questions of direct discrimination, see, eg, *R (E) v Governing Body of JFS* [2010] 2 AC 728 (Supreme Court of the United Kingdom).
[104] *Bull v Hall* (n 7) [33].
[105] ibid [36].
[106] ibid [44], [51].

Lee involved a bakery business run by Colin and Karen McArthur (the bakers), whose name is derived from Genesis 49:20: 'Bread from Asher shall be rich and he shall yield royal dainties'.[107] The bakers were Christians who believed that sex between a man and woman within marriage was the only form of full sexual expression consistent with Biblical teaching (and therefore acceptable to God), and that only marriage between a man and a woman was consistent with Biblical teaching (and therefore acceptable to God).[108] Gareth Lee (the customer) was a gay man who went to the shop and placed an order for a cake to be iced with his design: a picture of characters 'Bert and Ernie', the logo of QueerSpace (an LGBT community organisation in Belfast), and the text 'Support Gay Marriage'.[109] Karen McArthur took the order and the customer paid for the cake, but the bakers decided that they could not in conscience produce a cake with that text.[110] Karen McArthur telephoned the customer and explained that his order could not be fulfilled because they were a Christian business.[111] He received a refund and the image was returned.[112]

In Northern Ireland, discrimination in the provision of goods, facilities or services on the ground of religious belief or political opinion was prohibited by the Fair Employment and Treatment (Northern Ireland) Order 1998 (FETO).[113] Discrimination in the provision of goods, facilities or services on grounds of sexual orientation was prohibited by the Equality Act (Sexual Orientation) Regulations (Northern Ireland) 2006.[114] The customer complained to the Equality Commission for Northern Ireland about the order cancellation.[115] The lower courts found that there was direct discrimination on the grounds of sexual orientation, and it was not necessary to read down the legislation for compatibility with the rights of the bakery owners under Articles 9 and 10 of the European Convention on Human Rights.[116] However, the UK Supreme Court, in a judgment written by Lady Hale (with whom Lord Mance, Lord Kerr, Lord Hodge and Lady Black agreed), unanimously allowed an appeal.

As the primary judge had not found that the customer was refused service because of his sexual orientation,[117] Lady Hale reasoned as follows in rejecting the claim for direct discrimination on the basis of sexual orientation:

> This was a case of associative discrimination [that is, discrimination due to association with the gay and bisexual community] or it was nothing. It would be unwise in the context of this particular case to attempt to define the closeness of the association which

[107] *Lee* (n 7) [9].
[108] ibid.
[109] ibid [12].
[110] ibid.
[111] ibid.
[112] ibid.
[113] SI 1998/3162 (NI 21); ibid [3].
[114] SI 2006/439; ibid.
[115] ibid [14].
[116] ibid [2].
[117] ibid [22].

> justifies such a finding. Not only did the District Judge not make such a finding in this case, the association would not have been close enough for her to do so. In a nutshell, the objection was to the message and not to any particular person or persons.[118]

Turning to discrimination on the ground of political opinion, Lady Hale considered that similar considerations applied, since

> [t]he objection was not to [the customer] because he, or anyone with whom he associated, held a political opinion supporting gay marriage. The objection was to being required to promote the message on the cake. The less favourable treatment was afforded to the message not to the man.[119]

However, she accepted that there was a 'much closer association between the political opinions of the man and the message that he wishes to promote, such that it could be argued that they are "indissociable" for the purpose of direct discrimination on the ground of political opinion'.[120] In view of this, Lady Hale considered the effect of the European Convention on Human Rights. Article 9 was engaged in this case.[121] Given section 3 of the Human Rights Act 1998, the non-discrimination law 'should not be read or given effect in such a way as to compel providers of goods, facilities and services to express a message with which they disagree, unless justification is shown for doing so'.[122]

III. Compatibility Analysis

In *Masterpiece Cakeshop*, Ginsburg J expressed agreement with parts of Kennedy J's opinion, for example the statement that

> it is a general rule that [religious and philosophical] objections do not allow business owners and other actors in the economy and in society to deny protected persons equal access to goods and services under a neutral and generally applicable public accommodations law.[123]

But she added: 'I strongly disagree, however, with the Court's conclusion that [the same-sex couple] should lose this case'.[124] That was because

> [t]he different outcomes the Court features do not evidence hostility to religion of the kind we have previously held to signal a free-exercise violation, nor do the comments

[118] ibid [34].
[119] ibid [47].
[120] ibid [48].
[121] ibid [49].
[122] ibid [56]. Subsequently, the customer brought a case to the European Court of Human Rights, but this case was ruled inadmissible due to a failure to exhaust domestic remedies, since he had not argued human rights grounds before the domestic courts: see *Lee v United Kingdom* App no 18860/19 (ECtHR, 6 January 2022).
[123] *Masterpiece Cakeshop* (n 6) 1748 (quoting 1727).
[124] ibid.

by one or two members of one of the four decisionmaking entities considering this case justify reversing the judgment below.[125]

Ginsburg J's concerns about the US Supreme Court's decision in *Masterpiece Cakeshop* do not seem misplaced. In substance, the baker was permitted by force of the First Amendment to discriminate against a same-sex couple in the provision of a wedding cake because of comments by a public official or the Commission's handling of other, procedurally unrelated cases – an outcome that may seem intuitively unsatisfactory. The first question of the framework, compatibility, asks whether the activity sought to be protected from state action by the claim to liberty of conscience entailed interference with the basic liberties of others, and seeks to resolve any such clash. Exploring this question helps to illustrate why the US Supreme Court's decision in *Masterpiece Cakeshop*, and indeed also its decision in *Fulton*, raise such obvious difficulties.

Importantly, although all four cases considered in this chapter concern the interaction of non-discrimination law with liberty of conscience, there are distinctions between the cases. Specifically, it will be argued that although *Masterpiece Cakeshop*, *Fulton* and *Bull* all implicate the basic liberty of non-discrimination because they involve discrimination towards same-sex couples on the basis of sexual orientation, the UK Supreme Court in *Lee* was correct to find that there was no discrimination on the ground of sexual orientation on the facts of that case. Nor, indeed, was there any discrimination on the ground of political opinion – the objection was not to attributes of the customer, but to the message that the cake was required to bear. Accordingly, there appears to have been no clash between the basic liberties in *Lee*, and the moral position was that the liberty of conscience claim in that case should succeed, subject to necessity. However, in respect of *Masterpiece Cakeshop*, *Fulton* and *Bull*, the application of the framework suggests that the preferable moral position was that the same-sex couple should prevail in all three of these cases.

Turning to *Masterpiece Cakeshop*, the claim made by the baker under the Free Exercise Clause of the First Amendment was to an exemption from Colorado discrimination law in order to protect the baker's refusal to provide a wedding cake to a same-sex couple. The baker's action of refusing to sell a wedding cake to a same-sex couple, when he was willing to sell such cakes to opposite-sex couples, interfered with the basic liberty of non-discrimination of the same-sex couple. Because of this, a clash exists between the baker's claim to liberty of conscience and the basic liberty of non-discrimination. The clash between these two basic liberties of liberty of conscience and non-discrimination requires that the circumstances be carefully considered to determine how to construe them conformably with one another.

The first issue is whether the baker's claim to liberty of conscience fell within the central range of application of that basic liberty. The central range is discerned

[125] ibid 1749.

by reference to the exercise and development of the moral powers – to enable citizens to judge right and justice and to pursue a conception of the good. It is easy to imagine that activities connected with dissemination of religious doctrine, such as the staffing of a church, or perhaps even religious schooling, might be within the central range of application of liberty of conscience because they are important to those moral powers. However, the operation of a bakery – an activity in the commercial sphere that has nothing specifically to do with religious belief or other comprehensive doctrines – is not nearly so facilitative of the exercise and development of the moral powers (even if it may be itself informed by such exercise and development). Observing religious convictions in that context is therefore generally not within the central range of application of liberty of conscience.

Moreover, the requirement that he not discriminate against a same-sex couple in the selling of a wedding cake is not a very extensive limitation of the baker's liberty of conscience that would go to the central range of application for that reason. On the one hand, the baker was being required to do something contrary to his convictions, that is, to provide a form of support for a same-sex wedding. It was not simply a time and place restriction. But the baker remained free to hold and express his religious convictions. He was not compelled to write a message that was contrary to his convictions, as distinct from *Lee*; he was simply being required to provide a product that was identical to that provided to opposite-sex couples. As far as restrictions on the baker's religious freedom might go, this was a slight one.[126]

[126] In reaching this result, I agree with Adenitire's conclusion that the baker's claim is at the 'periphery' of liberty of conscience. Adenitire argues that in this type of situation the baker's concern is merely to avoid 'complicity in immorality/sinfulness' (namely, that of same-sex marriage), and it is because of this that the claim is at the periphery of the right and should be defeated by a 'dignitary' harm caused to the same-sex couple that goes to the core of non-discrimination: Adenitire, *A General Right to Conscientious Exemption* (n 40) 280. See also D NeJaime and RB Siegel, 'Conscience Wars: Complicity-Based Conscience Claims in Religion and Politics' (2015) 124 *Yale Law Journal* 2516; T Poston, 'Religious Conscience and the Private Market' in K Vallier and M Weber (eds), *Religious Exemptions* (Oxford: Oxford University Press, 2018). However, for my part, I am not so sure that a claim relating to 'complicity' is necessarily always at the periphery of liberty of conscience. Such a claim, if it affected, for example, religious worship, might well be within the central range of application, depending on the circumstances. An example illustrates this. Imagine an illiberal state Intolerantia divided between two religions, Majoritism (believed by 80% of the country) and Minoritism (believed by 20%). In this state Minoritism is subject to increasing persecution by the state. One of the tenets of Minoritism is that music should not be played during its worship services under any circumstances. The Parliament of Intolerantia, which is dominated by members of the Majoritism religion, passes a law that compels its citizens to contact a special government agency whenever members of the Minoritism gather for a worship service, notifying the agency of the location and time of the service. Upon receiving the notification, the government agency then dispatches musicians to the location of the worship service, who play music during it in a way that members of the Minoritism religion consider sinful. In this scenario, even a member of that religion participating herself in the worship service is under a legal obligation to notify the government agency of it, which would make her 'complicit' in the government agency's action of playing music at the service. It therefore goes against the conscientious beliefs of the believer to notify the government agency as required by the law. The interference with liberty of conscience embodied by this law is within the central range of liberty of conscience because although it could be portrayed as merely involving the believer's 'complicity' in the immoral action of a third party – namely, that of the government agency – that immoral action significantly affects religious worship.

The next issue is whether non-discrimination in this context (purchasing a wedding cake) was within the central range of non-discrimination. This is again determined by reference to the development and exercise of the moral powers. Discrimination in the selling of a cake might not seem to be as serious to the development and exercise of the moral powers as, for example, discrimination in education, or in political organising. On one perspective, the result is simply inconvenience, which may be addressed by going to another baker. For example, Alito J, who was in the majority in *Masterpiece Cakeshop*, has commented extra-curially that there was 'no reason to think that [the baker's] stand would deprive any same-sex couple of a wedding cake. The couple that came to his shop was given a free cake by another bakery, and celebrity chefs have jumped to the couple's defense'.[127]

But, contrary to the view of Alito J, the issue is not simply whether or not the same-sex couple was able to get a cake. As discussed earlier in this chapter, the sense of exclusion that may result from being denied service on the basis of sexual orientation should not be overlooked. The sense of alienation from the community – of being a second-class citizen – that potentially ensues from discrimination in a public context could have considerable impacts on the exercise and development of the moral powers, including at the psychological level. Indeed, except where the discrimination is of a truly trivial nature, it is difficult to see how direct discrimination in this context would ever be outside the central range of application of that basic liberty – and there is no doubt that this constituted direct discrimination. As NeJaime and Siegel put it, '[t]he argument that the Court should only consider material harms is at odds with the origins of [US] public accommodations laws and [its] civil rights tradition'.[128]

Nor, however, are the material impacts always, or necessarily, negligible. Alito J seems to assume that it will always be easy for a same-sex couple denied service to obtain another cake, but that depends on how many bakeries there are in a given town and their disposition towards same-sex couples. It is far from inconceivable that, if enabled by the law to discriminate, in some towns many bakeries might adopt a hostile stance to serving wedding cakes to same-sex couples. Alito J seems to imagine the objection exclusively as that of one baker – but if permitted, there is no reason to think that it cannot scale up. Moreover, even if the same-sex couple is able to find another baker, this may still entail time and hassle which should not be required to be endured in circumstances of direct discrimination. For all these reasons, put in terms of the facts of the case, the baker's claim to liberty of conscience intersected, outside its central range of application, with the right to

[127] Federalist Society, 'Address by Justice Samuel Alito [2020 National Lawyers Convention]' https://www.youtube.com/watch?v=VMnukCVIZWQ. See also RT Anderson, 'Disagreement Is Not Always Discrimination: On *Masterpiece Cakeshop* and the Analogy to Interracial Marriage' (2018) 16 *Georgetown Journal of Law & Public Policy* 123.

[128] D NeJaime and R Siegel, 'Religious Exemptions and Antidiscrimination Law in *Masterpiece Cakeshop*' (2018) 128 *Yale Law Journal Forum* 201, 214.

non-discrimination in public contexts of the same-sex couple, within its central range of application.

This ends the inquiry at the first stage, because we do not construe liberty of conscience outside its central range of application as extending to interfere with other basic liberties within their central range. As explained in Chapter 4, the issue that the US Supreme Court focused on – whether the baker's free exercise of religion was limited pursuant to neutral state action – does not arise within the framework. Construed according to compatibility, his right to liberty of conscience was not limited at all, because interpreting that right conformably with other basic liberties reads it as not extending to his action of refusing to sell a wedding cake to a same-sex couple. In the absence of any burden on liberty of conscience properly construed, the framework suggests that the inquiry should end with the defeat of the conscience claim.

A similar analysis applies in respect of *Bull*. Managing a hotel is an activity that lies within the commercial sphere, and has little connection with the exercise and development of the two moral powers – the same, in that regard, as the selling of a wedding cake. As has been explained above, the UK Supreme Court divided on the question of whether the action of the hotel owners was direct or indirect discrimination. Lady Hale explained her reasoning in reaching the conclusion that it was direct discrimination as follows:

> I have the greatest difficulty in seeing how discriminating between a married and a civilly partnered person can be anything other than direct discrimination on grounds of sexual orientation. At present marriage is only available between a man and a woman and civil partnership is only available between two people of the same sex. We can, I think, leave aside that some people of homosexual orientation can and do get married, while it may well be that some people of heterosexual orientation can and do enter civil partnerships. Sexual relations are not a pre-condition of the validity of either. The principal purpose of each institution is to provide a legal framework within which loving, stable and committed adult relationships can flourish. I would therefore regard the criterion of marriage or civil partnership as indissociable from the sexual orientation of those who qualify to enter it. More importantly, there is an exact correspondence between the advantage conferred and the disadvantage imposed in allowing a double bed to the one and denying it to the other.[129]

Lord Kerr placed emphasis on regulation 3(4) of the Equality Act (Sexual Orientation) Regulations 2007, which provided that, in assessing discrimination, 'the fact that one of the persons … is a civil partner while the other is married shall not be treated as a material difference in the relevant circumstances', and observed that '[i]n concrete terms the effect of regulation 3(4) in the present case is that when Mr Preddy and Mr Hall arrived at Mr and Mrs Bull's hotel, their situation was the legal equivalent of that of a married couple'.[130] Thus, it was said to follow that 'Mr and Mrs Bull may not … legally assert that they treated Mr Preddy and

[129] *Bull v Hall* (n 7) [29].
[130] ibid [59].

Mr Hall differently because they were not married for, in law, they are to be regarded as the same as a married couple' and 'the only remaining basis on which they were treated less favourably was their sexual orientation'.[131] Finally, Lord Toulson agreed that it was direct discrimination, explaining that

> it is true that in the case of unmarried heterosexuals it is not their sexual orientation which causes Mr and Mrs Bull to treat them differently from married heterosexuals, but the fact that the couple have not chosen to marry. But it is a non sequitur to reason from this that the differential treatment of persons in a civil partnership from that of married heterosexuals (or, similarly, of same sex married couples from opposite sex married couples) is not due to their sexual orientation, when that is the very factor which separates them.[132]

However, Lord Neuberger disagreed on this point on the basis that there was not an 'exact correspondence between the criterion and the protected characteristic' as required for direct discrimination.[133] Lord Hughes similarly considered that as the ground for the discrimination was unmarried status, it was a case of indirect discrimination.[134] For the purposes of compatibility analysis, this may not be a critical issue, since even if it was indirect discrimination, it might be indirect discrimination that sufficiently affected the exercise and development of the moral powers that it went to the central range of that basic liberty. However, the better view is that the married couples only requirement for double bedded rooms amounted to proxy discrimination under the framework: it operated as an effective proxy for same-sex couples, since *all* same-sex couples were unable to satisfy this requirement.[135] As with *Masterpiece Cakeshop*, the refusal of service to the customers fell within the central range of the basic liberty of non-discrimination because of the nature of such treatment in a public context. The UK Supreme Court was morally correct to find for the customers because the clash was between one basic liberty within its central range and another outside its central range.

The position in *Fulton* may be slightly more complex, at both ends of the compatibility inquiry – the nature of the liberty of conscience claim and the nature of the non-discrimination claim. On the one hand, it is not quite as clear as in *Masterpiece Cakeshop* and *Bull* that the liberty of conscience claim in relation to refusing same-sex couples certification as foster parents lay outside the central range of application of that basic liberty. The judgments in *Fulton*, particularly that of Alito J, highlighted the long history of foster care services provided by the

[131] ibid [60].
[132] ibid [68].
[133] ibid [74]–[76].
[134] ibid [91].
[135] For an analysis of *Bull* in the light of *Bostock* that suggests that there was direct discrimination on the basis of sex, rather than sexual orientation, see DJ Hill, 'Is Sexual-Orientation Discrimination a Form of Sex Discrimination?' (2020) 41 *Liverpool Law Review* 357. However, it is open to question whether the mental gymnastics that Gorsuch J performed in *Bostock* are necessary or desirable in the context of the UK case law, given that the Equality Act 2010 offers express protection on the basis of sexual orientation.

Catholic Church, spanning centuries, and the importance of such services to those of the Christian faith.[136] This might be thought to create more of a connection between the activity of providing foster care services and religion, drawing it closer to the central range of application of liberty of conscience and strengthening the liberty of conscience claim.

However, while perhaps not as clear cut as the preceding two cases, it remains unlikely that this activity falls within the central range of application of liberty of conscience. Providing foster care services may be important to the Christian faith, but it has little to do with either of the moral powers. Unlike, for example, religious teaching or worship, it does not directly enable citizens to judge right and justice and to pursue a conception of the good, even if this action may be the *result* of pursuing a conception of the good that has been adopted on a religious basis. Although potentially directed at more charitable ends than the purely commercial activities in *Masterpiece Cakeshop* and *Bull*, it remains, like selling cakes and hotel rooms, an activity that takes place in wider society – indeed in partnership with the City government – and away from the core features of religious practice. It falls within the scope of liberty of conscience, but outside the central range of application of that basic liberty.

Another difficulty with *Fulton* arises in respect of whether there was discrimination towards same-sex couples at all, within the meaning of the relevant statute. The definition of public accommodations was '[a]ny place, provider or public conveyance, whether licensed or not, which solicits or accepts the patronage or trade of the public or whose goods, services, facilities, privileges, advantages or accommodations are extended, offered, sold, or otherwise made available to the public'.[137] Roberts CJ found in *Fulton* that certification was not '"made available to the public" in the usual sense of the words' because it 'involves a customized and selective assessment that bears little resemblance to staying in a hotel, eating at a restaurant, or riding a bus'.[138] However, it is less than clear why the provision of a customised and selective assessment removes a service from the scope of non-discrimination law. Gorsuch J, in his opinion concurring in the judgment, was critical of this aspect of Roberts CJ's reasoning.[139] Nonetheless, Roberts CJ elaborated as follows on this rather counterintuitive point:

> The process takes three to six months. Applicants must pass background checks and a medical exam. Foster agencies are required to conduct an intensive home study during which they evaluate, among other things, applicants' 'mental and emotional adjustment,' 'community ties with family, friends, and neighbors,' and '[e]xisting family relationships, attitudes and expectations regarding the applicant's own children and parent/child relationships.' … Such inquiries would raise eyebrows at the local bus station. And agencies understandably approach this sensitive process from different angles. As the City itself explains to prospective foster parents, '[e]ach agency has slightly different requirements,

[136] *Fulton* (n 6) 1884–85.
[137] ibid 1880.
[138] ibid.
[139] ibid 1927.

> specialties, and training programs.' … All of this confirms that the one-size-fits-all public accommodations model is a poor match for the foster care system.[140]

This analysis is strange, because the existence of a customised and selective process leading to the provision of a service does not seem to mean that the service is not made available to the public. Medical services, such as in vitro fertilisation (IVF), may also necessarily involve selectiveness and customisation before the provision of the services, yet it would be odd to suggest that those services are not made available to the public. They are made available to the public because any member of the public can be considered for them. Whether she receives them will depend on other factors, but it would justly be regarded as wrong to turn a member of the public away at the outset on the basis of a protected characteristic. The same might be said to be true of admissions to university and other educational institutions – these, too, are selective, but are clearly made available to the public. Within the moral framework outlined in this book, there is little doubt that applications for certification as foster parents take place in a public context. Accordingly, the same considerations as in the other cases bring the circumstances within the central range of application of non-discrimination.

Finally, in *Lee* the UK Supreme Court was surely correct to conclude that there was no discrimination. Although there was a denial of service in a public context, it was not on the basis of any personal attribute – as Lady Hale explained, the objection was to the message, not the customer; there was no discrimination on the basis of the customer's sexual orientation or political opinion (when this law was read compatibly with Article 9), and the basic liberty of non-discrimination was not implicated in this case. However, the basic liberty of liberty of conscience was implicated, albeit not in its central range given the commercial context. To ask the bakers to prepare a cake bearing a message opposed to their religious convictions would have been a violation of their right to liberty of conscience (a point that is discussed further in the next section of this chapter). As Hunter-Henin puts it, the 'distinction drawn in *Ashers Bakery* between an objection to a message and an objection to the messenger is of imperative application in liberal democracies'.[141] That is because '[f]orcing a religious service provider to endorse a message he/she objects to would betray the goal of an enriching pluralism by denying any expression to minority views in commercial contexts'.[142]

To conclude this is in no way to diminish the important rights of a gay customer to receive services without suffering discrimination, but merely to avoid transgressing the limits of the concept. As Lady Hale explained in the case:

> In reaching the conclusion that there was no discrimination on grounds of sexual orientation in this case, I do not seek to minimise or disparage the very real problem of

[140] ibid 1880.

[141] M Hunter-Henin, *Why Religious Freedom Matters for Democracy: Comparative Reflections from Britain and France for a Democratic 'Vivre Ensemble'* (Oxford: Hart Publishing, 2020) 172.

[142] ibid.

> discrimination against gay people. Nor do I ignore the very full and careful consideration which was given to the development of the law in this area, to which Mr Allen drew our attention at considerable length. Everyone, as article 1 of the Universal Declaration of Human Rights put it 70 years ago is 'born free and equal in dignity and rights'. Experience has shown that the providers of employment, education, accommodation, goods, facilities and services do not always treat people with equal dignity and respect, especially if they have certain personal characteristics which are now protected by the law. It is deeply humiliating, and an affront to human dignity, to deny someone a service because of that person's race, gender, disability, sexual orientation or any of the other protected personal characteristics. But that is not what happened in this case and it does the project of equal treatment no favours to seek to extend it beyond its proper scope.[143]

Accordingly, some commentators have welcomed *Lee*. Hambler points out, correctly, that the judgment 'does not … unwind other controversial decisions such as [*Bull*]', and '[i]t is too early to assume that the modest gains for religious freedom resulting from this decision represent a significant change in judicial approach and indeed there are no real grounds to suppose that it will'.[144] Indeed, *Lee* is consistent with *Bull*, and does not represent a departure from existing legal principle.[145] For this reason, it seems too much to hope, as Leigh does, that there might be some 'de-escalation' of the 'culture war' as a result – the underlying tensions remain even if some matters are demarcated by the decision.[146] Sarah Fraser Butlin echoes the view that *Lee* struck an appropriate balance that avoids overreach:

> This is a very vexed area, but broadly the judgment represents a careful balancing exercise between protection from discrimination and the rights of religious people not to be compelled to act against their conscience. … The decision of the Supreme Court constitutes a vital affirmation of the fundamental importance of freedom of conscience and of speech. While many would disagree with the stance of the McArthurs, the judgment represents an important waymark in the equality project, achieving a difficult balance between protecting minority groups from discrimination and ensuring religious freedom. This balance is essential if we are to live in a truly plural and diverse society.[147]

While the outcomes of the two UK Supreme Court cases were morally correct according to the framework, compatibility analysis lays bare the shortcomings of the jurisprudence of the US Supreme Court, particularly in *Masterpiece Cakeshop*.[148]

[143] *Lee* (n 7) [35].

[144] A Hambler, 'Cake, Compelled Speech, and a Modest Step Forward for Religious Liberty: The Supreme Court Decision in *Lee v Ashers*' (2018) 181 *Law & Justice* 156, 169–70.

[145] See similarly C McCrudden, 'The *Gay Cake* Case: What the Supreme Court Did, and Didn't, Decide in *Ashers*' (2020) 9 *Oxford Journal of Law and Religion* 238, 269; EML Ho, 'Marking the Internal and External Limits of Discrimination Law in *Lee v Ashers Baking Company*' (2021) 6 *Cambridge Law Review* 203.

[146] I Leigh, '*Lee v Ashers Baking Company*: Crumbs of Comfort in the Culture War' in R Barker et al (eds), *Law and Religion in the Commonwealth: The Evolution of Case Law* (Oxford: Hart Publishing, 2022) 79.

[147] SF Butlin, 'Cakes in the Supreme Court' (2019) 78 *Cambridge Law Journal* 280, 283.

[148] For a comparison between *Masterpiece Cakeshop* and *Lee*, preferring the latter, see R Reyes, '*Masterpiece Cakeshop* and *Ashers Baking Company*: A Comparative Analysis of Constitutional Confections' (2020) 16 *Stanford Journal of Civil Rights & Civil Liberties* 113.

Unlike the analysis above, the majority in that case did not sufficiently grapple with the fact that the baker's religious freedom claim, being in the commercial sphere, was outside the central range of application. Indeed, in the opinion of the Court, Kennedy J criticised the comments of a member of the Commission that he perceived to have 'endorsed the view that religious beliefs cannot legitimately be carried into the public sphere or commercial domain, implying that religious beliefs and persons are less than fully welcome in Colorado's business community'.[149]

But the issue at stake is not whether religious beliefs can be carried into the public sphere or commercial domain, or whether religious people are 'welcome' in Colorado's business community. The issue is whether, in carrying those beliefs into the commercial domain, as religious people are entitled to do, they should also be entitled to exemptions from laws that protect others in that domain. The case for such exemptions is surely weaker than where a law interferes with matters central to religious organisation or practice. Similarly, although in *Fulton* the activity of certifying foster parents might have been considered less remote from religious practice than selling cakes, it nonetheless fell outside the central range. In both cases, the majority allowed the claim to prevail even though it was far removed from a claim made in respect of, for example, the staffing of churches, which would be significantly more important to liberty of conscience. Compatibility analysis draws attention to this issue, as the remoteness of the religious activity forms a key part of the reasoning.

Further, the majority's reasoning in *Masterpiece Cakeshop* and *Fulton* did not involve any meaningful consideration of the rights of others (similarly to the US cases relating to coronavirus restrictions considered in Chapter 5), a point that is made apparent by the way that such consideration is essential within the moral framework in its compatibility analysis. In that sense, these cases differed significantly from the careful consideration of the rights of others (namely, their right to non-discrimination) in *Bull* and *Lee*. It is true that the opinion of the US Supreme Court in *Masterpiece Cakeshop* made several statements that emphasised that discrimination towards same-sex couples in the commercial sphere was wrong, some of which was in turn quoted in *Fulton* by Roberts CJ.[150] Kennedy J accepted that this was a principle that needed to be reconciled against religious freedom, writing as follows:

> The case presents difficult questions as to the proper reconciliation of at least two principles. The first is the authority of a State and its governmental entities to protect the rights and dignity of gay persons who are, or wish to be, married but who face discrimination when they seek goods or services. The second is the right of all persons to exercise fundamental freedoms under the First Amendment, as applied to the States through the Fourteenth Amendment.[151]

[149] *Masterpiece Cakeshop* (n 6) 1729.

[150] *Fulton* (n 6) 1882.

[151] *Masterpiece Cakeshop* (n 6) 1723–24. For discussion of these dicta, see LG Sager and N Tebbe, 'The Reality Principle' (2019) 34 *Constitutional Commentary* 171.

But in practice, Kennedy J did not give this consideration – 'the dignity of gay persons' – any weight, subordinating it to such matters as a commissioner's critical comments and other, procedurally unrelated decisions of the Commission. He identified the tension that 'gay persons and gay couples cannot be treated as social outcasts or as inferior in dignity and worth', but religious and philosophical objections to gay marriage were also protected under the First Amendment.[152] However, he did not 'reconcile' this tension, instead disposing of the case on another basis. The same criticisms may be made of the judgment of Roberts CJ in *Fulton*, which merely paid lip service to the rights of same-sex couples, before finding against them on the substance. Viewed through the lens of the framework's compatibility analysis, the impact on the rights of others (here, same-sex couples' right to non-discrimination) should have been decisive, as it was in *Bull*. The majority in both *Masterpiece Cakeshop* and *Fulton* failed to sufficiently appreciate the fundamental importance of the right to non-discrimination – which, as has been seen, was violated in a central, rather than remote, way – and to demonstrate appropriate concern for the harm caused to same-sex couples. Indeed, the opinion of the Court in *Fulton* sought problematically to dilute the effect of non-discrimination law in Philadelphia through a puzzling recasting of the concept of public accommodations.

In summary, compatibility analysis produces clear results when applied to the four cases under consideration in this chapter. In *Masterpiece Cakeshop*, *Fulton* and *Bull*, the interference with the basic liberty of non-discrimination – which went to the central range of application of that basic liberty – entailed by the actions that were the subject of claims to liberty of conscience was critical. Because the actions for which protection was sought on the basis of liberty of conscience were outside the central range of application of that basic liberty, being in the commercial or charitable sphere, the claim to liberty of conscience would be defeated under the framework. The exception is *Lee*, because there was no genuine clash of rights in that case, since non-discrimination was not implicated at all. Whereas the UK Supreme Court's approach aligned with the moral framework, that of the US Supreme Court proves problematic under the framework. As has been seen, issues arise both with the test applied by the US courts and the way in which they applied it in these cases.

IV. Necessity Analysis

The conclusion under compatibility means that the liberty of conscience claims in *Masterpiece Cakeshop*, *Fulton* and *Bull* should all fail according to the moral framework set out in this book. However, for completeness, it is desirable to assess the position under necessity in the common interest as well, to consider whether

[152] *Masterpiece Cakeshop* (n 6) 1727.

the same result is arrived at there. There is a strong argument that the conscience claims would also fail at this stage of the framework. Significantly, the inquiry as to neutrality and general applicability that the US Supreme Court focused on would not be relevant to assessing necessity. What matters in the necessity analysis is not whether the law is neutral and of general applicability or not, but whether its burden on religious freedom is justified. This requires a tailored limitation that pursues a purpose in the common interest.

It is convenient first to turn to *Masterpiece Cakeshop*. Was the purpose of the state action sufficient, in the sense of being in the common interest? The importance of non-discrimination is considerable. Non-discrimination is not merely a benefit to the 'net sum of social and economic advantages for society as a whole',[153] but an important moral idea in its own right that is important to social harmony. Adenitire writes that

> [t]he main problem with LGB customers being turned away from providers of commercial services is not that offence and humiliation is caused. It is that the law forgoes the basic commitment of a liberal society: that each member of the political community is of equal worth irrespective of their personal identity.[154]

Thus, it is 'a form of social harm which undermines the equal social standing of members of a section of the political community'.[155]

Indeed, the opinion of the Court acknowledged the importance of non-discrimination. Kennedy J said that 'it is a general rule that [religious and philosophical] objections do not allow business owners and other actors in the economy and in society to deny protected persons equal access to goods and services under a neutral and generally applicable public accommodations law'.[156] That is necessary to spare gay persons from 'indignities when they seek goods and services in an open market'.[157] Thus, he said as follows:

> When it comes to weddings, it can be assumed that a member of the clergy who objects to gay marriage on moral and religious grounds could not be compelled to perform the ceremony without denial of his or her right to the free exercise of religion. This refusal would be well understood in our constitutional order as an exercise of religion, an exercise that gay persons could recognize and accept without serious diminishment to their own dignity and worth. Yet if that exception were not confined, then a long list of persons who provide goods and services for marriages and weddings might refuse to do so for gay persons, thus resulting in a community-wide stigma inconsistent with the history and dynamics of civil rights laws that ensure equal access to goods, services, and public accommodations.[158]

[153] Rawls, *Justice as Fairness: A Restatement* (n 9) 111.
[154] Adenitire, *A General Right to Conscientious Exemption* (n 40) 282.
[155] ibid 283.
[156] *Masterpiece Cakeshop* (n 6) 1727.
[157] ibid 1732.
[158] ibid 1727.

These considerations offer good reason to conclude that reasonably tailored non-discrimination laws are necessary in a common interest in social harmony, at least in respect of a claim to liberty of conscience that is outside the central range of application of that basic liberty. The analysis might differ if the baker's claim had been within the central range of application of liberty of conscience – for example, if it had related to the staffing of churches. If the concern about neutrality (as no purpose to limit exercise) is set aside, this result seems to follow from the reasoning in the opinion of the Court and its acknowledgment of the importance of non-discrimination towards same-sex couples. Thus, the moral framework suggests that the baker's claim in *Masterpiece Cakeshop* should fail at both stages.

The analysis set out by the US Supreme Court in *Fulton* is at least more thorough than that in *Masterpiece Cakeshop* because Roberts CJ's judgment did not skip the strict scrutiny stage. As a result, his judgment expressly addressed the question of justification, acknowledging 'the interest of the City in the equal treatment of prospective foster parents and foster children', but nonetheless it did so in a very brief and superficial way.[159] Roberts CJ analysed the question as follows:

> We do not doubt that this interest is a weighty one, for '[o]ur society has come to the recognition that gay persons and gay couples cannot be treated as social outcasts or as inferior in dignity and worth.' … On the facts of this case, however, this interest cannot justify denying CSS an exception for its religious exercise. The creation of a system of exceptions under the contract undermines the City's contention that its non-discrimination policies can brook no departures. … The City offers no compelling reason why it has a particular interest in denying an exception to CSS while making them available to others.[160]

However, the bare possibility of exceptions hardly seems to be a sufficient reason to displace non-discrimination law in favour of liberty of conscience. Indeed, the extreme understanding of general applicability demonstrated by Roberts CJ's judgment in *Fulton* – in substance, that *any* law with exceptions is not generally applicable, and therefore fails the first stage of the *Smith-Lukumi* test – seems to wreak potential havoc. Pill observes that virtually any law would fail this test:

> Every law either includes statutory exemptions for at least some kinds of behavior that violate the prescribed general rule, or else allows for officials to use discretion to grant exemptions in cases that warrant special consideration given countervailing concerns. Such exemptions inevitably undermine the narrow and specific policy aims served by the rule, yet they are given because the legislature or relevant executive official determines that doing so serves other, weightier values or policy goods.[161]

The majority in *Fulton* sought to evade the task of reconciling the conflicting values, but in the moral analysis, the claim to liberty of conscience, outside its

[159] *Fulton* (n 6) 1882.

[160] ibid 1882.

[161] SC Pill, 'The False Promise of Expanded Religious Liberty Rights after the COVID-19 Cases and *Fulton v City of Philadelphia*' (2023) 31 *William & Mary Bill of Rights Journal* 825, 873.

central range, should be overridden by non-discrimination law that is necessary in the common interest. The same considerations about what is necessary in the common interest apply in respect of *Bull*, in which the UK Supreme Court reached the morally preferable position by siding with the hotel customers, and in *Lee*, where there was ultimately no clash between non-discrimination and conscience. René Reyes observes that the UK Supreme Court's analysis was more developed in *Lee* than that of the US Supreme Court in *Masterpiece Cakeshop*, commenting that: '*Ashers Baking Company* offers considerably more engagement with several issues left unresolved in *Masterpiece Cakeshop*, making the US Supreme Court's analysis look all the more "massively under-proved" by comparison.'[162] Lady Hale in *Bull* persuasively acknowledged the importance of non-discrimination law for same-sex couples as follows:

> Sexual orientation is a core component of a person's identity which requires fulfilment through relationships with others of the same orientation. As Justice Sachs of the South African Constitutional Court movingly put it in *National Coalition for Gay and Lesbian Equality v Minister of Justice*, 1999 (1) SA 6, para 117: 'While recognising the unique worth of each person, the Constitution does not presuppose that a holder of rights is an isolated, lonely and abstract figure possessing a disembodied and socially disconnected self. It acknowledges that people live in their bodies, their communities, their cultures, their places and their times. The expression of sexuality requires a partner, real or imagined.'
>
> Heterosexuals have known this about themselves and been able to fulfil themselves in this way throughout history. Homosexuals have also known this about themselves but were long denied the possibility of fulfilling themselves through relationships with others. This was an affront to their dignity as human beings which our law has now (some would say belatedly) recognised. Homosexuals can enjoy the same freedom and the same relationships as any others. But we should not underestimate the continuing legacy of those centuries of discrimination, persecution even, which is still going on in many parts of the world. It is no doubt for that reason that Strasbourg requires 'very weighty reasons' to justify discrimination on grounds of sexual orientation. It is for that reason that we should be slow to accept that prohibiting hotel keepers from discriminating against homosexuals is a disproportionate limitation on their right to manifest their religion.[163]

Viewed against such considerations, the framework's necessity analysis makes evident the oddness of the US Supreme Court's focus on neutrality and general applicability (as addressed in relation to neutrality in Chapter 4). That the Court's focus on these concepts allowed it to avoid core issues, leaving them for another day, is express. As Kennedy J put it in *Masterpiece Cakeshop*, '[t]he outcome of cases like this in other circumstances must await further elaboration in the courts.'[164] Similarly, Gorsuch J's concurrence in *Fulton* complained that the ruling could be

[162] Reyes (n 148) 115.
[163] *Bull v Hall* (n 7) [52]–[53].
[164] *Masterpiece Cakeshop* (n 6) 1732.

worked around with minor changes to the contract between CSS and the City, by eliminating the possibility of individualised exceptions.[165] Both cases, therefore, dodged the question of the necessity of the non-discrimination law at issue.

Instead, the US Supreme Court's analysis made central issues that should arguably have been peripheral. In *Masterpiece Cakeshop*, Kennedy J reasoned in relation to the Commissioner's critical comments as follows:

> To describe a man's faith as 'one of the most despicable pieces of rhetoric that people can use' is to disparage his religion in at least two distinct ways: by describing it as despicable, and also by characterizing it as merely rhetorical – something insubstantial and even insincere. The commissioner even went so far as to compare [the baker's] invocation of his sincerely held religious beliefs to defenses of slavery and the Holocaust. This sentiment is inappropriate for a Commission charged with the solemn responsibility of fair and neutral enforcement of Colorado's antidiscrimination law – a law that protects against discrimination on the basis of religion as well as sexual orientation.[166]

Kagan J, with whom Breyer J joined, similarly concurred on the basis of the Commissioner's statements. She said that 'state actors cannot show hostility to religious views; rather, they must give those views "neutral and respectful consideration"'.[167] However, one possible reading of the Commissioner's comments is that, while potentially overstated, they correctly perceived that religious freedom, if not in some way limited, could be viewed as a licence to discriminate. But the artlessness of the Commissioner's remarks sufficed to establish unconstitutionality, even though there is no provision of the US Constitution that prohibits exaggerated or impolitic rhetoric by public officials. As Ginsburg J said, '[w]hatever one may think of the statements in historical context, I see no reason why the comments of one or two Commissioners should be taken to overcome [the baker's] refusal to sell a wedding cake to [the same-sex couple]'.[168] It seems odd for it to become, in effect, permissible to discriminate just because a public official makes an errant remark handling the complaint.

In *Masterpiece Cakeshop*, Kennedy J also pointed to the fact that the Commission had previously found that no discrimination occurred when bakers refused to

[165] *Fulton* (n 6) 1929–30.

[166] *Masterpiece Cakeshop* (n 6) 1729.

[167] ibid 1732.

[168] ibid 1751. Whether the remarks signified hostility or animus may not be altogether clear. However, assuming this to be so, Samuel Marcosson argues that they violated a 'principle' that 'governments may not make decisions affecting a fundamental right on the basis of intolerance of or hostility towards the group exercising the right': SA Marcosson, '*Masterpiece Cakeshop* and Tolerance as a Constitutional Mandate: Strategic Compromise in the Enactment of Civil Rights Laws' (2020) 15 *Duke Journal of Constitutional Law & Public Policy* 139, 141. For the reasons given in Chapter 4, I consider that tests that focus on the government's purposes in this way misdirect the inquiry. As I explained there, some religious practices may conceivably merit targeting. Indeed, in particularly extreme cases, they may even merit hostility or animus. Is hostility or animus towards, for example, the practices of a religious group that involve an act of terrorism wrong? The relevant question is not the government's purposes, but whether there is an adequate justification for the limitation, as judged in the framework through the necessity stage.

supply cakes criticising gay marriage; this seemed, according to him, to be inconsistent with the result in the baker's case.[169] Gorsuch J, with whom Alito J joined, also said that the Commission 'failed to act neutrally toward [the baker's] religious faith', '[m]aybe most notably' because 'the Commission allowed three other bakers to refuse a customer's request that would have required them to violate their secular commitments' while 'den[ying] the same accommodation to [the baker]'.[170] Thomas J, with whom Gorsuch J joined, claimed that 'the Commission treated [the baker's] case differently from a similar case involving three other bakers, for reasons that can only be explained by hostility toward [the baker's] religion'.[171]

However, as the analysis of *Lee* indicates, that objection to a message, rather than the attributes of the customer, is not discrimination under the basic liberty in the moral framework. Even if the decisions of the Commission were inconsistent with each other – which might suggest that the Commission got it wrong in some other cases – that does not appear to offer a reason why it is permissible to discriminate against a same-sex couple. In any case, the claim that there was such an inconsistency between the decisions is doubtful. For example, Gorsuch J found that these cases (refusing to provide cakes expressing criticism of same-sex marriage and refusing to provide a cake for a same-sex wedding) 'share all legally salient features' because '[i]n both cases, it was the kind of cake, not the kind of customer, that mattered to the bakers'.[172]

This analysis seems to overlook that an ordinary wedding cake arguably has no political message, while a cake with an anti-gay marriage statement clearly has one.[173] The point is the subject of some debate in the literature. For example, Laycock claims that 'with or without words or symbols … the cake [requested by the same-sex couple in *Masterpiece Cakeshop*] sends a celebratory message in support of a same-sex wedding'.[174] However, such reasoning elides important distinctions. A cake – like any other aspect of a wedding, from the food to the decorations – may be *used* by its purchasers for the purpose of celebration (or indeed in any possible way, which may be unknown to the seller). But in the absence of text or symbols stating or referencing any particular ideas, it seems wrong to say that the cake itself bears a political message.

[169] *Masterpiece Cakeshop* (n 6) 1730.
[170] ibid 1734.
[171] ibid 1740.
[172] ibid 1735–36.
[173] A baker might understandably decline to create a cake bearing a political message – and being required by non-discrimination law to write a political message that the baker opposes can amount to compelled speech, infringing the baker's First Amendment rights: see J Hart, 'When the First Amendment Compels an Offensive Result: *Masterpiece Cakeshop, Ltd v Colorado Civil Rights Commission*' (2018) 79 *Louisiana Law Review* 419; AS Greene, '*Barnette* and *Masterpiece Cakeshop*: Some Unanswered Questions' (2019) 13 *FIU Law Review* 667. The freedom of expression issue presented by these types of cases is beyond the scope of this book.
[174] D Laycock, 'The Broader Implications of Masterpiece Cakeshop' [2019] *Brigham Young University Law Review* 167, 188.

Other members of the US Supreme Court noticed this difference. Kagan J said that the anti-gay marriage cakes would not have been 'made for any customer', and thus 'the bakers did not single out [the customer] because of his religion, but instead treated him in the same way they would have treated anyone else'.[175] Meanwhile, 'the same-sex couple in this case requested a wedding cake that [the baker] would have made for an opposite-sex couple'.[176] Ginsburg J said that 'the cases the Court aligns are hardly comparable' since '[t]he bakers would have refused to make a cake with [the customer's] requested message for any customer, regardless of his or her religion'.[177] In contrast, '[the baker] would not sell to [the same-sex couple], for no reason other than their sexual orientation, a cake of the kind he regularly sold to others'.[178]

In reality, neither the statements of the Commissioner nor the 'inconsistent' procedurally unrelated decisions are morally relevant to the necessity issue. As Klint Alexander writes, 'the Supreme Court, in the end, failed to resolve the conflict between the principles of religious freedom and nondiscrimination in this particular case'.[179] In other words, 'the Supreme Court ultimately dodged the question, instead focusing on procedural irregularities with the case and the Colorado Commission's dismissive attitude towards a cakeshop owner's claim of religious freedom under the First Amendment'.[180] The same distraction is apparent in *Fulton*, in which the power to grant exceptions under the contract between CSS and the City in effect enabled discrimination towards same-sex couples to take place.

In contrast, in *Lee*, there is no plausible suggestion that necessity in the common interest would justify the interference with liberty of conscience in the circumstances of that case. In rejecting the claim of discrimination on the ground of political opinion, Lady Hale cogently explained the effect of Article 9 of the European Convention on Human Rights, in a way that aligns with necessity analysis under the framework in this book:

> Articles 9 and 10 are, of course, qualified rights which may be limited or restricted in accordance with the law and insofar as this is necessary in a democratic society in pursuit of a legitimate aim. It is, of course, the case that businesses offering services to the public are not entitled to discriminate on certain grounds. The bakery could not refuse to provide a cake – or any other of their products – to Mr Lee because he was a gay man or because he supported gay marriage. But that important fact does not amount to a justification for something completely different – obliging them to supply a cake iced with a message with which they profoundly disagreed. In my view they

[175] *Masterpiece Cakeshop* (n 6) 1733.
[176] ibid.
[177] ibid 1750.
[178] ibid.
[179] KW Alexander, 'The Masterpiece Cakeshop Decision and the Clash between Nondiscrimination and Religious Freedom' (2019) 71 *Oklahoma Law Review* 1069, 1070. See similarly TC Berg, '*Masterpiece Cakeshop*: A *Romer* for Religious Objectors?' [2018] *Cato Supreme Court Review* 139, 139–40; ML Movsesian, '*Masterpiece Cakeshop* and the Future of Religious Freedom' (2019) 42 *Harvard Journal of Law & Public Policy* 711, 750.
[180] Alexander (n 179) 1107.

would be entitled to refuse to do that whatever the message conveyed by the icing on the cake – support for living in sin, support for a particular political party, support for a particular religious denomination. The fact that this particular message had to do with sexual orientation is irrelevant to the [FETO] claim.

Under section 3(1) of the Human Rights Act 1998, all legislation is, so far as it is possible to do so, to be read and given effect in a way which is compatible with the Convention rights. I have already indicated my doubts about whether this was discrimination against Mr Lee on the grounds of his political opinions, but have acknowledged the possibility that it might be. But in my view, FETO should not be read or given effect in such a way as to compel providers of goods, facilities and services to express a message with which they disagree, unless justification is shown for doing so.[181]

Although decided on free speech, not free exercise, grounds, the 2023 decision of *303 Creative LLC v Elenis* reinforces this analysis.[182] In this case, the US Supreme Court held that it violated the Free Speech Clause of the First Amendment for a website designer to be compelled by non-discrimination law to provide a website for a same-sex wedding. Freedom of expression arises as an additional issue in some of the cases considered in this chapter, but is not specifically addressed as a topic in this book, so I do not engage in any detailed analysis of *303*. However, it is worth noting that the decision turned on similar questions to *Lee*, inasmuch as the critical issue was the expressive content for Free Speech Clause purposes of the activity. This kind of compelled speech remains fundamentally different from providing a cake with no message, as in *Masterpiece Cakeshop*, or hotel accommodation, as in *Bull*.[183]

In summary, necessity analysis confirms the outcomes achieved under compatibility analysis. In *Masterpiece Cakeshop* and *Fulton*, the strict scrutiny analysis was either skipped altogether or half baked. This aspect of the test, applied properly, should have yielded similar results to the necessity analysis in the framework, so the flaw here is with how the courts applied the test more than the test itself. In *Bull* and *Lee*, the dicta of Lady Hale reflect the same kind of considerations as the necessity stage of the framework, in acknowledging the importance of Article 9 of the European Convention on Human Rights while also its limitations as against the public interest. Once again, the UK Supreme Court's approach was generally consistent with the moral framework, while that of the US Supreme Court failed to reflect the moral position, largely because of the test of neutrality and general applicability following *Smith*, and the lack of attention paid to the strict scrutiny test.

[181] *Lee* (n 7) [55]–[56].

[182] (2023) 143 S Ct 2298 (Supreme Court of the United States).

[183] For debate over this case, see CJ Russo, 'Point: The Supreme Court Gets It Right in *303 Creative v Elenis*: People of Faith Cannot Be Compelled to Create Expressive Messages Violating Their Religious Beliefs' (2024) 49 *University of Dayton Law Review* 1; JC Sun, 'Counterpoint to: "The Supreme Court Gets It Right in *303 Creative v Elenis*: People of Faith Cannot Be Compelled to Create Expressive Messages Violating Their Religious Beliefs" – The Privilege to Silence "Customized" Speech: The Website Kerfuffle in *303 Creative v Elenis*' (2024) 49 *University of Dayton Law Review* 14.

V. Conclusion

In this chapter, I have applied the moral framework developed in this book to four cases – two decisions of the US Supreme Court and two of the UK Supreme Court. The analysis suggests that the US Supreme Court decisions in *Masterpiece Cakeshop* and *Fulton* did not reflect the moral position, because the Court failed to appreciate the impact of the religious activity for which the claim was made on the rights of others. Diverted by the issues of the neutrality and general applicability of the impugned law, the majority of the Court placed too little emphasis on the fundamental importance of non-discrimination and the harm that discrimination causes. That analysis resolves the case on compatibility alone. But even if that were not the case, the same result can be reached at the necessity stage. In contrast, the UK Supreme Court's decisions in *Bull* and *Lee* were consistent with the framework in this book.

7

Conclusion

In this book I set out an analysis of the justification and limits of liberty of conscience. By understanding the theoretical foundations of liberty of conscience, we can better understand how it can be limited, and how such limitations may be applied in difficult cases, including in cases where there are complex interactions between liberty of conscience, the rights of others, and the common interest. The problem of liberty of conscience is its enormous potential breadth – liberty of conscience claims can extend to virtually any action or inaction. The solution, I suggest, is not to deny the fundamental importance of liberty of conscience, but to establish principled limits that are consistent with the underlying rationale for the right.

The rationale that I advance is based on Rawls's concept of moral personality, which refers to the capacity for a conception of the good and the capacity for a sense of justice.[1] This rationale is distinct from approaches that focus on autonomy, neutrality, dignity, or group rights, all of which have potential difficulties. Even without employing a social contract approach, Rawls's concept of the moral powers illuminates the basis for liberty of conscience, because this right is important to moral personality: there is a sufficient tendency that interference with this right will impair the exercise and development of both moral powers. Paired with Darwall's concept of recognition respect,[2] respect for free and equal citizens as moral persons supports the protection of liberty of conscience. Legal officials, too, owe duties of recognition respect, and should give effect to liberty of conscience through law.

Morally, then, liberty of conscience is an important right that is relevant to our capacities. However, certain limits also flow from its status as derivable from moral personality. One limit is its possible interaction with other rights also derivable from moral personality. Since these have the same underlying rationale as liberty of conscience – that they are necessary for the exercise and development of the moral powers – it makes sense that they are on equal footing, rather than occupying differing positions in a hierarchy of rights. That makes rendering the basic liberties consistently with one another, an issue that I term compatibility (following Rawls), an important question. Rawls's concept of the central range of

[1] J Rawls, *A Theory of Justice (Revised Edition)* (Cambridge, MA: Harvard University Press, 1999) 442.

[2] SL Darwall, 'Two Kinds of Respect' (1977) 88 *Ethics* 36.

application of a basic liberty,[3] discernible by reference to the proximity between the exercise of the basic liberty and the moral powers, assists in this compatibility exercise.

The other possible limit relates to the common interest. Rawls acknowledges that the common interest in, for example, public order and security is important to the liberties of all; in essence, it underpins the basic liberties, and is a premise for the exercise and development of the moral powers.[4] Accordingly, a sufficiently strong argument that a state measure is in the common interest should suffice to serve as an alternative basis for limiting liberty of conscience. Rawls does not explain in much detail how to determine what is in the common interest. I suggest that the idea of necessity is applicable here, and some form of balancing test is required to assess necessity claims. Although the framework is not strongly prescriptive of the type of test, I favour a means-end test over the kind of balancing undertaken in proportionality. In contrast, the concept of neutrality is not used to assess liberty of conscience in the framework established in this book. There is a need to disambiguate neutrality, but considering the US Supreme Court's case law focusing on whether a law has the purpose of restricting religious exercise,[5] this type of neutrality test focuses on less relevant matters compared with the test offered by the framework.

In applying this moral framework to assess case studies in US and UK law, it is necessary to consider two other potential basic liberties: integrity of the person and non-discrimination. I argue that both of these rights should be considered basic liberties at the same level as liberty of conscience, and this much is fairly clear as they are derivable in the same way as liberty of conscience. Specifically, there is a sufficient tendency that interference with either of these rights will undermine the exercise and development of the moral powers. In this regard, my position is slightly different from Rawls, since although Rawls accepts that physical and psychological integrity of the person is a basic liberty,[6] he considers non-discrimination (in the form of fair equality of opportunity) to be an aspect of the second principle of justice, not the first principle of justice (the liberty principle).[7]

In the first case study addressing coronavirus restrictions and liberty of conscience, in both US and UK law challenges to restrictions on places of worship have enjoyed some success under the First Amendment to the US Constitution and the UK Human Rights Act respectively.[8] Applying the framework, I argue that

[3] Rawls, *A Theory of Justice (Revised Edition)* (n 1) 54.

[4] ibid 186–89.

[5] *Church of the Lukumi Babalu Aye v City of Hialeah* (1993) 508 US 520 (Supreme Court of the United States).

[6] See, eg, J Rawls, *Justice as Fairness: A Restatement* (E Kelly ed, Cambridge, MA: Harvard University Press, 2001) 44.

[7] See, eg, J Rawls, *Political Liberalism* (New York: Columbia University Press, 2005) 363–64.

[8] See, eg, *Roman Catholic Diocese v Cuomo* (2020) 141 S Ct 63 (Supreme Court of the United States); *Philip v Scottish Ministers* [2021] SLT 559 (Outer House of the Court of Session).

in the circumstances of the pandemic, temporary limitations on religious practice could be justified both by the rights of others (recalling that integrity of the person, which is threatened by the spread of a virus, has the status of a basic liberty) and the common interest (since the pandemic threatened public health) – at least where it was possible to move many aspects of religious worship online, and subject to an assessment of whether the means employed were necessary for these purposes. In the cases considered, the means arguably met this standard, casting doubt on the results in some of the decisions in the US and UK, which failed to align with the preferable moral position.

In the second case study, concerning non-discrimination requirements in respect of same-sex couples and liberty of conscience, the US and UK diverged significantly.[9] The US cases handed significant victories to religious freedom claimants, while in the UK it was clear that the same-sex couples' rights to non-discrimination prevailed, at least where discrimination actually occurred. The moral framework applied in this book confirms the approach in the UK and raises doubts about that in the US. Once again, both the rights of others (the right to non-discrimination, another basic liberty) and the common interest in social harmony justified the defeat of liberty of conscience claims, in circumstances where the claim went to the central range of application of non-discrimination but not the central range of application of liberty of conscience because it related to, for example, the commercial sphere. However, the result would be different in matters more central to religious worship and organisation.

Some larger themes and implications emerge from this analysis. First, the potential breadth of liberty of conscience is both the problem posed by this right and also the solution, as it means that it will often be overcome in conflicts of rights, as shown by compatibility analysis. Conscientious belief can extend to virtually anything, and thus a claim to liberty of conscience can cover virtually any action or inaction. That presents the difficulty that has been the focus of this book: how to place limits on such a potentially broad right. However, it also means that claims to liberty of conscience sometimes travel well outside what we have called the central range of application of this basic liberty, and can be limited on that basis. The concept of the central range of application, adopted from Rawls's work and discussed in this book especially in the context of compatibility analysis, proves critical to an understanding of how to address liberty of conscience claims under the moral framework.

Depending on the beliefs in question, liberty of conscience has the potential to clash with a great many rights belonging to others. However, the more remote manifestations of beliefs, such as adhering to one's own religious doctrine in the commercial sphere, are difficult to view as within this central range of application

[9] See *Bull v Hall* [2013] 1 WLR 3741 (Supreme Court of the United Kingdom); *Masterpiece Cakeshop v Colorado Civil Rights Commission* (2018) 584 US 617 (Supreme Court of the United States); *Lee v Ashers Baking Company Ltd* [2020] AC 413 (Supreme Court of the United Kingdom); *Fulton v City of Philadelphia* (2021) 141 S Ct 1868 (Supreme Court of the United States).

of liberty of conscience. Although not entirely disconnected from them, they are rather far removed from the development and exercise of the moral powers. These outer reaches of liberty of conscience, beyond the central range of application, are often where clashes with other rights occur. Although the basic liberties are formally equal (there is no hierarchy of basic liberties), the consequence is that in practice liberty of conscience might sometimes have to yield to the other basic liberties, because they may not be as expansive beyond their central ranges of application.

This point proved significant to both of the case studies in this book. In neither case study did the relevant interference with liberty of conscience go to its central range of application, though the matter was close to the borderline in the coronavirus restrictions case study in Chapter 5. In that case study, there was no doubt that the closure of places of worship was a significant interference, but the fact that the restrictions were temporary and worship could largely go ahead online meant that the interference did not impair the exercise and development of the moral powers enough to go to the central range (whereas a non-temporary closure or even a closure without the possibility of online worship very likely would have gone to the central range of application, potentially shifting the terms of the analysis).

In respect of the case study in Chapter 6, the instances of discrimination towards same-sex couples were in the commercial sphere – selling a cake, running a hotel, and arranging foster care. These were outside the central range of application of liberty of conscience as interference with them would have a limited impact on the exercise and development of the moral powers. As such, in each of the case studies, the claims to liberty of conscience were overcome by the interference posed by the activity to the basic liberties of integrity of the person (through the possibility of propagation of the coronavirus, risking death) and non-discrimination (through direct discrimination in a public context) respectively, which went to the central range of application of the basic liberty and more seriously threatened moral personality. This fact allowed both case studies to be resolved on the basis of compatibility.

A second corollary of this book is that the rights of others serve as a key basis on which liberty of conscience may be limited. Because other rights are derivable on a similar basis to liberty of conscience – that is, they are derivable from considerations of recognition respect for moral personality – liberty of conscience may sometimes have to give way to those rights, in compatibility analysis, when they are more centrally affected. The compatibility approach is one in which the rights in conflict are delimited at a deontological and definitional level to be read consistently with one another, rather than overridden.

Sometimes the issue of adjudicating a religious freedom claim is thought of as being merely about the balance struck between the claim and the state interest.[10] However, to do so overlooks a morally relevant aspect of the inquiry. The current

[10] See, eg, D Laycock and TC Berg, 'Protecting Free Exercise under *Smith* and after *Smith*' [2021] *Cato Supreme Court Review* 33, 41–60.

law often involves this omission. In the US cases, such as *Roman Catholic Diocese* and *Masterpiece Cakeshop*, there is a lack of opportunity to consider the rights of others because of the test employed – involving neutrality, general applicability and strict scrutiny.[11] In the result, the US Supreme Court in both the coronavirus cases and the non-discrimination cases failed to pay sufficient regard to the rights of others, despite their importance in the circumstances. This omission seems to impoverish the analysis, by depriving courts of what may sometimes be an intuitive and important basis on which to limit liberty of conscience.

In the UK cases, consideration of the rights of others is at least possible – unsurprisingly, given the express mention of these rights under Article 9(2) of the European Convention on Human Rights – but it nonetheless sometimes does not occur, with *Philip* serving as a salient example of the omission of this consideration. In contrast, in the non-discrimination cases such as *Bull*, the UK courts seemed well aware of the importance of the non-discrimination rights that were in conflict with the right to liberty of conscience. However, there may be a risk in the UK case law of subsuming the rights of others into the proportionality assessment. This is preferable to ignoring them altogether as in the US law, but there could be a concern that they are given less attention than in a freestanding assessment of compatibility with the rights of others. Acknowledging the rights of others can be important symbolically.[12] The rights of others can represent a convincing reason to limit a liberty of conscience claim, if those other rights are more significantly impaired by the religious practice sought to be protected than the right to liberty of conscience. They might sometimes offer a more principled and intelligible basis on which to reject a religious freedom claim than balancing because the latter may be viewed as a contestable exercise of judicial discretion.

The value of considering the rights of others is reinforced by other cases. For example, in *Christian Education South Africa v Minister of Education*,[13] a South African case referred to previously in Chapter 2, a ban on corporal punishment in schools was challenged by an association of Christian schools on the basis of

[11] Tebbe suggests that solicitude for harm to others is implicit in some of the US Supreme Court's case law, but refers only to some older cases: see N Tebbe, *Religious Freedom in an Egalitarian Age* (Cambridge, MA: Harvard University Press, 2017) 58–59. Although the rights of others may be theoretically relevant to the strict scrutiny analysis which was centred in pre-*Smith* cases, the more recent cases studied in the case studies in Chapters 5 and 6 demonstrate the Court's current tendency not to pay heed to the rights of others.

[12] Compatibility analysis may also make a practical difference in some cases, because it is at least theoretically possible to conceive of claims to liberty of conscience where the rights of others are affected, but the common interest is weak. Consider a fictional country Flammabilia. In one part of the country, a new religion exists called Burnism. As one of its central planks of doctrine, Burnism calls for the burning of toxic substances, releasing noxious smoke. The adherents of the religion wear gas masks to avoid adverse health effects from this. Further, due to the remoteness of the small community of Burnism adherents, the smoke does not affect anyone other than one unfortunate neighbour towards whom the smoke is frequently carried by the wind. A law that targets the practices of this religion might not be defensible on the grounds of the common interest because only one person is adversely affected by the religious practice, and (let us assume) there happens to be very little environmental damage. But it could be justified due to the right to integrity of the person of the neighbour.

[13] (2000) (4) SA 757 (Constitutional Court of South Africa).

religious freedom under section 15 of the Constitution of the Republic of South Africa (among other grounds). The respondent Minister of Education, defending the constitutionality of the ban, argued that the governing provision was section 31(1) for cultural, religious and linguistic communities, which was subject to a qualification in section 31(2) that such rights 'may not be exercised in a manner inconsistent with any provision of the Bill of Rights'.[14] The Minister therefore contended that that 'since corporal punishment at school violates the right to equality and the right to dignity, it forfeits any claim to constitutional regard'.[15]

Sachs J in the Constitutional Court of South Africa adopted the approach 'most favourable to the appellant' and 'assume[d] without deciding that appellant's religious rights under sections 15 and 31(1) are both in issue' (the section 15 religious freedom right not being subject to section 31(2)) and further 'that corporal punishment as practiced by the appellant's members is not "inconsistent with any provision of the Bill of Rights" as contemplated by section 31(2)'.[16] Because of these assumptions, Sachs J eschewed consideration of the rights of others and proceeded directly to a balancing analysis, on the basis of which he upheld the law as proportionate. Yet this balancing analysis could be objected to as overly discretionary, which the looseness of the concluding statement seems to illustrate: '[w]hen all [the] factors are weighed together, the scales come down firmly in favour of upholding the generality of the law in the face of the appellant's claim for a constitutionally compelled exemption'.[17]

Although the decision in *Christian Education* is no doubt correct, and the approach of Sachs J understandable given the mechanics of sections 15 and 31, it would likely have been more intuitive and symbolically powerful if the case had been decided on the basis of the rights of others – that is, the inconsistency of corporal punishment with the other provisions of the Bill of Rights in South Africa protecting, for example, freedom and security of the person under section 12 and the rights of children under section 28. The South African Court's approach forms an interesting contrast with that of the UK House of Lords in *R (Williamson) v Secretary of State for Education and Employment*,[18] in which the rights of others were the basis on which a law prohibiting corporal punishment was found to be proportionate under Article 9. Lord Nicholls explained that 'in a pluralist society a balance has to be held between freedom to practise one's own beliefs and the interests of others affected by those practices'.[19] The interference with the manifestation of the claimants' beliefs by the law prohibiting corporal punishment at school was 'necessary in a democratic society … for the protection of the rights and freedoms of others'.[20] *Williamson* therefore illustrates the way in which the rights of others

[14] ibid [8].
[15] ibid [17].
[16] ibid [27].
[17] ibid [52].
[18] [2005] 2 AC 246 (United Kingdom House of Lords).
[19] ibid [17].
[20] ibid [49].

can be addressed within the proportionality test. Lord Nicholls went on to elaborate on this analysis as follows:

> The statutory ban pursues a legitimate aim: children are vulnerable, and the aim of the legislation is to protect them and promote their wellbeing. Corporal punishment involves deliberately inflicting physical violence. The legislation is intended to protect children against the distress, pain and other harmful effects this infliction of physical violence may cause. That corporal punishment may have these harmful effects is self-evident.
>
> Further, the means chosen to achieve this aim are appropriate and not disproportionate in their adverse impact on parents who believe that carefully-controlled administration of corporal punishment to a mild degree can be beneficial, for this reason: the legislature was entitled to take the view that, overall and balancing the conflicting considerations, all corporal punishment of children at school is undesirable and unnecessary and that other, non-violent means of discipline are available and preferable.[21]

Lastly, the moral framework's focus on necessity in the common interest points to the relevance of a balancing exercise of some description. As has been explained, this operates as a kind of consequentialist override of the deontological position embodied by a rights claim.[22] The common interest is relevant as a possible basis for the limitation of liberty of conscience because the common interest underpins all basic liberties and the exercise and development of the moral powers. Moreover, this focus implies some kind of assessment of what is necessary in the common interest. Although the exact form of that assessment is not prescribed by the framework, the preferable form that it may take is means-ends analysis, due to problems with the breadth of the final balancing stage of structured proportionality.

In the case studies, I conclude that both the coronavirus restrictions and the non-discrimination measures were necessary in the common interest, because of the dire threat to public health posed by the coronavirus pandemic, at least prior to the achievement of widespread vaccination, and that to social harmony posed by discrimination on the grounds of sexual orientation. These matters lay in the common interest as generally affecting the members of a society. Both the UK and US law on liberty of conscience contain a balancing assessment – in the former the test is proportionality and in the latter it is strict scrutiny. However, the US courts have lately neglected the strict scrutiny analysis in favour of questions of neutrality and general applicability, following *Smith*.[23] In contrast, in the UK law, balancing remains central through the proportionality test.

The analysis in the case studies reinforces the desirability of focusing attention on the necessity of a law interfering with liberty of conscience as distinct from assessing the attributes of the law. The attention given by the US courts to

[21] ibid [49]–[50].

[22] See generally MH Kramer, 'Looking Back and Looking Ahead: Replies to the Contributors' in M McBride and VAJ Kurki (eds), *Without Trimmings: The Legal, Moral, and Political Philosophy of Matthew Kramer* (Oxford: Oxford University Press, 2022) 489.

[23] *Employment Division v Smith* (1990) 494 US 872.

neutrality as no purpose to limit exercise is morally suboptimal. It addresses less relevant matters, given the possibility of a law placing an unnecessary burden on liberty of conscience despite a lack of a 'problematic' purpose, and of a law placing a necessary burden on liberty of conscience despite the presence of a 'problematic' purpose. Further, the test is practically unworkable. It turns on virtually indeterminate questions of the similarity or difference of the regulation of secular and religious activities. Writing in the context of the coronavirus restriction cases considered by the US Supreme Court, Berg explains this point as follows:

> Reading 'neutrality and general applicability' to require close review whenever the state exempts any meaningful number of comparable secular activities can give substantial protection to religious freedom. But the pandemic cases also revealed the downsides to that approach. It calls on judges to make contentious, potentially resentment-provoking judgments about whether religious activities are being treated as well as various secular activities. Those threshold disputes could be avoided if courts simply required government to show 'compelling,' or at least strong, reasons for significant restrictions on in-person worship – while tempering that standard, as Roberts suggested, with reasonable deference to officials' expertise in 'dynamic and fact-intensive' circumstances. Carefully considered restrictions on in-person worship would likely have survived under such an approach.[24]

Interestingly, in *Fulton* Alito J (with whom Gorsuch J and Thomas J joined) wrote a lengthy concurring opinion contending that *Smith* should be overturned. He explained his view of the effect of the decision in *Smith* as follows:

> In [*Smith*], the Court abruptly pushed aside nearly 40 years of precedent and held that the First Amendment's Free Exercise Clause tolerates any rule that categorically prohibits or commands specified conduct so long as it does not target religious practice. Even if a rule serves no important purpose and has a devastating effect on religious freedom, the Constitution, according to *Smith*, provides no protection.[25]

The test in *Sherbert v Verner* proceeded directly to strict scrutiny in circumstances of a 'substantial' burden on free exercise, asking whether the burdening law was narrowly tailored to a compelling state interest.[26] On its face, this test is friendlier to the claimant than under *Smith*. One example of a successful challenge was *Wisconsin v Yoder*,[27] which related to an Amish religious objection to compulsory education beyond the eighth grade. However, in the period in which the *Sherbert* test was applied by the US Supreme Court, religious freedom claimants were only

[24] TC Berg, 'Religious Freedom Amid the Tumult' (2022) 17 *University of St Thomas Law Journal* 735, 742.

[25] *Fulton v City of Philadelphia* (2021) 141 S Ct 1868 (Supreme Court of the United States). This call for a reconsideration of *Smith* was rejected by the opinion of the Court, while Barrett J concurred with that opinion, expressing some concerns about *Smith* but uncertainty as to what would replace it, and finding that it was not necessary at present to resolve the question (Kavanaugh J joined this concurrence and Breyer J joined all except the first paragraph in which Barrett J questioned *Smith*). For analysis of Barrett J's concerns about what would replace *Smith*, see CC Lund, 'Answers to *Fulton*'s Questions' (2023) 108 *Iowa Law Review* 2075.

[26] (1963) 374 US 398 (Supreme Court of the United States).

[27] (1972) 406 US 205 (Supreme Court of the United States).

periodically successful. Michael McConnell explains that, in this time, 'the Supreme Court only rarely sided with the free exercise claimant [because it] generally found either that the free exercise right was not burdened or that the government interest was compelling'.[28] That may reflect a difference in the mindset of those members of the Court towards religious freedom, but it may also be the result of focusing attention on the strict scrutiny analysis. Under the *Smith* test, even though the strict scrutiny stage remains, it has either been skipped altogether (as in *Masterpiece Cakeshop*) or passed through cursorily (as in *Roman Catholic Diocese*), an apparent afterthought to the main question of neutrality and general applicability. In the case studies, laws that seemingly should have been upheld under strict scrutiny were struck down as the court sped breezily through this important analysis.

Thus, it may be that restoring strict scrutiny to its central position could lead to more cautious free exercise jurisprudence – depending, at least, on how it is applied. In particular, Alito J's assumption that if the *Sherbert* test had been applied in *Fulton*, matters would have resolved in favour of the free exercise claim seems wrong. Addressing the issues squarely under the *Sherbert* test might instead have led to a better outcome. As David Beck observes, '[h]ad the *Fulton* Court overruled the *Smith* analysis and reverted to the previous test found in *Sherbert v Verner*, while also holding that the protection of the LGBTQ+ community from stigma is a compelling state interest, the City would have prevailed'.[29] Indeed, '[p]rotecting the LGBTQ+ community from stigma and discrimination is a compelling state interest'.[30] That is all the more so given evidence gathered by Netta Barak-Corren that discrimination towards same-sex couples has increased in the US following the decision in *Masterpiece Cakeshop*.[31]

Although the UK's proportionality test is preferable to the approach in *Smith*, that is not to say that it is without problems. The main difficulty with it is the incommensurability involved in the final balancing stage of the test. The way that incommensurable matters are weighed against each other at this stage is apparent from the reasoning of the Outer House of the Court of Session in *Philip*. Lord Braid, in finding that the coronavirus restrictions in Scotland failed the final balancing stage of the proportionality test, pointed to factors such as the 'severity of Covid-19 and the threats posed by the new variant' on the one hand (which he said he did 'not underplay in the slightest') and the 'importance of the affected right' (Article 9) on the other hand.[32] With discretion to weigh these incommensurable factors however he pleased, Lord Braid concluded as follows:

[28] MW McConnell, 'Free Exercise Revisionism and the *Smith* Decision' (1990) 57 *University of Chicago Law Review* 1109, 1110.

[29] D Beck, '*Fulton v City of Philadelphia*: Religious Objectors, Historically Marginalized Communities, and a Missed Opportunity' (2021) 68 *Loyola Law Review* 95, 97.

[30] ibid 123.

[31] N Barak-Corren, 'Religious Exemptions Increase Discrimination toward Same-Sex Couples: Evidence from *Masterpiece Cakeshop*' (2021) 50 *Journal of Legal Studies* 75; N Barak-Corren, 'A License to Discriminate? The Market Response to *Masterpiece Cakeshop*' (2021) 56 *Harvard Civil Rights-Civil Liberties Law Review* 315.

[32] *Philip v Scottish Ministers* 2021 SLT 559 (Outer House of the Court of Session) [118]–[125].

> [T]he apparent under-playing of the importance of the article 9 right in comparison with other activities, coupled with the blanket ban on *all* forms of worship, including private prayer, communion, confession and baptism, lead me to the conclusion that even if *some* enforced restriction on the right to worship was justified by the situation in December 2020/January 2021, the Regulations in the form they were passed did have a disproportionate effect and thus that they also fail the fourth stage of the assessment.[33]

Accordingly, although it is clear from the analysis in this book that an assessment of necessity is, and should be, an important aspect of assessing liberty of conscience claims, it remains open to debate what the appropriate test is. The pre-*Smith* US case law, governed by the test in *Sherbert*, applied a means-end test of strict scrutiny. This test has much to commend it, and the analysis in this book suggests that it is superior to the test under *Smith*. For that reason, I agree with Alito J in *Fulton* that the *Smith* test should be discarded and the earlier test recovered. The 2025 decision of *Mahmoud v Taylor*,[34] in which the US Supreme Court applied *Wisconsin v Yoder* – and stated that when 'a law imposes a burden of the same character as that in *Yoder*, strict scrutiny is appropriate regardless of whether the law is neutral or generally applicable' – further suggests that *Smith* may be on life support. Although proportionality in the UK has significant advantages over the current US case law, it also has drawbacks, and the analysis in *Philip* helps to illustrate the high level of judicial discretion entailed by the final balancing stage of structured proportionality. It would be better for the UK to adopt a means-end test as well, as in the necessity stage of structured proportionality.

Needless to say, many stones are left unturned in this book, but the moral framework set out in Chapters 2, 3 and 4 I hope may provide helpful conceptual resources for other issues. For example, the analysis of discrimination towards same-sex couples could be applied beyond 'public accommodations' to situations such as religious objections by public officials to same-sex marriage, or issues relating to employment. The analysis of coronavirus restrictions may also have implications for issues such as vaccine mandates, though these mandates pose a more difficult question than restrictions on attendance at places of worship: whereas limitations on association clearly prevent transmission, it is doubtful whether vaccination actually prevents transmission and protects others.[35] Thus, the rights of others loomed less large in respect of this question than in respect of public health measures designed to protect the public from the transmission

[33] ibid [126].

[34] (2025) 145 S Ct 2332 (Supreme Court of the United States) 2361.

[35] C Stokel-Walker, 'What Do We Know about Covid Vaccines and Preventing Transmission?' (2022) 376 *British Medical Journal* o298. See generally *Does 1–3 v Mills* (2021) 142 S Ct 17; *Dr A v Hochul* (2021) 142 S Ct 552; *National Federation of Independent Business v Department of Labor* (2022) 142 S Ct 661; *Biden v Missouri* (2022) 142 S Ct 647. Some human rights scholars have argued in support of mandatory vaccination: see J King et al, 'Mandatory COVID-19 Vaccination and Human Rights' (2022) 399 *The Lancet* 220. At the time of writing, the constitutionality of vaccine mandates remains a current issue: K Dallas, 'Will the Supreme Court Reenter the Vaccine Wars?' (*SCOTUSblog*, 6 August 2025) www.scotusblog.com/2025/08/supreme-court-covid-vaccine-mandates/.

of the virus, and the liberty of conscience claim may be stronger. That is all the more so given that both the adenovirus and mRNA coronavirus vaccines have had patchy safety records. In another context, the heightening clash between the Establishment Clause jurisprudence in the US – which previously mandated a strong separation between church and state, as set out in the 1971 case of *Lemon v Kurtzman*[36] – and the new directions of Free Exercise jurisprudence under the current US Supreme Court majority offer another area of potential analysis.

The book's analysis might also be extended to other human rights by reference to the consideration of recognition respect for moral personality utilised in respect of liberty of conscience in Chapter 2 of the book, and in respect of integrity of the person and non-discrimination in Chapters 5 and 6 of the book. Liberty of conscience is not the only right explicable by reference to recognition respect for moral personality, as many human rights that should be recognised as fundamental are explicable through this concept. Rawls's own list of basic liberties is an example of this, but his list is likely to be overly short and might be thought to overlook some rights that are necessary for the exercise and development of the moral powers. With the proper scope of human rights and constitutional rights an enduring area of controversy in many countries, the foundation of human rights (as well as the question of whether there needs to be such a foundation at all) remains an important debate with political significance.

Much of the controversy surrounding the protection of human rights in the UK and elsewhere concerns the view expressed by some that judges might use rights to 'trump' the interests of the public as notionally expressed through the decisions of the Westminster Parliament. Contrary to some views, I do not consider it persuasive to argue that the common interest represents such an invariably compelling consideration that it must always sweep aside the rights of individuals. However, there are some circumstances when the common interest is indeed compelling, as this book has established. An account based on the Rawlsian concept of moral personality therefore sheds significant light on the justification and limits of liberty of conscience.

[36] (1971) 403 US 602 (Supreme Court of the United States).

BIBLIOGRAPHY

Abbey, R, 'Rawlsian Resources for Animal Ethics' (2007) 12 *Ethics and the Environment* 1

Ackerman, B, 'The Emergency Constitution' (2004) 113 *Yale Law Journal* 1029

Adenitire, J, 'Conscientious Exemptions: From Toleration to Neutrality; From Neutrality to Respect' (2017) 6 *Oxford Journal of Law and Religion* 268

—— (ed), *Religious Beliefs and Conscientious Exemptions in a Liberal State* (Oxford: Hart Publishing, 2019)

—— *A General Right to Conscientious Exemption: Beyond Religious Privilege* (Cambridge: Cambridge University Press, 2020)

Adenitire, JO and Fasel, R, *Animals and the Constitution: Towards Sentience-Based Constitutionalism* (Oxford: Oxford University Press, 2025)

Ahdar, R and Leigh, I, 'Is Establishment Consistent with Religious Freedom?' (2004) 49 *McGill Law Journal* 635

Ahmed, F, 'The Autonomy Rationale for Religious Freedom' (2017) 80 *Modern Law Review* 238

—— 'What Establishment Expresses' (2022) 20 *International Journal of Constitutional Law* 818

Al-Astewani, A, 'To Open or Close? COVID-19, Mosques and the Role of Religious Authority within the British Muslim Community: A Socio-Legal Analysis' (2021) 12 *Religions* 11

Alexander, KW, 'The *Masterpiece Cakeshop* Decision and the Clash between Nondiscrimination and Religious Freedom' (2019) 71 *Oklahoma Law Review* 1069

Alexander, L, 'What Makes Wrongful Discrimination Wrongful? Biases, Preferences, Stereotypes, and Proxies' (1992) 14 *University of Pennsylvania Law Review* 149

Anderson, RT, 'Disagreement Is Not Always Discrimination: On *Masterpiece Cakeshop* and the Analogy to Interracial Marriage' (2018) 16 *Georgetown Journal of Law & Public Policy* 123

Androutsopoulos, G, 'The Right of Religious Freedom in Light of the Coronavirus Pandemic: The Greek Case' (2021) 10 *Laws* 14

Arneson, RJ, 'Against Rawlsian Equality of Opportunity' (1999) 93 *Philosophical Studies* 77

—— 'What Is Wrongful Discrimination?' (2006) 43 *San Diego Law Review* 775

Babie, PT, '*Adelaide Company of Jehovah's Witnesses v Commonwealth*: Balancing Free Exercise and Public Order' in R Barker et al (eds), *Law and Religion in the Commonwealth: The Evolution of Case Law* (Oxford: Hart Publishing, 2022)

Baffelli, E, 'Did Aum Shinrikyō Really End?' in M Stausberg et al (eds), *The Demise of Religion: How Religions End, Die, or Dissipate* (London: Bloomsbury, 2020)

—— 'Fear and the Construction of Minority Religions in Japan' (2023) 51 *Religion, State & Society* 223

Baggaley, RF et al, 'Impact of the COVID-19 Pandemic on Communal Religious Worshippers' Mental Health and the Benefits of Positive Religious Coping' (2024) 10 *Heliyon* e39093

Baldwin, G, 'The Pandemic and the First Amendment' *UK Constitutional Law Association Blog* (8 December 2020) https://ukconstitutionallaw.org/2020/12/08/guy-baldwin-the-pandemic-and-the-first-amendment/

—— 'Banning Public Worship during the Pandemic?' *UK Constitutional Law Association Blog* (12 April 2021) https://ukconstitutionallaw.org/2021/04/12/guy-baldwin-banning-public-worship-during-the-pandemic/

—— 'Review of *A General Right to Conscientious Exemption: Beyond Religious Privilege*. By John Adenitire' (2022) 81 *Cambridge Law Journal* 430

—— 'The Coronavirus Pandemic and Religious Freedom: Judicial Decisions in the United States and United Kingdom' (2021) 26 *Judicial Review* 297

—— 'Freedom of Religion under the Australian Constitution: Is Proportionality the Answer?' (2023) 3 *Australian Journal of Law and Religion* 20
—— 'Rawls and Animal Moral Personality' (2023) 13 *Animals* 1238
—— 'A Chance to Close the Proportionality Chapter in Australian Constitutional Law?' *AUSPUBLAW* (17 November 2023) https://www.auspublaw.org/blog/2023/11/a-chance-to-close-the-proportionality-chapter-in-australian-constitutional-law
—— 'Support for Terrorism and Freedom of Association' [2024] 4 *European Human Rights Law Review* 342
—— 'Positive Obligations to Protect the Public under Human Rights Law' (2025) 30 *Judicial Review* 232
—— 'The Lawfulness of Citizenship Deprivation: Comparing Australia and the UK' (2025) 14 *Laws* 12
Baldwin, G and Hatano, A, 'The Diffusion of Religious Freedom in Japan' (2026) 21 *Asian Journal of Comparative Law* (forthcoming)
Barak, A, *Proportionality: Constitutional Rights and Their Limitations* (Cambridge: Cambridge University Press, 2012)
Barak-Corren, N, 'A License to Discriminate? The Market Response to *Masterpiece Cakeshop*' (2021) 56 *Harvard Civil Rights-Civil Liberties Law Review* 315
—— 'Religious Exemptions Increase Discrimination toward Same-Sex Couples: Evidence from *Masterpiece Cakeshop*' (2021) 50 *Journal of Legal Studies* 75
Barclay, SH, 'The Religion Clauses after *Kennedy v Bremerton School District*' (2023) 108 *Iowa Law Review* 2097
Beck, D, '*Fulton v City of Philadelphia*: Religious Objectors, Historically Marginalized Communities, and a Missed Opportunity' (2021) 68 *Loyola Law Review* 95
Beck, L, 'The Case against Improper Purpose as the Touchstone for Invalidity under Section 116 of the Australian Constitution' (2016) 44 *Federal Law Review* 505
—— '*Attorney-General (Victoria) Ex Rel Black v Commonwealth*: The High Court's Attempt to Make the Establishment Clause of the Australian Constitution Mean Very Little' in R Barker, PT Babie and N Foster (eds), *Law and Religion in the Commonwealth* (Oxford: Hart Publishing, 2022)
Bendor, AL and Sela, T, 'How Proportional Is Proportionality?' (2015) 13 *International Journal of Constitutional Law* 530
Berg, TC, '*Masterpiece Cakeshop*: A *Romer* for Religious Objectors' [2018] *Cato Supreme Court Review* 139
—— 'Religious Freedom Amid the Tumult' (2022) 17 *University of St Thomas Law Journal* 735
Bhargava, R, 'What Is Indian Secularism and What Is It For?' (2002) 1 *India Review* 1
Bielefeldt, H, Ghanea, N and Wiener, M, *Freedom of Religion or Belief: An International Law Commentary* (Oxford: Oxford University Press, 2016)
Billingham, P, 'Exemptions for Religious Groups and the Problem of Internal Dissent' in J Adenitire (ed), *Religious Beliefs and Conscientious Exemptions in a Liberal State* (Oxford: Hart Publishing, 2019)
Bird, B, 'COVID-19 and Religious Freedom in Canada' (2022) 64 *Journal of Church and State* 621
Blackman, J, 'The "Essential" Free Exercise Clause' (2021) 44 *Harvard Journal of Law & Public Policy* 637
Brady, KA, *The Distinctiveness of Religion in American Law: Rethinking Religion Clause Jurisprudence* (Cambridge: Cambridge University Press, 2015)
—— 'The Disappearance of Religion from Debates about Religious Accommodation' (2017) 20 *Lewis & Clark Law Review* 1093
Brennan, J, 'Against the Moral Powers Test of Basic Liberty' (2020) 28 *European Journal of Philosophy* 492
Brest, P, 'Foreword: In Defense of the Antidiscrimination Principle' (1976) 90 *Harvard Law Review* 1
Bridge, D, 'Religious Freedom or Libertarianism: What Explains State Enactments of Religious Freedom Restoration Act Laws?' (2014) 56 *Journal of Church and State* 347

Brown, J and Kirk-Wade, E, *Coronavirus: A History of 'Lockdown Laws' in England* (London: House of Commons Library, 2021)
Buchanan, A, *Justice, Legitimacy, and International Relations: Moral Foundations for International Law* (Oxford: Oxford University Press, 2004)
Burke, C, 'COVID-19 and Korea: Viral Xenophobia through a Legal Lens' (2023) 16 *International Journal for Religious Freedom* 91
Butlin, SF, 'Cakes in the Supreme Court (2019) 78 *Cambridge Law Journal* 280
Caney, S, 'Global Poverty and Human Rights: The Case for Positive Duties' in T Pogge (ed), *Freedom from Poverty as a Human Right: Who Owes What to the Very Poor?* (Oxford: Oxford University Press, 2007)
Carter, I, 'Respect and the Basis of Equality' (2011) 121 *Ethics* 538
Chang, R, 'Incommensurability (and Incomparability)' in H LaFollette (ed), *The International Encyclopedia of Ethics* (Oxford: Blackwell, 2013)
Chapman, NS, 'The Case for the Current Free Exercise Regime' (2023) 108 *Iowa Law Review* 2115
Chordia, S, *Proportionality in Australian Constitutional Law* (Alexandria, NSW: Federation Press, 2020)
Clough, A, 'Finding the Balance: Intoxication and Consent' (2019) 40 *Liverpool Law Review* 49
Cochrane, A, 'From Human Rights to Sentient Rights' (2013) 16 *Critical Review of International Social and Political Philosophy* 655
—— *Sentientist Politics: A Theory of Global Inter-Species Justice* (Oxford: Oxford University Press, 2018)
Cohen, AJ, 'What Toleration Is' (2004) 115 *Ethics* 6878
'Constitutional Constraints on Free Exercise Analogies' (2021) 134 *Harvard Law Review* 1782
Corbin, CM, 'Religious Liberty in a Pandemic' (2020) 70 *Duke Law Journal Online* 1
Cornell, D, *The Imaginary Domain: Abortion, Pornography and Sexual Harassment* (Abingdon: Routledge, 1995)
Corvino, J, 'Is Religion Special? Exemptions, Conscience and the Culture Wars' in J Adenitire (ed), *Religious Beliefs and Conscientious Exemptions in a Liberal State* (Oxford: Hart Publishing, 2019)
Council of Europe, 'Derogations Covid-19' https://www.coe.int/en/web/conventions/derogations-covid-19
Cowan, DE and Bromley, DG, *Cults and New Religions: A Brief History*, 2nd edn (Chichester: Wiley, 2015)
Cranmer, F, 'Can Secular Non-Natural Persons Be Said to Have a "Conscience"?' in J Adenitire (ed), *Religious Beliefs and Conscientious Exemptions in a Liberal State* (Oxford: Hart Publishing, 2019)
Cross, FB, *Constitutions and Religious Freedom* (Cambridge: Cambridge University Press, 2015)
Cruft, R, Liao, SM and Renzo, M (eds), *Philosophical Foundations of Human Rights* (Oxford: Oxford University Press, 2015)
Cupit, G, 'The Basis of Equality' (2000) 75 *Philosophy* 105
Dallas, K, 'Will the Supreme Court Reenter the Vaccine Wars?' *SCOTUSblog* (6 August 2025) https://www.scotusblog.com/2025/08/supreme-court-covid-vaccine-mandates/
Daly, E, 'The Ambiguous Reach of Constitutional Secularism in Republican France: Revisiting the Idea of Laïcité and Political Liberalism as Alternatives' (2012) 32 *Oxford Journal of Legal Studies* 583
Darwall, SL, 'Two Kinds of Respect' (1977) 88 *Ethics* 36
Dindjer, H, 'The New Legal Anti-Positivism' (2020) 26 *Legal Theory* 181
Donaldson, S and Kymlicka, W, *Zoopolis: A Political Theory of Animal Rights* (Oxford: Oxford University Press, 2011)
Douek, E, 'All Out of Proportion: The Ongoing Disagreement about Structured Proportionality in Australia' (2019) 47 *Federal Law Review* 551
Dreisbach, DL, *Thomas Jefferson and the Wall of Separation between Church and State* (New York: New York University Press, 2002)

Du Plessis, GA and Portaru, A, 'Restrictions to Religious Worship during COVID-19: A Bird's-Eye View of Court Decisions from Selected European Countries and the European Court of Human Rights' (2022) 64 *Journal of Church and State* 641
Dworkin, R, *Law's Empire* (Cambridge, MA: Harvard University Press, 1986)
—— *Justice for Hedgehogs* (Cambridge, MA: Harvard University Press, 2013)
—— *Taking Rights Seriously* (London: Bloomsbury, 2013)
Edmundson, WA, *John Rawls: Reticent Socialist* (Cambridge: Cambridge University Press, 2017)
Eidelson, B, *Discrimination and Disrespect* (Oxford: Oxford University Press, 2015)
Eisgruber, CL and Sager, LG, *Religious Freedom and the Constitution* (Cambridge, MA: Harvard University Press, 2010)
Endicott, T, 'Proportionality and Incommensurability' in G Huscroft, BW Miller and G Webber (eds), *Proportionality and the Rule of Law: Rights, Justification, Reasoning* (Cambridge: Cambridge University Press, 2014)
Evans, C, *Freedom of Religion under the European Convention on Human Rights* (Oxford: Oxford University Press, 2001)
Fallon, Jr RH, 'Strict Judicial Scrutiny' (2007) 54 *UCLA Law Review* 1267
Fasel, RN, 'The Old "New" Dignitarianism' (2019) 25 *Res Publica* 531
—— *More Equal Than Others: Humans and the Rights of Other Animals* (Oxford: Oxford University Press, 2024)
Federalist Society, 'Address by Justice Samuel Alito [2020 National Lawyers Convention]' https://www.youtube.com/watch?v=VMnukCVIZWQ
Feldman, D, 'Secrecy, Dignity, or Autonomy? Views of Privacy as a Civil Liberty' (1994) 47 *Current Legal Problems* 41
—— 'Public Law and Freedom of Religion: General Conclusions' (2005) 17 *European Review of Public Law* 735
—— 'Rights to Life, Physical and Moral Integrity, Freedom of Lifestyle and Religion or Belief' in D Feldman (ed), *English Public Law*, 2nd edn (Oxford: Oxford University Press, 2009)
Ferejohn, J and Pasquino, P, 'The Law of the Exception: A Typology of Emergency Powers' (2004) 2 *International Journal of Constitutional Law* 210
Finnis, JM, 'Does Free Exercise of Religion Deserve Constitutional Mention?' (2009) 54 *American Journal of Jurisprudence* 41
Floris, G, 'Contingency, Arbitrariness, and the Basis of Moral Equality' (2023) 36 *Ratio* 224
Fone, B, *Homophobia: A History* (New York: Henry Holt, 2000)
Fornerod, A, 'Freedom of Worship during a Public Health State of Emergency in France' (2021) 10 *Laws* 15
Forrester, K, *In the Shadow of Justice: Postwar Liberalism and the Remaking of Political Philosophy* (Princeton, NJ: Princeton University Press, 2019)
Fredman, S, 'Tolerating the Intolerant: Religious Freedom, Complicity, and the Right to Equality' (2020) 9 *Oxford Journal of Law and Religion* 305
Freeman III, GC, 'The Misguided Search for the Constitutional Definition of "Religion"' (1983) 71 *Georgetown Law Review* 1519
Freeman, S, *Rawls* (Abingdon: Routledge, 2007)
Galloway, RW, 'Means-Ends Scrutiny in American Constitutional Law' (1988) 21 *Loyola of Los Angeles Law Review* 449
García Oliva, J and Hall, H, 'Same-Sex Marriage: An Inevitable Challenge to Religious Liberty and Establishment?' (2014) 3 *Oxford Journal of Law and Religion* 25
—— *Religion, Law and the Constitution: Balancing Beliefs in Britain* (Abingdon: Routledge, 2017)
—— *Constitutional Culture, Independence, and Rights: Insights from Quebec, Scotland, and Catalonia* (Toronto: University of Toronto Press, 2023)
Gardner, J, 'On the Ground of Her Sex(uality)' (1998) 18 *Oxford Journal of Legal Studies* 167
Girgis, GM, 'What Is a "Substantial Burden" on Religion Under RFRA and the First Amendment?' (2020) 97 *Washington University Law Review* 1755

Gowder, P, 'Why Majority Religions Should Not Be Accommodated' (2023) 108 *Iowa Law Review* 2153
Greenawalt, K, *Religion and the Constitution: Free Exercise and Fairness* (Princeton, NJ: Princeton University Press, 2006)
Greene, A, *Emergency Powers in a Time of Pandemic* (Bristol: Bristol University Press, 2020)
—— 'Closing Places of Worship and COVID-19: Towards a Culture of Justification?' (2021) 25 *Edinburgh Law Review* 393
Greene, AS, 'Barnette and Masterpiece Cakeshop: Some Unanswered Questions' (2019) 13 *FIU Law Review* 667
Greene, JK, *How Rights Went Wrong: Why Our Obsession with Rights Is Tearing America Apart* (Boston, MA: Houghton Mifflin Harcourt 2021)
Gross, O and Aoláin, FN, *Law in Times of Crisis: Emergency Powers in Theory and Practice* (Cambridge: Cambridge University Press, 2006)
Gunn, TJ, 'Religious Freedom and Laïcité: A Comparison of the United States and France' (2004) *Brigham Young University Law Review* 419
Gur-Arye, M and Shakargy, S, 'Solidarity, Religious Freedom and COVID-19: The Case of the Ultra-Orthodox Sects in Israel' (2021) 50 *Netherlands Journal of Legal Philosophy* 203
Habermas, J, 'Religious Tolerance – The Pacemaker for Cultural Rights' (2004) 79 *Philosophy* 5
Hambler, A, 'Cake, Compelled Speech, and a Modest Step Forward for Religious Liberty: The Supreme Court Decision in *Lee v Ashers*' (2018) 181 *Law & Justice* 156
Hamilton, MA, 'Federalism and the Public Good: The True Story behind the Religious Land Use and Institutionalized Persons Act' (2003) 78 *Indiana Law Journal* 311
Hart, HLA, 'Rawls on Liberty and Its Priority' (1973) 40 *University of Chicago Law Review* 534
—— *The Concept of Law*, 3rd edn (Oxford: Oxford University Press, 2012)
Hart, J, 'When the First Amendment Compels an Offensive Result: *Masterpiece Cakeshop, Ltd v Colorado Civil Rights Commission*' (2018) 79 *Louisiana Law Review* 419
Hellman, D, *When Is Discrimination Wrong?* (Cambridge, MA: Harvard University Press, 2008)
Herring, J and Wall, J, 'The Nature and Significance of the Right to Bodily Integrity' (2017) 76 *Cambridge Law Journal* 566
Hill, DJ, 'Is Sexual-Orientation Discrimination a Form of Sex Discrimination?' (2020) 41 *Liverpool Law Review* 357
Hirschl, R, *Comparative Matters: The Renaissance of Comparative Constitutional Law* (Oxford: Oxford University Press, 2014)
Ho, EML, 'Marking the Internal and External Limits of Discrimination Law in *Lee v Ashers Baking Company*' (2021) 6 *Cambridge Law Review* 203
Hobbes, T, *Leviathan or The Matter, Forme and Power of a Commonwealth Ecclesiasticall and Civil* (1651)
Hohfeld, WN, 'Some Fundamental Legal Conceptions as Applied in Judicial Reasoning' (1913) 23 *Yale Law Journal* 16
—— 'Fundamental Legal Conceptions as Applied in Judicial Reasoning' (1917) 26 *Yale Law Journal* 710
Hughes, K, 'A Behavioural Understanding of Privacy and Its Implications for Privacy Law' (2012) 75 *Modern Law Review* 806
—— 'The Public Figure Doctrine and the Right to Privacy' (2019) 78 *Cambridge Law Journal* 70
Hunter-Henin, M, 'Why the French Don't Like the Burqa: Laïcité, National Identity and Religious Freedom' (2012) 61 *International and Comparative Law Quarterly* 613
—— *Why Religious Freedom Matters for Democracy: Comparative Reflections from Britain and France for a Democratic 'Vivre Ensemble'* (Oxford: Hart Publishing, 2020)
Huscroft, G, Miller, BW and Webber, G, 'Introduction' in G Huscroft, BW Miller and G Webber (eds), *Proportionality and the Rule of Law: Rights, Justification, Reasoning* (Cambridge: Cambridge University Press, 2014)

Husi, S, 'Why We (Almost Certainly) Are Not Moral Equals' (2017) 21 *Journal of Ethics* 375
Inazu, J, 'COVID-19, Churches, and Culture Wars' (2022) 18 *University of St Thomas Law Journal* 307
Jackson, VC, 'Comparative Constitutional Law: Methodologies' in M Rosenfeld and A Sajó (eds), *Oxford Handbook of Comparative Constitutional Law* (Oxford: Oxford University Press, 2012)
Järvinen, P, and Vikman, V, '*Pasquinelli and Others v San Marino* – The Momentous Competing Interests of the Community as a Whole against Healthcare Workers Refusing the Covid-19 Vaccine' (*Strasbourg Observers*, 4 October 2024) https://strasbourgobservers.com/2024/10/04/pasquinelli-and-others-v-san-marino-the-momentous-competing-interests-of-the-community-as-a-whole-against-healthcare-workers-refusing-the-covid-19-vaccine/
Jones, P, 'Conscientious Claims, Ill-Founded Belief and Religious Exemption' in J Adenitire (ed), *Religious Beliefs and Conscientious Exemptions in a Liberal State* (Oxford: Hart Publishing, 2019)
Kavanagh, A, 'What's So Weak about "Weak-Form Review"? The Case of the UK Human Rights Act 1998' (2015) 13 *International Journal of Constitutional Law* 1008
Kenny, D, 'Examining Constitutional Culture: Assisted Suicide in Ireland and Canada' (2022) 17 *Journal of Comparative Law* 85
Kenyon, C, 'Flattening-the-Curve Associated with Reduced Covid-19 Case Fatality Rates – An Ecological Analysis of 65 Countries' (2020) 81 *Journal of Infection* E89
Khaitan, T and Norton, JC, 'The Right to Freedom of Religion and the Right against Religious Discrimination: Theoretical Distinctions' (2019) 17 *International Journal of Constitutional Law* 1125
King, J, Ferraz, OLM and Jones, A, 'Mandatory COVID-19 Vaccination and Human Rights' (2022) 399 *Lancet* 220
King, J and Ferraz, OLM (eds), *Comparing Covid Laws: A Critical Global Survey* (Oxford: Oxford University Press, 2026)
Koppelman, A, 'A Rawlsian Defence of Special Treatment for Religion' in C Laborde and A Bardon (eds), *Religion in Liberal Political Philosophy* (Oxford: Oxford University Press, 2017)
—— *Gay Rights vs Religious Liberty? The Unnecessary Conflict* (Oxford: Oxford University Press, 2020)
—— 'The Increasingly Dangerous Variants of the "Most-Favored-Nation" Theory of Religious Liberty' (2023) 108 *Iowa Law Review* 2237
Kramer, MH, 'Getting Rights Right' in MH Kramer (ed), *Rights, Wrongs and Responsibilities* (London: Palgrave Macmillan, 2001)
—— *In Defense of Legal Positivism: Law without Trimmings* (Oxford: Oxford University Press, 2003)
—— 'Rights in Legal and Political Philosophy' in GA Caldeira, RD Kelemen and KE Whittington (eds), *The Oxford Handbook of Law and Politics* (Oxford: Oxford University Press, 2008)
—— 'Michael Moore on Torture, Morality, and Law' (2012) 25 *Ratio Juris* 472
—— *Torture and Moral Integrity: A Philosophical Enquiry* (Oxford: Oxford University Press, 2014)
—— *Liberalism with Excellence* (Oxford: Oxford University Press, 2017)
—— 'Looking Back and Looking Ahead: Replies to the Contributors' in M McBride and VAJ Kurki (eds), *Without Trimmings: The Legal, Moral, and Political Philosophy of Matthew Kramer* (Oxford: Oxford University Press, 2022)
Kramer, MH, Simmonds, N and Steiner, H, *A Debate over Rights: Philosophical Enquiries* (Oxford: Oxford University Press, 2000)
Laborde, C, 'Political Liberalism and Religion: On Separation and Establishment' (2013) 21 *Journal of Political Philosophy* 67
—— *Liberalism's Religion* (Cambridge, MA: Harvard University Press, 2017)
Laycock, D, 'The Religious Freedom Restoration Act' (1993) *Brigham Young University Law Review* 221
—— 'Church Autonomy Revisited' (2009) 7 *Georgetown Journal of Law & Public Policy* 253
—— 'The Broader Implications of *Masterpiece Cakeshop*' (2019) *Brigham Young University Law Review* 167
—— 'The Remnants of Free Exercise' [1990] *Supreme Court Review* 1

Laycock, D and Berg, TC, 'Protecting Free Exercise under *Smith* and after *Smith*' [2021] *Cato Supreme Court Review* 33
Lee, WE, 'The Conscience of Corporations and the Right Not to Speak' (2019) 43 *Harvard Journal of Law & Public Policy* 155
Leigh, I, 'The Courts and Conscience Claims' in J Adenitire (ed), *Religious Beliefs and Conscientious Exemptions in a Liberal State* (Oxford: Hart Publishing, 2019)
—— '*Lee v Ashers Baking Company*: Crumbs of Comfort in the Culture War' in R Barker, PT Babie and N Foster (eds), *Law and Religion in the Commonwealth: The Evolution of Case Law* (Oxford: Hart Publishing, 2022)
Leigh, I and Hambler, A, 'Religious Symbols, Conscience, and the Rights of Others' (2014) 3 *Oxford Journal of Law and Religion* 2
Leiter, B, *Why Tolerate Religion?* (Princeton, NJ: Princeton University Press, 2012)
—— 'Constitutional Law, Moral Judgment, and the Supreme Court as Super-Legislature' (2015) 66 *Hastings Law Journal* 1601
Leupp, GP, *Male Colors: The Construction of Homosexuality in Tokugawa Japan* (Berkeley, CA: University of California Press, 1997)
Levine, SJ, 'The Supreme Court's Hands-Off Approach to Religious Questions in the Era of Covid-19 and Beyond' (2022) 24 *Journal of Constitutional Law* 276
Lindblom, L, 'In Defense of Rawlsian Fair Equality of Opportunity' (2018) 47 *Philosophical Papers* 235
Linton, PB, 'Religious Freedom Claims and Defenses under State Constitutions' (2013) 7 *University of St Thomas Journal of Law and Public Policy* 103
Lippert-Rasmussen, K, *Born Free and Equal? A Philosophical Inquiry Into the Nature of Discrimination* (Oxford: Oxford University Press, 2014)
—— *Making Sense of Affirmative Action* (Oxford: Oxford University Press, 2020)
Locke, J, *First Letter Concerning Toleration* (William Popple tr, 1689)
Lund, CC, 'Answers to *Fulton's* Questions' (2023) 108 *Iowa Law Review* 2075
Macklem, T, 'Faith as a Secular Value' (2000) 45 *McGill Law Journal* 1
Maclure, J and Taylor, C, *Secularism and Freedom of Conscience* (Jane Marie Todd tr, Cambridge, MA: Harvard University Press, 2011)
Marcosson, SA, '*Masterpiece Cakeshop* and Tolerance as a Constitutional Mandate: Strategic Compromise in the Enactment of Civil Rights Laws' (2020) 15 *Duke Journal of Constitutional Law & Public Policy* 139
McConnell, MW, 'Free Exercise Revisionism and the *Smith* Decision' (1990) 57 *University of Chicago Law Review* 1109
McCrudden, C, 'In Pursuit of Human Dignity: An Introduction to Current Debates' in C McCrudden (ed), *Understanding Human Dignity* (Oxford: Oxford University Press, 2013)
—— *Litigating Religions: An Essay on Human Rights, Courts, and Beliefs* (Oxford: Oxford University Press, 2018)
—— 'The *Gay Cake* Case: What the Supreme Court Did, and Didn't, Decide in *Ashers*' (2020) 9 *Oxford Journal of Law and Religion* 238
McGowan, J, 'Public Health, Proportionality, and the "Freedom of Halie Kirk": On *Philip v Scottish Ministers*' [2022] *Public Law* 545
McNally, MD, *Defend the Sacred: Native American Religious Freedom beyond the First Amendment* (Princeton, NJ: Princeton University Press, 2020)
Michaels, R, 'The Functional Method of Comparative Law' in M Reimann and R Zimmerman (eds), *Oxford Handbook of Comparative Law*, 2nd edn (Oxford: Oxford University Press, 2019)
Miklosi, Z, 'The Problem of Equal Moral Status' (2022) 21 *Politics, Philosophy & Economics* 372
Mikoski, C, 'Churches and COVID-19: Key Trends in Congregational Life since the Pandemic' (2025) 16 *Religions* 759
Mill, JS, *On Liberty*, 4th edn (London: Longmans, Green, Reader and Dyer, 1869)
Miller, D, *Principles of Social Justice* (Cambridge, MA: Harvard University Press, 2001)
—— 'What's Wrong with Religious Establishment?' (2021) 15 *Criminal Law and Philosophy* 75

Minow, M, 'Tolerance in an Age of Terror' (2007) 16 *Southern California Interdisciplinary Law Journal* 453
Moon, R, 'Conscience in the Image of Religion' in J Adenitire (ed), *Religious Beliefs and Conscientious Exemptions in a Liberal State* (Oxford: Hart Publishing, 2019)
Moore, MS, *Placing Blame: A General Theory of the Criminal Law* (Oxford: Clarendon, 1997)
—— 'Patrolling the Borders of Consequentialist Justifications: The Scope of Agent-Relative Restrictions' (2008) 27 *Law and Philosophy* 35
Moore, VL and Graham, LD, '*R (Gardner and Harris) v Secretary of State for Health and Social Care and Others* [2022] EWHC 967: Scant Regard for Covid-19 Risk to Care Homes' (2022) 30 *Medical Law Review* 734
Movsesian, ML, '*Masterpiece Cakeshop* and the Future of Religious Freedom' (2019) 42 *Harvard Journal of Law & Public Policy* 711
—— 'Law, Religion, and the COVID-19 Crisis' (2022) 37 *Journal of Law and Religion* 9
Nagel, T, *Equality and Partiality* (Oxford: Oxford University Press, 1991)
National Inquiry into the Separation of Aboriginal and Torres Strait Islander Children from Their Families, *Bringing Them Home* (Commonwealth of Australia, 1997)
Nehushtan, Y, *Intolerant Religion in a Tolerant-Liberal Democracy* (Oxford: Hart Publishing, 2015)
—— 'Review of Adenitire, John, *A General Right to Conscientious Exemption: Beyond Religious Privilege*' (2022) 84 *Modern Law Review* 1097
NeJaime, D and Siegel, RB, 'Conscience Wars: Complicity-Based Conscience Claims in Religion and Politics' (2015) 124 *Yale Law Journal* 2516
—— 'Conscience Wars in Transnational Perspective: Religious Liberty, Third-Party Harm, and Pluralism' in S Mancini and M Rosenfeld (eds), *The Conscience Wars: Rethinking the Balance between Religion, Identity, and Equality* (Cambridge: Cambridge University Press, 2018)
—— 'Religious Exemptions and Antidiscrimination Law in *Masterpiece Cakeshop*' (2018) 128 *Yale Law Journal Forum* 201
Neo, JL, 'Definitional Imbroglios: A Critique of the Definition of Religion and Essential Practice Tests in Religious Freedom Adjudication' (2018) 16 *International Journal of Constitutional Law* 574
Nickel, JW, 'Who Needs Freedom of Religion?' (2005) 76 *University of Colorado Law Review* 941
Norrie, KM, '*Lee v Ashers Baking Co Ltd*' (2019) 1 *Juridical Review* 88
Norton, JC, *The Freedom of Religious Organizations* (Oxford: Oxford University Press, 2016)
Nussbaum, MC, 'Capabilities and Human Rights' (1998) 66 *Fordham Law Review* 273
—— *Women and Human Development: The Capabilities Approach* (Cambridge: Cambridge University Press, 2000)
—— *Liberty of Conscience: In Defense of America's Tradition of Religious Equality* (New York: Basic Books, 2008)
—— *Justice for Animals: Our Collective Responsibility* (New York: Simon & Schuster, 2023)
Okumura, T, et al, 'Report on 640 Victims of the Tokyo Subway Sarin Attack' (1996) 28 *Annals of Emergency Medicine* 129
Oleske, Jr JM, 'Free Exercise (Dis)Honesty' [2019] *Wisconsin Law Review* 689
Parr, T and Slavny, A, 'Rescuing Basic Equality' (2019) 100 *Pacific Philosophical Quarterly* 837
Patosalmi, M, 'Bodily Integrity and Conceptions of Subjectivity' (2009) 24 *Hypatia* 125
Patten, A, *Equal Recognition: The Moral Foundations of Minority Rights* (Princeton, NJ: Princeton University Press, 2014)
—— 'Religious Exemptions and Fairness' in C Laborde and A Bardon (eds), *Religion in Liberal Political Philosophy* (Oxford: Oxford University Press, 2017)
Pearson, M, *Proportionality, Equality Laws, and Religion: Conflicts in England, Canada, and the USA* (Abingdon: Routledge, 2019)
Peffer, RG, 'Towards a More Adequate Rawlsian Theory of Social Justice' (2017) 75 *Pacific Philosophical Quarterly* 251
Petri, DP and Flores, T, 'The Impact of COVID-19 on Religious Regulation in Colombia, Cuba, Mexico, and Nicaragua' (2023) 16 *International Journal for Religious Freedom* 31

Phuong, NT, 'Religion, Law, State, and Covid-19 in Vietnam' (2020) 8 *Journal of Law, Religion and State* 284
Pill, SC, 'The False Promise of Expanded Religious Liberty Rights after the COVID-19 Cases and Fulton v City of Philadelphia' (2023) 31 *William & Mary Bill of Rights Journal* 825
Piwko, AM, 'Islam and the COVID-19 Pandemic: Between Religious Practice and Health Protection' (2021) 60 *Journal of Religion and Health* 3291
Pogge, T, *Realizing Rawls* (Ithaca, NY: Cornell University Press, 1989)
Posner, RA, *Not a Suicide Pact: The Constitution in a Time of National Emergency* (Oxford: Oxford University Press, 2006)
Poston, T, 'Religious Conscience and the Private Market' in K Vallier and M Weber (eds), *Religious Exemptions* (Oxford: Oxford University Press, 2018)
Pratiwi, CS, 'Indonesia's Legal Policies amid Covid-19' (2022) 6 *Journal of Southeast Asian Human Rights* 182
Rawls, J, *A Theory of Justice* (Cambridge, MA: Harvard University Press, 1971)
—— *A Theory of Justice (Revised Edition)* (Cambridge, MA: Harvard University Press, 1999)
—— *Justice as Fairness: A Restatement* (E Kelly ed, Cambridge, MA: Harvard University Press, 2001)
—— *The Law of Peoples* (Cambridge, MA: Harvard University Press, 2001)
—— *Political Liberalism* (New York: Columbia University Press, 2005)
Raz, J, *The Morality of Freedom* (Oxford: Oxford University Press, 1986)
Raza, F, 'Limitations to the Right to Religious Freedom: Rethinking Key Approaches' (2020) 9 *Oxford Journal of Law and Religion* 435
Reiss, DR and Thomas, M, 'More Than a Mask: Stay-at-Home Orders and Religious Freedom' (2020) 57 *San Diego Law Review* 947
Reyes, R, '*Masterpiece Cakeshop* and *Ashers Baking Company*: A Comparative Analysis of Constitutional Confections' (2020) 16 *Stanford Journal of Civil Rights & Civil Liberties* 113
Rodrigo Lara, B, 'Two Years Later: A Critical Analysis of the Impact of Spanish Law about COVID-19 on Religious Freedom' (2022) 64 *Journal of Church and State* 683
Rorty, R, 'Human Rights, Rationality, and Sentimentality' (1998) 318 *Headline Series* 116
Rothschild, Z, 'Free Exercise's Lingering Ambiguity' (2020) 11 *California Law Review Online* 282
—— 'Free Exercise Partisanship' (2022) 107 *Cornell Law Review* 1067
—— 'Individualized Exemptions, Vaccine Mandates, and the New Free Exercise Clause' (2022) 131 *Yale Law Journal Forum* 1106
Russo, CJ, 'Point: The Supreme Court Gets It Right in *303 Creative v Elenis*: People of Faith Cannot Be Compelled to Create Expressive Messages Violating Their Religious Beliefs' (2024) 49 *University of Dayton Law Review* 1
Sager, LG and Tebbe, N, 'The Reality Principle' [2019] *Constitutional Commentary* 171
Sandel, M, 'Religious Liberty – Freedom of Conscience or Freedom of Choice?' [1989] *Utah Law Review* 597
Saunders, BB, and Meagher, D, 'Taking Seriously the Free Exercise of Religion under the Australian Constitution' (2021) 43 *Sydney Law Review* 287
Segall, E, *Supreme Myths: Why the Supreme Court Is Not a Court and Its Justices Are Not Judges* (Westport, CT: Praeger, 2012)
Shah, T, Farr, T and Friedman, J (eds), *Religious Freedom and Gay Rights: Emerging Conflicts in the United States and Europe* (Oxford: Oxford University Press, 2016)
Shelby, T, 'Race and Ethnicity, Race and Social Justice: Rawlsian Considerations' (2004) 72 *Fordham Law Review* 1697
Shemudara, OT and Ayeni, VO, 'Law and Religion: The Challenges of Citizens as a Result of Covid-19 Pandemic in Nigeria' (2021) 3 *International Review of Law and Jurisprudence* 166
Sher, G, *Equality for Inegalitarians* (Cambridge: Cambridge University Press, 2014)
Shiffrin, SV, 'Race and Ethnicity, Race, Labor, and the Fair Equality of Opportunity Principle' (2004) 72 *Fordham Law Review* 1643
Shue, H, *Basic Rights: Subsistence, Affluence, and US Foreign Policy: 40th Anniversary Edition* (Princeton, NJ: Princeton University Press, 2020)

Singer, P, *Animal Liberation*, revsd edn (London: Bodley Head, 2015)
—— *Animal Liberation Now* (London: Bodley Head, 2023)
Sirota, L and Baldwin, G, 'Can States Throw Away the Key? Critiquing Human Rights Law Approaches to Whole Life Sentences' [2026] 3 *European Human Rights Law Review* 340
Skoczylas, Ł, 'Restrictions on Religious Practices in Selected European Countries during the COVID-19 Pandemic: A Legal-Sociological Study from Poland's Experiences' (2023) 7 *Society Register* 35
Smilansky, S, 'Should We Sacrifice the Utilitarians First?' (2020) 70 *Philosophical Quarterly* 281
Smith, SD, 'The Rise and Fall of Religious Freedom in Constitutional Discourse' (1991) 140 *University of Pennsylvania Law Review* 149
Snow, DA and Byrd, SC, 'Ideology, Framing Processes, and Islamic Terrorist Movements' (2007) 12 *Mobilization: An International Quarterly Review* 119
Steinhoff, U, *Do All Persons Have Equal Moral Worth? On 'Basic Equality' and Equal Respect and Concern* (Oxford: Oxford University Press, 2014)
Stokel-Walker, C, 'What Do We Know about Covid Vaccines and Preventing Transmission?' (2022) 376 *British Medical Journal* o298
Strasser, M, 'COVID-19, Free Exercise, and Most Favored Nation Status' (2023) 27 *Lewis & Clark Law Review* 1
Stucki, S, 'Towards a Theory of Legal Animal Rights: Simple and Fundamental Rights' (2020) 40 *Oxford Journal of Legal Studies* 533
Su, A, 'Judging Religious Sincerity' (2016) 5 *Oxford Journal of Law and Religion* 28
Sugiyama, A et al, 'The Tokyo Subway Sarin Attack Has Long-Term Effects on Survivors: A 10-Year Study Started 5 Years after the Terrorist Incident' (2020) 15 *PLoS ONE* e0234967
Sun, JC, 'Counterpoint to: "The Supreme Court Gets It Right in *303 Creative v Elenis*: People of Faith Cannot Be Compelled to Create Expressive Messages Violating Their Religious Beliefs" – The Privilege to Silence "Customized" Speech: The Website Kerfuffle in *303 Creative v Elenis*' (2024) 49 *University of Dayton Law Review* 14
Sunstein, CR, 'Our Anti-*Korematsu*' (2021) 1 *American Journal of Law and Equality* 221
Tasioulas, J, 'Human Rights, Universality, and the Values of Personhood: Retracting Griffin's Steps' (2002) 10 *European Journal of Philosophy* 79
Taylor, PM, *Freedom of Religion: UN and European Human Rights Law and Practice* (Cambridge: Cambridge University Press, 2005)
Tebbe, N, *Religious Freedom in an Egalitarian Age* (Cambridge, MA: Harvard University Press, 2017)
Tengatenga, J, Duley, SMT and Tengatenga, CJ, '*Zimitsani Moto*: Understanding the Malawi COVID-19 Response' (2021) 10 *Laws* 20
Tomasi, J, *Free Market Fairness* (Princeton, NJ: Princeton University Press, 2012)
Trispiotis, I, 'Religious Freedom and Religious Antidiscrimination' (2019) 82 *Modern Law Review* 864
Tsakyrakis, S, 'Proportionality: An Assault on Human Rights?' (2009) 7 *International Journal of Constitutional Law* 468
Tushnet, M, 'Some Reflections on Method in Comparative Constitutional Law' in S Choudhry (ed), *The Migration of Constitutional Ideas* (Cambridge: Cambridge University Press, 2007)
—— 'The Political Constitutional of Emergency Powers: Parliamentary and Separation-of-Powers Regulation' (2007) 3 *International Journal of Law in Context* 275
Urbina, FJ, 'Incommensurability and Balancing' (2015) 35 *Oxford Journal of Legal Studies* 575
Van Wees, N, 'Judicial Review of Legislators' Motives' (2017) 45 *Federal Law Review* 681
Vermeule, A, *Common Good Constitutionalism* (Cambridge: Polity Press, 2022)
Vickers, L, *Religious Freedom, Religious Discrimination and the Workplace*, 2nd edn (Oxford, Hart Publishing, 2016)
Vinx, L, *Hans Kelsen's Pure Theory of Law: Legality and Legitimacy* (Oxford: Oxford University Press, 2007)
Von Platz, J, 'Are Economic Liberties Basic Rights?' (2013) 13 *Politics, Philosophy & Economics* 23
Waldron, J, 'Indirect Discrimination' in S Guest and A Milne (eds), *Equality and Discrimination: Essays in Freedom and Justice* (Stuttgart: F Steiner, 1985)

—— 'The Core of the Case against Judicial Review' (2006) 115 *Yale Law Journal* 1346
—— *The Harm in Hate Speech* (Cambridge, MA: Harvard University Press, 2012)
Wang, EH, 'To Prohibit Free Exercise: A Proposal for Judging Substantial Burdens on Religion' (2023) 72 *Emory Law Journal* 723
Weinrib, J, *Dimensions of Dignity: The Theory and Practice of Modern Constitutional Law* (Cambridge: Cambridge University Press, 2016)
Whittington, KE, *Political Foundations of Judicial Supremacy: The Presidency, the Supreme Court, and Constitutional Leadership in US History* (Princeton, NJ: Princeton University Press, 2009)
Wintemute, R, 'Accommodating Religious Beliefs: Harm, Clothing or Symbols, and Refusals to Serve Others' (2014) 77 *Modern Law Review* 223
Young, AL, *Parliamentary Sovereignty and the Human Rights Act* (Oxford: Oxford University Press, 2009)
—— *Democratic Dialogue and the Constitution* (Oxford: Oxford University Press, 2017)
Zuolo, F, 'Misadventures of Sentience: Animals and the Basis of Equality' (2019) 9 *Animals* 1044

INDEX

Adenitire, John, 7, 11, 21–22, 24, 46, 49–50, 131, 153–54
animal sacrifice, 61–62, 77–78, 83
animals:
  moral personality, 39–40
  prevention of cruelty to animals, 77–78
Australia, 44–45
  neutrality as right of free exercise, 71, 73, 78–79, 80–81, 84, 85
autonomy-based justifications, 18–20, 25, 32, 130

balancing rights and freedoms, 3, 163–64
  compatibility with basic liberties of others, 54–62
  corporal punishment at school
    right to equality and right to dignity, 165–67
  freedom of speech, 58–59
  human dignity, 60–61
  necessity in the common interest, 67–70
  privacy, 58
  rights of animals, 61–62
  socio-economic rights, 58
balancing of incommensurables, 68–70, 116, 169–70
  see also balancing rights and freedoms; proportionality
burden on holding or manifestation of conscientious belief, 51–54

Canada
  neutrality, 71–73
  capacity, 161–62
  capacity for a conception of the good, 3, 25, 28–30, 32, 35–36, 41–42, 90–91, 129–30, 143–44, 148, 161
  capacity for a sense of justice, 3, 25, 28, 29, 30, 37–40, 61, 161
  integrity of the person, 93
choice, 18–20, 32–36, 41–43, 47–48, 56, 130
Civil Rights Act 1964 (USA), 8
common law, 12
  bodily integrity, 100–1
  state protection of citizens from physical harm, 89
compatibility with basic liberties of others, 54–58, 93, 161–62
  coronavirus and lockdown restrictions
    ECHR, 101–6, 110
    UK, 101, 103–4, 105, 108–10
    US, 100–1, 108–10
  freedom of speech, 58–59
  human dignity, 60–61
  privacy, 58
  non-discrimination and same-sex couples, 131–32
    UK, 146–47, 149–51, 152
    US, 142–46, 147–49, 151–52
  rights of animals, 61–62
  socio-economic rights, 58
comprehensive doctrines, 7, 25, 26, 32, 143–44
conscientious belief, 4, 6–7, 20–25
  choice, 35–36, 41–43
  intolerance, 45–47
  manifestations of conscientious belief, 43–45
    non-negligible burden, 51–54
consent:
  capacity, 92–93
  integrity of the person, 92–93
constitutional and human rights protections, 2
  state protection of citizens from physical harm, 89
coronavirus, 2, 3, 87–89, 119–20, 162–63
  compatibility with basic liberties of others, 54–58, 93
    ECHR, 101–6, 110
    UK, 101, 103–4, 105, 108–10
    US, 100–1, 108–10
  ECHR
    right to life (Art. 2) and limitations to Art. 9, 101–6, 110
  necessity in the common interest, 111, 167
    neutrality and general applicability test (US), 111–13, 114–18
    proportionality test (UK), 113–14, 116–17, 118–19
  UK
    case law, 97–100, 103–6
    proportionality test, 113–14, 116–17, 118–19
    rights of others, relevance of, 101–10
  US
    case law, 94–97, 100–1, 120
    neutrality and general applicability test, 111–13, 114–18
    rights of others, irrelevance of, 100–1
  see also lockdown restrictions

Darwall, Steven L, 1
  recognition respect, 47, 161
    appraisal respect distinguished, 31, 33–34
due process, 10
Dworkin, Ronald, 13–14, 59, 67, 127–28

Equality Act (Sexual Orientation) Regulations (Northern Ireland) 2006, 141
Equality Act (Sexual Orientation) Regulations 2007, 146–47
Equality Act 2010 (UK), 8, 41, 52–53, 139–40
European Convention on Human Rights (ECHR):
  coronavirus and lockdown restrictions
    compatibility with basic liberties of others, 101–6, 110
    right to life (Art. 2) and limitations to Art. 9, 101–6, 110
  freedom of thought, belief and religion (Art.9), 9–10
    absolute nature of *forum internum*, 9
    qualified nature of *forum externum, 9*
  necessity in the common interests, 158–59
  non-discrimination and same-sex couples, 158–59
  right to life (Art. 2)
    coronavirus and limitations to Art. 9, 101–6, 110
  secular beliefs, 11, 25
exemptions, 3, 45–46, 84–85, 138–39, 151, 154

fair equality of opportunity, 27, 30, 123–24, 162
Feldman, David, 19–20, 34–35
First Amendment (US Constitution), 5–6, 8, 120, 138, 143, 151–52, 158, 162–63
  Establishment Clause, 10
  Free Exercise Clause, 10, 13, 43, 61–62, 76, 94, 138, 143, 168
  Free Speech Clause, 138, 159
  neutrality test, 79
forum internum (internal belief) and *forum externum* (manifestations of belief) distinguished, 9, 43–45, 52–53
Fourteenth Amendment (US Constitution), 151
  Due Process Clause, 10
freedom of speech, 5–6, 27, 30, 58–59, 138, 159

harm to others, 54, 165
  direct and indirect harm, 49–50, 66
Hobbes, Thomas, 89
Hohfeld, Wesley Newcomb, 5–6
human dignity, 60–61, 150
Human Rights Act 1998 (UK), 6, 8, 9, 13
  non-discrimination, 142, 158–59

integrity of the person, 27, 30, 58–60, 88–89, 89–94
  bodily integrity and physical inviolability, 92
  capacity, 93
  case law, 94–97
  compatibility with basic liberties of others, 100–1, 106, 109–10
  consent, 92–93
  harmfulness of interference, 91–94
  intention by others, relationship with, 93–94
  justification of integrity, 92
  potential limitations for compatibility and necessity, 93
  recognition respect for moral personality, 90–91
intention by others:
  integrity of the person, relationship with, 93–94
internal belief (*forum internum*) and manifestations of belief (*forum externum*) distinguished, 9, 43–45, 52–53
intolerance, 45–47, 123

Japan
  Aum Shinrikyo religious group, 82–83
  religious establishment, 75–76
Jefferson, Thomas, 1, 74
justifications for liberty of conscience, 17–18, 25–26, 161
  autonomy-based justifications, 18–20
  enabling pluralism and minimising marginalisation, 22–23
  group/collective rights, 22–24
  individual rights, 17–22
  limitations, 22
  non-interference/state neutrality justifications, 21–22
  religious and non-religious beliefs distinguished, 23–24
  toleration-based justifications, 20–21

laïcité, 74
  see also non-establishment
legal immunity, 5
  liberty of conscience in law as Hohfeldian immunity, 5–6
legal power, 5
legal privileges, 5
legal rights, 5, 126–27
liberty of conscience and non-discrimination distinguished, 7–8
liberty principle, 4, 26–27, 54–55, 63, 89, 123
limitations, 161
  balancing rights and freedoms, 3, 22
  compatibility with basic liberties of others, 54–58, 93
    freedom of speech, 58–59
    human dignity, 60–61
    privacy, 58
    rights of animals, 61–62
    socio-economic rights, 58
  ECHR
    right to life (Art. 2) and limitations to Art. 9, 101–6, 110
  justifications for liberty of conscience, 22
  necessity in the common interest, 62–67, 93
    evaluative assessment, 67–70
  potential limitations for compatibility and necessity, 93
  right to life (ECHR Art. 2) and limitations to ECHR Art. 9, 101–6, 110
lockdown restrictions, 2, 3, 162–63
  compatibility with basic liberties of others, 54–58, 93

ECHR, 101–6, 110
UK, 101, 103–4, 105, 108–10
US, 100–1, 108–10
necessity in the common interest, 111
neutrality and general applicability test (US), 111–13, 114–18
proportionality test (UK), 113–14, 116–17, 118–19
strict scrutiny test (US), 115, 116
Locke, John, 18–19, 20–21, 25, 42, 45, 65–66, 75

manifestation of religion or beliefs, 43–45
burden on holding or manifestation of conscientious belief, 51–54
internal belief (*forum internum*) distinguished, 43–45, 52–53
non-negligible burden, 51–54
qualified nature, 9–10
marginalisation:
enabling pluralism and minimising marginalisation, 22–23
means and ends test, 68–70, 103, 116, 119, 167
moral personality, 3, 161
moral power
capacity for a conception of the good, 3, 25, 28–30, 32, 35–36, 41–42, 90–91, 129–30, 143–44, 148, 161
capacity for a sense of justice, 3, 25, 28, 29, 30, 37–40, 61, 161
non-human animals, 39–40
principles of justice
fair equality of opportunity, 27, 30, 123–24, 162
liberty principle, 4, 26–27, 54–55, 63, 89, 123
Rawls, 26–30
'basis of equality' argument, 37–38
capacity concept, 38
recognition respect, 30–37
non-discrimination, 128–32
moral powers:
capacity for a conception of the good, 3, 25, 28–30, 32, 35–36, 41–42, 90–91, 129–30, 143–44, 148, 161
capacity for a sense of justice, 3, 25, 28, 29, 30, 37–40, 61, 161

necessity in the common interest, 62–67, 162
coronavirus and lockdown restrictions, 111, 167
neutrality and general applicability test (US), 111–13, 114–18
proportionality test (UK), 113–14, 116–17, 118–19
strict scrutiny (US), 111, 115–16
evaluative assessment, 67–70
non-discrimination and same-sex couples, 131–32, 152–53, 167
ECHR, 158–59
neutrality and general applicability test (US), 152–53, 154, 155–57, 159
proportionality test (UK), 155
strict scrutiny (US), 154, 159
UK case law, 157, 158–59
US case law, 153–59
neutrality:
lockdown restrictions, 111
neutrality and general applicability test (US), 111–13, 114–18
neutrality explained, 71–72
favour and hinder, 71
neutrality of purpose and effect, 72–73
neutrality of justification and neutrality of effect, 73
non-establishment, 73, 74–76
Smith-Lukumi test (US), 94, 100, 110, 113–15, 116, 119, 122, 154
state neutrality justifications, 21–22
non-discrimination, 123–24, 163
compatibility with other basic liberties, 131–32
UK, 146–47, 149–51, 152
US, 142–46, 147–49, 151–52
denial of service or opportunity, 126–27
direct discrimination, 126
indirect discrimination, 126
liberty of conscience distinguished, 7–8
material harm, 129–30
mental state or 'animus', 132–33
nature of discrimination, 124–26
necessity in the common interest, 131–32, 152–53, 167
ECHR, 158–59
neutrality and general applicability (US), 152–54, 155–57, 159
proportionality test (UK), 155
strict scrutiny test (US), 154, 159
UK law, 157, 158–59
psychological harm, 129, 130–31
social conditions informing what is wrongful discrimination, 133–35
unfairness of discrimination, 126–27
UK case law, 135, 139–42
US case law, 135–39
neutrality and general applicability, 137–39
strict scrutiny, 139
non-establishment, 71, 72, 73, 74–76, 85
non-interference justifications, 21–22
non-negligible burden on conscientious belief, 51–54
Nussbaum, Martha, 1, 7, 21, 23, 33–34, 44, 50, 92

objections to protection of liberty of conscience, 41
conscientious belief as a choice, 41–43
conscientious belief as intolerant, 45–47
internal belief (*forum internum*) versus manifestations of belief (*forum externum*), 43–45

pluralism, 11, 17, 44, 149, 166–67
duty of neutral pluralism, 21–23, 24
enabling pluralism and minimising marginalisation, 22–23

principles of justice (Rawls):
fair equality of opportunity, 27, 30, 123–24, 162
liberty principle, 4, 26–27, 54–55, 63, 89, 123
proportionality, 67–70
lockdown restrictions, 2, 3, 169–70
necessity analysis and proportionality test in UK, 113–14, 116–17, 118–19
non-discrimination and same-sex couples, 155
see also balancing of incommensurables; balancing rights and freedoms
public interest, 1, 22, 49–50, 105–6, 109, 159

qualified nature of liberty of conscience, 3, 9

Rawls, John, 1, 3
basic liberty, liberty of conscience as, 3, 5
comprehensive doctrines, 7, 25, 26, 32
'duty of others' aspect of liberty of conscience, 6
moral personality, 3, 26–30
'basis of equality' argument, 37–38
capacity concept, 38
non-human animals, 39–40
recognition respect, 30–37
moral powers
capacity for a conception of the good, 3, 25, 28–30, 32, 35–36, 41–42, 90–91, 129–30, 143–44, 148, 161
capacity for a sense of justice, 3, 25, 28, 29, 30, 37–40, 61, 161
principles of justice
fair equality of opportunity, 27, 30, 123–24, 162
liberty principle, 4, 26–27, 54–55, 63, 89, 123
recognition respect, 30–37, 47, 161
appraisal respect distinguished, 31, 33–34
moral personality, 30–37
non-discrimination, 128–32
non-discrimination, 128–32
religious and non-religious beliefs distinguished, 6–7, 23–24, 33–34, 45–47, 52–53
Religious Freedom Restoration Act 1993 (USA), 8, 10, 52
Religious Land Use and Institutionalized Persons Act 2000 (USA), 8, 10
respect-based account of liberty of conscience:
recognition respect, 30–37
right to liberty of conscience, 4–5
Hohfeld, 5–6
justifications, *see* justifications for liberty of conscience
legal immunity, 5–6
liberty of conscience and non-discrimination distinguished, 7–8
moral personality, *see* moral personality
nature of conscientious belief, 6–7
non-discrimination, 7–8
objections, 41
conscientious belief as a choice, 41–43
conscientious belief as intolerant, 45–47
internal belief (*forum internum*) versus manifestations of belief (*forum externum*), 43–45
recognition respect, 30–37, 47, 161
appraisal respect distinguished, 31, 33–34
moral personality, 30–37, 128–32
non-discrimination, 128–32
threshold requirement for liberty of conscience, 51–54
right to privacy, 58, 66
rights of animals, 61–62
rights of others, 1, 3–4, 34–35, 162–63, 164–67
compatibility with basic liberties of others, 55, 57, 70, 79–82, 83
coronavirus, 100–3, 106, 110
non-discrimination and same sex couples, 151–52
coronavirus and lockdown restrictions
UK, 101–10
US, 100–1
limitations, 49–51
non-discrimination, 46–47, 132
same sex couples, 122, 140, 151–52, 164–65
public interest, 1, 22, 49–50, 105–6, 109, 159
ritual slaughter, 61–62, 77–78, 83
ritual drug-taking:
peyote, 76, 80
rule of law, 26–27, 30, 102

same-sex couples, 2, 3, 121–22, 163
compatibility with basic liberties of others, 131–32
UK, 146–47, 149–51, 152
US, 142–46, 147–49, 151–52
non-discrimination in UK case law, 135, 139–42
proportionality, 155
non-discrimination in US case law
Colorado Anti-Discrimination Act, 136–37
neutrality and general applicability, 137–39
Philadelphia's Fair Practices Ordinance, 137–39
strict scrutiny, 139
secular beliefs, protection of, 74
ECHR, 11, 25
see also non-establishment
separation of church and state, *see* non-establishment
socio-economic rights, 58
South Africa
manifestation of conscientious belief, 43–44
rights of others, 42–43, 165–67
sexual orientation, 155
state neutrality justifications, 21–22
see also neutrality
strict scrutiny (US), 10, 68–69, 84–85
coronavirus and lockdown restrictions, 94–95, 96, 100–1, 111, 115–16, 164–65, 167, 168–70
foster carers, 138–39
non-discrimination and same-sex couples, 154, 159, 164–65, 167, 168–70

terrorism, 82–83, 110
threshold requirement for liberty of conscience, 51–54
toleration-based justifications, 20–21, 25, 34

United Kingdom
case law, 97–100, 103–6, 135, 139–42
Church of England, 75–76
compatibility with basic liberties of others
coronavirus and lockdown restrictions, 101, 103–4, 105, 108–10
non-discrimination and same-sex couples, 146–47, 149–51, 152
coronavirus and lockdown restrictions, 2, 3, 87–89, 119–20, 162–63
case law, 97–100
compatibility with basic liberties of others, 101, 103–4, 105, 108–10
necessity analysis and proportionality test, 113–14, 116–17, 118–19
Equality Act 2010, 8, 41, 52–53, 139–40
Health Protection (Coronavirus) (Restrictions and Requirements) (Local Levels) (Scotland) Amendment (No 11) Regulations 2021, 98–100
Health Protection (Coronavirus, Restrictions) (England) Regulations 2020, 97
Human Rights Act 1998, 6, 8, 9, 13
non-discrimination, 142, 158–59
lockdown restrictions, 2, 3, 162–63
compatibility with basic liberties of others, 101, 103–4, 105, 108–10
necessity in the common interest, 111
proportionality test, 113–14, 116–17, 118–19
necessity in the common interest, 62–67, 111, 157, 158–59, 162, 167
coronavirus and lockdown restrictions, 111, 113–14, 116–17, 118–19, 167
proportionality test, 113–14, 116–17, 118–19, 155
non-discrimination and same-sex couples, 123–24, 157, 158–59, 163
compatibility with other basic liberties,146–47, 149–51, 152
proportionality test, 155
proportionality test, 67–70
lockdown restrictions, 2, 3, 169–70
necessity analysis, 113–14, 116–17, 118–19
rights of others, 1, 3–4, 162–63, 164–67
coronavirus and lockdown restrictions, 101–10
relevance of, 101–10
same-sex couples, 2, 3, 121–22, 163
compatibility with basic liberties of others, 146–47, 149–51, 152
non-discrimination, 135, 139–40, 141–42, 155
United States:
case law, 94–97, 135, 136–39, 143
Civil Rights Act 1964, 8
Colorado Anti-Discrimination Act, 136–37
compatibility with basic liberties of others
coronavirus and lockdown restrictions, 100–1, 108–10
non-discrimination and same-sex couples, 142–46, 147–49, 151–52
coronavirus and lockdown restrictions, 2, 3, 87–89, 100–1, 119–20, 162–63
case law, 94–97
compatibility with basic liberties of others, 100–1, 108–10
necessity in the common interest, 111–13, 114–18, 167
neutrality and general applicability test, 111–13, 114–18
rights of others, irrelevance of, 100–1
strict scrutiny, 111, 115–16
First Amendment (US Constitution), 5–6, 8, 120, 151–52, 158, 162–63
Establishment Clause, 10
Free Exercise Clause, 10, 13, 43, 61–62, 76, 94, 138, 143, 168
Free Speech Clause, 138, 159
neutrality test, 79
Fourteenth Amendment (US Constitution), 151
Due Process Clause, 10
lockdown restrictions, 2, 3, 162–63
compatibility with basic liberties of others, 100–1, 108–10
necessity in the common interest, 111–13, 114–18
neutrality and general applicability test, 111–13, 114–18
strict scrutiny test, 115, 116
means and ends test, 68–69
necessity in the common interest, 62–67, 162
coronavirus and lockdown restrictions, 111–13, 114–18, 167
neutrality and general applicability test, 111–13, 114–18, 152–53, 154, 155–57, 159
non-discrimination and same-sex couples, 131–32, 152–53, 154, 155–57, 159, 167
strict scrutiny, 111, 115–16, 154, 159
US case law, 153–59
neutrality
lockdown restrictions, 111–13, 114–18
neutrality and general applicability test (US), 111–13, 114–18
neutrality as right of free exercise, 76–78, 79, 80, 81–85
non-discrimination, 123–24, 163
case law, 135–39
Colorado Anti-Discrimination Act, 136–37
compatibility with other basic liberties, 142–46, 147–49, 151–52
necessity in the common interest, 131–32, 152–54, 155–57, 159, 167
neutrality and general applicability, 137–39, 152–54, 155–57, 159

Philadelphia's Fair Practices Ordinance, 137–39
strict scrutiny, 139, 154, 159
neutrality and general applicability, 137–39
Philadelphia's Fair Practices Ordinance, 137–39
Religious Freedom Restoration Act 1993 (USA), 8, 10, 52
Religious Land Use and Institutionalized Persons Act 2000 (USA), 8, 10
rights of others
coronavirus and lockdown restrictions, 100–1
same-sex couples, 2, 3, 121–22, 163
case law, 135–39
Colorado Anti-Discrimination Act, 136–37
compatibility with basic liberties of others, 142–46, 147–49, 151–52
neutrality and general applicability, 137–39
non-discrimination in US case law, 135–39
Philadelphia's Fair Practices Ordinance, 137–39
strict scrutiny, 139
Smith-Lukumi test, 94, 100, 110, 113–15, 116, 119, 122, 154
strict scrutiny, 10, 68–69, 84–85
coronavirus and lockdown restrictions, 94–95, 96, 100–1, 111, 115–16, 164–65, 167, 168–70
foster carers, 138–39
non-discrimination and same-sex couples, 154, 159, 164–65, 167, 168–70
'wall of separation', 74

veil of ignorance, 26–28, 30–31, 123–24

'wall of separation', 74
see also non-establishment

www.ingramcontent.com/pod-product-compliance
Ingram Content Group UK Ltd.
Pitfield, Milton Keynes, MK11 3LW, UK
UKHW021703250926
475906UK00003B/66

9 781509 985272